KU-628-505

CAKES
REGIONAL
AND
TRADITIONAL

CAKES
REGIONAL
AND
TRADITIONAL

JULIE DUFF

GRUB STREET • LONDON

In memory of Judith

With thanks to Malcolm, my husband, for his love and unflagging tolerance of cakes. For two wonderful grandmothers, Elsie and Dora, who both loved cooking, giving me inspiration by example and allowing me to help even when very young. A mother, Thelma, who baked with enthusiasm, always ready to try out new recipes and just happened to make very good Rock Cakes!
My daughter Sian for gathering the information on spices. My son Andrew, for believing in my dream. Kate, Pippa and Sally without whose incredible support I would never have made cakes for our customers and finished the book on time. Peter for his help with research. Sian, Pippa, and Kate for helping me to bake the cakes for photography. Jenni Muir for pointing me in the right direction. Grub Street for giving me the opportunity of a lifetime and Anne Dolamore for her enthusiasm. And finally to Jess our beautiful Border Collie who faithfully lay at my feet whenever I sat writing, researching and drinking black coffee!

This paperback edition published in 2005 by
Grub Street
4 Rainham Close
London
SW11 6SS
Email: food@grubstreet.co.uk
www.grubstreet.co.uk

Reprinted 2008

Text copyright © Julie Duff 2005
Copyright this edition © Grub Street 2005
Photography by Michelle Garrett
Cover design by Hugh Adams, AB3 Design

British Library Cataloguing in Publication Data
Duff, Julie
Cakes: regional & traditional
1. Cake
I. Title
641.8'653

ISBN 978-1- 904943-19-8

All rights reserved. No part of this book may be reproduced or transmitted in any form or by any means, electronic or mechanical, including photocopying, recording or any information storage and retrieval system, without permission in writing from the publisher.

Printed and bound in India

CONTENTS

Of all the categories, this is probably my favourite, simply because there are not only some really delectable cakes but also some wonderful stories attached to them.

Probably the most difficult task has been selecting particular recipes, since so many of the cakes have several versions all claiming to be the 'original'. Whilst there may be some truth attached to such claims, I suspect that over many hundreds of years the origins of such cakes became blurred and many good and adventurous bakers have added their own little touches, which in turn became 'regional'.

Of course, a great many small cakes have their origins in festivals, fairs and wakes all of which were celebrated and enjoyed regionally. One which fits perfectly into this category would be Eccles Cakes, originally part of the food baked for wakes in the town of Eccles. Wakes were linked to various Church anniversaries, even though in the 16th and 17th centuries the Puritans verbally 'attacked' wakes and other noisy celebrations as they involved drinking and merry making on a disorderly scale, and would have included the eating of regional cakes. I have to admit they sound rather fun and no doubt the housewives and bakers thoroughly enjoyed preparing the 'traditional' edible delights.

Other such cakes are the Queen Cakes of England and the Queen Cakes of Ireland, which whilst having the same name, are actually completely different in appearance and character. The Irish Queen Cakes are very similar to Fairy Cakes, little sponge cakes cooked in a bun tin and finished with glace icing, whereas the English Queen Cakes, very popular in the 19th century, were traditionally baked in heart-shaped tins and un-iced but with the inclusion of a little lemon zest and fruit.

I hope you will enjoy some of the stories in this section, which in turn will tempt you to try baking them – although you could be forgiven if you choose to forego the Flead Cakes, that is unless you keep pigs in which case you have very little excuse.

**SMALL
REGIONAL CAKES**

SOUL CAKES

SHROPSHIRE AND CHESHIRE   *Makes 12*

Although there is no recorded baking of Soul Cakes since the 1850's, they did play an important part in All Soul's Day Celebrations on the 2nd November in Shropshire and Cheshire, when these simple buns were baked and given as gifts.

But interestingly last week I read in a newspaper that *A Dictionary of Sussex Dialect* states that on All Soul's Day people, dressed in black, held street collections to pay for masses for the dead and the collectors were traditionally offered Soul Cakes. So this custom clearly also had foundations in areas of the country other than Shropshire and Cheshire, although it may have been discontinued a lot earlier.

The slightly unorthodox method of making these buns is strictly in accordance with how they used to be made – so persevere. I must admit that when I baked this recipe I was rather satisfied with the result but it is important to remember that our view of baking has changed and perhaps today we have a tendency to prefer and expect something a little more elaborate.

I recently came across a modern day version of a Soul Cake recipe but feel that substituting it we lose something of historical value.

675 g/1 1/2 lb plain flour	25 g/1 oz yeast
1 teaspoon mixed spice	1 large egg
1 teaspoon allspice	Milk, to mix
115 g/4 oz butter	115 g/4 oz caster sugar

Preheat the oven to 200°C/400°F/Gas Mark 6.

Sift the flour and spice together in a bowl and rub in the butter to a fine breadcrumb texture. Cream the yeast together with the lightly beaten egg and a teaspoon of sugar and stir into the flour mixture. Add enough milk to form a soft dough, cover with a clean cloth and put aside in a warm place to rise for 30 minutes.

Finally add the remaining sugar to the dough, kneading gently before shaping into flat round buns, about 7.5 cm/3 inches in diameter.

Place on a greased baking tray and leave to rise for a further 20 minutes, then bake in the oven for 15 to 20 minutes or until well risen and golden.

Remove and place on wire rack to cool before eating. They may be split and buttered if preferred.

BIDDENDEN MAIDS CAKES

KENT   *Serves 6*

On Easter Monday in the village of Biddenden in Kent, these cakes formed part of an ancient custom known as the Biddenden Dole when they were handed out both to the needy and anyone else who may be watching the ceremony. Traditionally the cakes always have an imprint on one side of two ladies standing together, believed to have been Siamese twins named Eliza and Mary Chulkhurst, the founders of the Biddenden Dole; a sort of charity set up in their name with a legacy they left when they died at the age of 34 years. No one is really sure if this story of Eliza and Mary, who are supposed to have lived in the 12th century is true, but nonetheless it is a fascinating legend.

I understand that about 300 of these 'cakes' were made each year and distributed by the church wardens; prepared simply from flour and water, they are actually despite their name, more like a hard water biscuit than a cake. Sadly the ceremony caused such ructions that it was abandoned.

225 g/8 oz organic flour
7 tablespoons cold water

Preheat the oven to 140°C/275°F/Gas Mark 1.

Sift the flour into a medium sized bowl.

Add the water and stir to form a soft but workable dough. Form into a ball and roll out on a lightly floured surface to form an oblong approx. 30 x 10 cm/12 x 4 inches. Lift the cakes onto a greased baking tray.

Imprint the surface of the cakes with a design of your choice.

Bake in the centre of the oven for 15 to 20 minutes.

Allow to cool slightly before transferring to a cooling rack.

BATH BUNS

AVON AND SOMERSET   *Makes 8*

I rather like the idea that in the 18th century the Nelson family took the waters and ate Bath Buns in the City's Pump Room – their son Horatio Nelson, doubtless joining them when not at sea.

Thought to have been created by Dr W Oliver, who was also responsible for the famous Bath Oliver biscuits, Bath Buns can still be eaten in the Pump Room today or bought from bakers in the city.

Originally the round buns were scattered with caraway comfits (sugar-glazed caraway seeds), which are no longer available (though sugar-glazed fennel seeds, are sold in Indian food shops as mouth fresheners) but the buns are now normally topped with crushed lump sugar. Bath buns do not include dried fruit (although I have seen such variations on the basic recipe), but they do benefit from a little grated lemon peel or chopped candied mixed peel.

450 g/1 lb strong plain flour	**Glaze**
1/2 teaspoon salt	115 g/4 oz crushed lump sugar or
75 g/3 oz butter or lard	115 g/4 oz demerara sugar
75 g/3 oz sugar	150 ml/1/4 pint water
15 g/1/2 oz yeast	
2 eggs, lightly beaten	
150 ml/1/4 pint tepid milk	
50 g/2 oz chopped mixed peel, optional	

Preheat the oven to 220°C/425°F/Gas Mark 7.

Sieve flour and salt into a large bowl and rub in the fat. Stir in the sugar, reserving 1 teaspoonful.

Cream yeast with the remaining sugar and add the eggs and milk, mixing thoroughly. Add to the flour and fat together with mixed peel, if using.

Scoop the soft dough into a lightly greased bowl and put the bowl into a warm place to allow the mixture to rise and when doubled in size, turn onto a lightly floured surface and knead gently until smooth and elastic.

Divide into 8 equal segments, and place on a lightly-greased baking sheet, allowing them to be close enough to join together slightly when baked. Allow to rise for a further 20 minutes before placing in the centre of the oven. Bake for 10-15 minutes.

Prepare glaze by boiling water and sugar until thin syrup is formed. Immediately the buns are taken from the oven brush with the syrup, which will dry as the buns cool.

Sprinkle with crushed lump sugar, which is available from some food stores and delicatessens. If you are unable to obtain it, demerara sugar will be a fine substitute. Pull buns apart to serve.

HOPPER CAKES

Hoppers were baskets originally carried by farm workers as they walked the length and breadth of the ploughed fields broadcasting seed.

At the end of the sowing season, the farmer, his family and farm workers, gathered to share a celebration meal, the hoppers being lined with white cloths and filled with Hopper Cakes. Served with hot-spiced beer or ale, the small round cakes are in fact a variation of Plum Bread, fruitcake bread that is still extremely popular in Lincolnshire. Sadly with the advent of mechanisation, hoppers are rarely if ever used and subsequently the custom of Hopper Cakes died out.

The following recipe, a very typical Lincolnshire plum bread of the type used for Hopper Cakes, is from a handwritten cookery book of 1923.

350 g/12 oz plain flour	175 g/6 oz sultanas
1 tablespoon baking powder	50 g/2 oz chopped mixed peel
1/4 teaspoon salt	2 eggs, lightly beaten
1 teaspoon of ground ginger	Milk to mix
115 g/4 oz lard or butter	
175 g/6 oz sugar	**Topping**
175 g/6 oz currants	A little milk

Preheat the oven to 180°C/350°F/Gas Mark 4.

Sift the flour, baking powder, salt and ginger into a bowl and rub in the lard or butter to resemble fine breadcrumbs.

Stir in the sugar and fruits and then add the lightly beaten eggs, stir until the mixture forms a ball of dough. If the mixture is very stiff, add a little milk until a soft dough is formed.

Divide into 8 pieces, shaping them into rounds and place on a greased and lined baking tray, using a little of the milk, lightly brush the tops.

Leave for 20 minutes in a warm place before baking in the centre of the oven. The cakes will be cooked when well risen and golden brown, which will take approximately 20 to 25 minutes.

OAST CAKES OR HOPPING CAKES

KENT   *Makes 24 plus*

Hop Pickers put up with rather grim, cramped conditions during the annual 'migration' to the hop fields of Kent. They were often from London and the families working in the fields enjoyed nothing as much as a knees-up, appropriately called a 'Hopkin'.

During these lively evenings Oast Cakes, or Kentish Hopping Cakes as they were sometimes called, were part of the festive fare. Baked on very basic camp stoves or over open fires, they were fried in hot fat to seal them and give them a crisp golden brown appearance. Recipes vary a little in that alcohol was used to mix the dough, which might be parsnip wine or beer or ale, but somehow ale seems the most appropriate at a Hopkin. Little is heard of these cakes nowadays, mechanical picking having replaced the need for employing hop-picking gangs, but records in the Kent libraries clearly document the fun of 'Hopkins' and the rather plain little cakes which were such a tradition.

450 g/1 lb plain flour	50 g/2 oz lard
Pinch salt	100 g/4 oz currants
1 teaspoon baking powder	8 tablespoons ale

Sift the flour, salt and baking powder together in a bowl, add the lard and rub it in until it resembles fine breadcrumbs. Stir in the currants and mix it to stiff dough with the ale – adding a little more if it is too dry, until it forms manageable dough. Roll into balls of about 5 cm/2 inches in diameter.

Fry in hot fat until golden brown and eat whilst piping hot.

ECCLES CAKES

LANCASHIRE   *Makes 8-10*

In 1796 James Birch began baking cakes from his shop in Church Street, Eccles. Later the shop changed hands and in 1835 William Bradburn became the owner renaming it Bradburn's The Old Original Eccles Cake Shop.

First baked as part of the celebration of wakes (religious festivals), the cakes were banned along with such festivities in 1877, after it was decided that wakes had become too 'riotous'. Locals took little notice and Eccles Cakes made with flaky pastry (though there is much controversy about whether this should be puff pastry and indeed some recipes are made with puff so either will do), fruit and spices, continue to be enjoyed to this day.

Flaky Pastry
225 g/8 oz plain flour
Pinch of salt
175 g/6 oz cold butter
approx 6 tablespoons iced water

Filling
50 g/2 oz butter
40 g/1 1/2 oz pale muscovado sugar

50 g/2 oz mixed chopped peel
115 g/4 oz currants
1/2 teaspoon mixed spice
1/4 teaspoon ground nutmeg

Topping
1 egg white, lightly beaten
a little caster sugar

Pre-heat the oven to 220°C/ 425°F/Gas Mark 7.

To make the pastry, sift flour and salt into a medium bowl. Divide the butter into three and using a cheese grater, grate one portion into the flour, mix lightly together. Add the water until the mixture forms a soft but not sticky dough. Knead gently. Turn the pastry onto a lightly floured surface and roll into an oblong. Grate second portion of butter and sprinkle evenly over two-thirds of the surface. Fold unbuttered third over and bring final buttered third onto the top, pressing the edges to seal in the butter. Give pastry half-turn and roll again into an oblong. Repeat the process using last portion of butter. Leave pastry to rest for at least an hour before using. It is important to handle pastry lightly while making to keep it as cool as possible. On a lightly floured surface, roll out the pastry very thinly and cut into 13 cm/5 inch rounds.

Cream the butter and sugar in a bowl, and add the fruit and spices, mixing thoroughly. Place a tablespoon of the mixture in the centre of each pastry circle. Damp the edges and draw together to seal the filling. Turn cake over and roll gently to flatten slightly. Make two or three small slashes on the top.

Place them on a greased baking sheet and brush the top with the beaten egg white, then sprinkle with sugar. Bake in the centre of the oven for about 20 minutes or until puffed and golden. Remove carefully using a spatula and place on a wire rack to cool.

CHELSEA BUNS

LONDON
Makes 6

During the 17th and 18th centuries, the 'Chelsea Bun House' in Pimlico Road, near Sloane Square, was a popular destination for Londoners. Several generations of the Hand family owned the shop, one, Mr Richard Hand, was an officer in the militia who inevitably became known as Captain Bun. An eccentric chap, he walked around in a long dressing gown, wearing a fez – adding greatly to the pleasure of his customers. King George II and King George III with Queen Charlotte were often seen partaking of the highly acclaimed sticky, sugar coated, square, and lightly fruited, buns.

It is still possible to buy Chelsea Buns today but those mass-produced in supermarkets are often pretty uninteresting, so it is well worth trying this recipe.

Yeast batter
75 g/3 oz strong plain flour
I teaspoon caster sugar
15 g/1/2 oz fresh yeast
125 ml/4 fl oz tepid milk

Dough
175 g/6 oz strong plain flour
25 g/1 oz butter
I egg, lightly beaten

Filling
50 g/2 oz butter
50 g/2 oz pale muscovado sugar
50 g/2 oz currants
50 g/2 oz sultanas
25 g/1 oz chopped glace peel

Glaze
Honey

Preheat the oven to 200°C/400°F/Gas Mark 6.

Place all the ingredients for the batter in a large bowl and beat well with your bare hand until smooth. Leave in a warm place until frothy, about 30 minutes.

In a separate bowl place the flour and butter for the dough mix, and rub together until it resembles breadcrumbs. Add to the batter, together with the lightly beaten egg and whisk thoroughly, to ensure there are no lumps in the mixture; this may also be done with your hand, if preferred.

Lightly flour a work surface and turn the dough mixture out, kneading for about 10 minutes until it is elastic and smooth. Place in a lightly oiled bowl, cover with a cloth and leave to rise for 45 minutes or until the dough has doubled in size.

Turn out onto the floured surface and knead the dough lightly, rolling to a rectangular shape. Spread evenly with the diced butter, followed by the sugar, mixed peel and fruits. Roll into Swiss roll shape. Cut into 6 pieces. Place on a baking sheet, allowing room between them for expansion. Cover and allow to rise until the buns have doubled in size. Bake in the centre of the oven for 25 to 30 minutes until golden brown. Remove from the oven and brush with a little melted warm honey to glaze.

Leave to cool for 10 minutes and then remove to a wire rack to get cold.

DERBY CAKES

Makes about 12

Eaten straight from the oven, these cakes are particularly good with a morning coffee, as they are plain and almost shortbread-like in texture.

225 g/8 oz plain flour
115 g/4 oz butter
50 g/2 oz sugar
I large egg, lightly beaten
A little milk

Topping
White of an egg, well beaten

Preheat the oven to 160°C/325°F/Gas Mark 3.

Sift the flour into a bowl and add the butter, rubbing it into the flour with your fingers until it resembles fine breadcrumbs. Stir in the sugar and then the lightly beaten egg, to form a soft but not sticky dough, if necessary adding a little extra milk.

Form into a ball and then transferring to a lightly floured surface, roll the mixture gently until it forms quite a thin sheet. Then using cutters, transform the dough into shapes of your choice, transferring them carefully using a spatula, onto a greased and lightly floured baking tray. Finally, gently brush the tops of the cakes with the beaten white of egg, which will give the cakes an attractive glaze when cooked.

Bake in the centre of the oven for about 10 to 15 minutes or until golden brown.

Transfer to a wire rack to cool.

QUEEN CAKES

ENGLAND   *Makes 12*

Very much in favour during the 19th century, these little cakes were traditionally baked in heart-shaped tins and given the title 'Heart Cakes'. Simple to prepare.

115 g/4 oz butter	2 eggs beaten
115 g/4 oz caster sugar	50 g/2 oz sultanas or currants
115 g/4 oz plain flour	A little lemon zest
1/2 level teaspoon baking powder	

Preheat the oven to 375°F/190°C/Gas Mark 5.

Cream the butter and sugar until light and fluffy. Add the flour, baking powder and lightly beaten eggs a little at a time, folding in gently. The mixture should form a soft dropping consistency.

Add the dried fruit and lemon zest and spoon the mixture into small greaseproof cases on a bun tin, filling cases approximately two thirds full. Bake in the oven until well risen, golden and firm to touch. Cool on a wire rack.

IRELAND   *Makes approximately 12*

In Ireland, these celebrated little buns are to be found in most baker's shops. More akin to the English Fairy Cakes than the English Queen Cakes, they are a light sponge, sometimes with the addition of sultanas, but more often iced in pink or chocolate glace icing.

115 g/4 oz butter	**Topping**
115 g/4 oz caster sugar	Icing sugar
2 large eggs lightly beaten	A little cocoa or pink colouring
115 g/4 oz self raising flour	
1/2 teaspoon vanilla extract	

Preheat the oven to 190°C/375°F/Gas Mark 5.

Cream the butter and sugar until light and fluffy, add the eggs and flour alternately, beating gently until fully incorporated. Add the vanilla extract, stirring thoroughly.

Line a bun tin with greaseproof paper cases, spooning enough mixture into each case to fill them two thirds full. Bake in the centre of the oven for 15 to 20 minutes, or until well-risen and golden brown. They will feel firm to the touch if pressed lightly on top.

Leaving them in their paper cases, remove from bun tin and cool them on a wire rack. When cold, ice with the glace icing of your choice, which should be mixed to give a coating consistency and decorate with your chosen topping.

ST CATHERINE'S CAKES OR CATTERN CAKES

SOMERSET AND DEVON
Makes approximately 20-24

25th November is St Catherine's Day and my daughter, whose middle name is Catherine was actually born on the 25th November. I would like to be able to say that she was named after this saint, but actually it was pure coincidence as I only found out years later that it was St.Catherine's Day.

I have discovered that the famous Bonfire Night firework, the Catherine Wheel, is so named because of St Catherine's horrific, tortured death on a wheel. Since learning this I have never been able to view this rather spectacular firework in the same light.

Cattern Cakes, spiced currant pastries, are traditionally baked in the shape of a wheel and eaten on the Saint's Day, accompanied by cider. However in Somerset these delicious little cakes are baked and eaten on the 24th November, which is known as Cattern's Eve.

350 g/12 oz plain flour	25 g/1 oz candied peel
1 teaspoon bicarbonate soda	350 g/12 oz butter
1/2 teaspoon mixed spice	1 beaten egg
50 g/2 oz ground almonds	
350 g/12 oz caster sugar	**Glaze**
50 g/2 oz currants	1 lightly beaten egg
50 g/2 oz sultanas	2 tablespoons milk

Preheat the oven to 190°C/375°F/Gas Mark 5.

Sift the flour, bicarbonate of soda and spice into a large bowl. Add the ground almonds, caster sugar, currants, sultanas, candied peel and stir thoroughly.

In a small saucepan, melt the butter over a low heat and allow to cool slightly. Add to the dried ingredients together with the beaten egg, stirring with a pallet knife until the mixture forms a stiff dough.

Turn onto a lightly floured surface and knead gently until smooth, before rolling the dough into an oblong. Damp the top lightly with a little water and roll into a Swiss roll shape. Using a sharp knife, cut into slices approximately 10 mm/1/2 inch wide and arrange on a greased baking sheet, allowing space for expansion. Beat the egg and milk together and lightly brush over the top of the cakes, to glaze.

Place in the oven for approximately 15 minutes, watching carefully to see that they do not over brown.

Transfer the 'Catherine Wheels' onto a cooling rack using a spatula.

When cold, store in an airtight container.

BANBURY CAKES

OXFORDSHIRE   *Makes 8*

Ride a cock horse to Banbury Cross
To see a fine lady upon a white horse
With rings on her fingers and bells on her toes
She shall have music where-ever she goes

One of the first thoughts we have when Banbury is mentioned is Banbury Cross and a lady on a white horse, followed perhaps by the famous Banbury Cakes. Originally sold on fair days, Banbury Cakes are amongst the oldest English cakes; indeed a mention was made as far back as 1586 in T. Bright's *Treatise of Melancholy* and yet again in 1615 in *The English Huswife* by Gervaise Markham, although his recipe was rather different.

In Banbury Museum it is possible to see the actual round-lidded baskets once used to transport the cakes. Although the original 'Banbury Cake Shop', which dated from 1638, has now closed down, almost every bakery in the town still proudly produces these delicious little cakes, which are by far best eaten straight from the oven. Characterised by their flat oval shape, Banbury Cakes are made from flaky pastry filled with currants, butter, citrus peel, sugar, spices and rum, the sweet outer crust glazed with egg white and dredged with sugar forming a delectable sweet topping.

225 g/8 oz chilled Flaky Pastry (see page 30)

Filling
25 g/1 oz butter
12 g/¹/₂ oz plain flour
¹/₂ tsp mixed spice
115 g/4 oz currants

25 g/1 oz chopped mixed glace peel
50 g/2 oz soft brown sugar
2 tablespoons rum

Topping
1 beaten egg white
Caster sugar

Preheat the oven to 220°C/425°F/Gas Mark 7.

On a lightly floured surface, roll out the flaky pastry to 5 mm/¹/₂ inch thick before cutting into 7.5 cm/3 inch rounds.

To make the filling, melt the butter and stir in the flour and spice, cooking gently for a couple of minutes. Remove from the heat and stir in the remaining ingredients.

Place a tablespoonful of the filling in the centre of each of the pastry circles. Damp the edges of the circles and draw them together to form a ball. Turn the cakes over and gently roll each round into the traditional oblong shape, approximately 13 cm/5 inches x 6 cm/2¹/₂ inches. Make three cuts on the top of each cake and place them on a greased baking sheet.

Bake in the centre of the oven for 15 minutes, remove and brush the top with beaten egg white and dust with the caster sugar. Return to the oven for a further 5 minutes.

Remove the tray and lift the Banbury Cakes onto a cooling rack. Best eaten whilst still warm.

CHORLEY CAKES

LANCASHIRE   *Makes 6*

The history of these pastry cakes is unclear, probably dating back to medieval times perhaps even the Crusades. In Chapel Street in Chorley in the 1880's there is a record of a Mrs Corbett selling Chorley Cakes for 2d each from her shop. Varying in size from 20 cm/8 inches to smaller 8 cm/3 inches, they are described as an early convenience food.

Made from shortcrust pastry with a simple currant filling, Chorley Cakes are very akin to Eccles Cakes, without the spices or glace peel. Pale in appearance, the cakes are not egg washed before baking but simply dusted with icing sugar or sprinkled with caster sugar as soon as they are taken from the oven. Delicious eaten whilst still warm.

450 g/1 lb Shortcrust Pastry (see page 21)	**Topping**
115 g/4 oz currants	A little icing sugar or caster sugar

Preheat the oven to 180°C/350°F/Gas Mark 4.

Roll the pastry out to 5 mm/¼ inch thick and cut it into a circle about the size of a dinner plate. Sprinkle the currants into the centre of the circle and damping the edges, fold them into the centre. Turn over carefully and roll the circle until currants begin to peak through (rather like the Shy Cake, page 127). Lift onto a greased and floured baking sheet and brush the top with a little milk.

Bake in the centre of the oven for approximately 30 minutes until brown.

Remove from the oven and place on a cooling rack, sprinkle with icing sugar when cool.

HOT CROSS BUNS

LONDON   *Makes 12*

One a penny, Two a penny, Hot cross buns

This cry, which is now part of a children's game, originated from street sellers in London and paints a colourful history for the Hot Cross Bun.

Yeast buns have been eaten in England since medieval times, although a decree issued in 1592, during the reign of Elizabeth I, forbade bakers from selling spiced breads or buns, except on feast days such as Good Friday and Christmas.

However the custom of slicing crosses into the top of bread or buns (believed to ward off evil spirits) eventually discontinued after the Reformation and only remained on the top of Hot Cross Buns, where they became pastry or citrus peel crosses, being symbolic of the crucifix of Christ.

450 g/1 lb strong plain flour	150 ml/¼ pint tepid milk
2 teaspoons mixed spice	25 g/1 oz fresh yeast
½ teaspoon salt	1 teaspoon of caster sugar
50 g/2 oz butter	
50 g/2 oz caster sugar	**Glaze**
115 g/4 oz currants or sultanas	50 g/2 oz caster sugar
50 g/2 oz chopped mixed peel	2 tablespoons water
1 large egg	

Preheat the oven to 220°C/425°F/Gas Mark 7.

Sift the flour, spice and salt into a warmed bowl. Rub in the butter. Add the sugar, fruit and peel and stir to ensure they are well mixed together.

Beat the egg into the tepid milk.

In a small bowl cream the yeast with a teaspoon of caster sugar and pour on the milk and egg mixture stirring thoroughly.

Make a well in the middle of the flour and pour in the milk mixture. Stir well and turn the dough onto a lightly floured board. Knead for about ten minutes, the dough although fairly soft, should not be sticky.

Place the dough into a clean bowl, cover with cloth and leave in a warm place to double in size, about 1 hour. Turn the dough onto a floured surface and knead again for a few minutes, until smooth.

Cut into equal portions (approximately 12) rolling into bun shapes. Cut a cross into the top of each bun and lift them onto a lightly greased baking sheet. Cover with a cloth, leaving to rise until doubled in size. Bake in the oven until golden brown, about 15 to 20 minutes.

Whilst the buns are baking, make a glaze by gently dissolving the sugar in the water and allowing to boil for 1 minute. When the buns are taken from the oven, brush immediately with the glaze and transferring to a wire rack leave to cool.

DOUGHNUTS

ISLE OF WIGHT   *Makes 8*

Until I began researching these sugary, deep fried buns, I had no idea that they had such a long connection with Britain, having believed them to be French in origin, and indeed they probably were centuries ago. I discovered them however, time and again in old recipe books. Eliza Acton mentions them in her book of 1845 *Modern Cookery for Private Families*, and her excellent recipe even suggests that after deep frying they should be drained on clean straw!

Many cookery books of similar age mention the Isle of Wight and its particular recipe which includes cinnamon, cloves, mace and a few currants. Elizabeth David however suggests that candied peel could be used to replace the jam.

Legend has it that Bedfordshire used to have a strong connection with doughnuts at one time; large quantities were baked in Luton on Shrove Tuesday, where they were apparently consumed with relish. Sadly, my father-in-law John Duff, whose uncle was a baker in Bedford, seemed very puzzled by this tale and despite a lot of detective work I have been unable to confirm its accuracy.

450 g/1lb plain flour	2 large eggs, lightly beaten
1 sachet dried yeast	Oil for deep-frying
25 g/1 oz butter	Red jam
115 g/4 oz caster sugar	Caster sugar
12 tablespoons milk, lukewarm	

Sift the flour into a large bowl, stirring in the yeast.

Rub in the butter to form a breadcrumb texture. Stir in the sugar.

Make a well in the centre and add the milk and eggs, stirring with a pallet knife to form a dough.

On a lightly floured surface, knead the dough until smooth; this will take about 5 or 6 minutes.

Place the dough in a clean bowl and cover with a cloth, leaving in a warm place to double in size, approximately 1 hour.

Knead the dough lightly until smooth and then divide into equal pieces, rolling into balls. Flatten and place a little jam in the centre, forming the dough around the jam, to seal it into the centre of the doughnut.

Cover with a clean cloth and leave for a further 30 minutes until well risen.

In a suitable deep-frying pan, heat the oil to 160°C/325°F and add the doughnuts, three or four at a time, turning with a slotted spoon until golden brown. Drain on kitchen paper and then roll the doughnuts in the sugar, putting them onto a plate to cool.

Best eaten the same day, although I suspect it may be difficult to prevent this anyway.

FAT RASCALS

YORKSHIRE   ***Makes about 12***

A very well known Yorkshire speciality, which has been documented since the 1860's, this round tea cake is best described as a cross between a rock cake and a scone. Made with currants, sultanas and citrus peel they were originally conceived as a smaller, more easily managed version of a Yorkshire Turf Cake. The scone-like texture is delicious when eaten warm, split and buttered.

Whilst in Yorkshire recently I saw several variations of Fat Rascals, and many included cherries and almonds which had been placed on the top of the cakes before baking.

350 g/12 oz self-raising flour
75 g/3 oz lard or pork dripping
75 g/3 oz caster sugar

115 g/4 oz currants
150 ml/1/4 pint soured cream or buttermilk

Preheat the oven to 200°C/400°F/Gas Mark 6.

Sift flour into a bowl and rub in the lard or pork dripping until it resembles fine breadcrumbs.

Add the remaining dry ingredients and mix together with the soured cream or buttermilk to form a soft but not sticky, dough.

Roll out to about 2.5 cm/1 inch thick, cut into circles with a metal cutter. Lift onto a lightly greased baking tray and bake in the centre of the oven for about 10 minutes or until risen and golden brown.

Using a spatula, lift onto a wire rack and leave to cool.

COVENTRY GOD CAKES

Makes 8

These delicious little triangular puff pastry cakes originated in the 19th century when they were sold for godparents to give as blessings to their godchildren. Filled with either jam or mincemeat they were given at either Christmas or Easter. The shape of the triangle is said to signify the Holy Trinity.

It is doubtful however, that such a tradition is honoured today but it is certainly still possible to buy them from good baker's shops, albeit they may simply be called 'jam puffs'.

450 g/1lb Puff Pastry (see page 20)

Topping
Egg white
Caster sugar

Filling
Jam, red preferred

Preheat the oven to 200°C/400°F/Gas Mark 6.

Roll out puff pastry and cut into thin squares approx 10 cm/4 inches by 10 cm/4 inches. Put a generous teaspoon of jam into the centre of each square and brush the edges with a little water. Fold corner to corner to form a triangle, pressing the edges together to seal. Make two small slits in the top of each cake and lift them carefully onto a greased baking sheet.

Bake for 25-30 minutes in the centre of the oven until well puffed and golden brown, then remove the baking sheet from the oven and quickly brush the tops of the cakes with a little beaten egg white and sprinkle with sugar. Return them to the oven immediately for a further 5 minutes until the topping is set.

Lift carefully from the baking sheet and leave to cool on a wire rack. Do be careful not to eat these until they are cool, as the hot jam would scald your mouth.

HUFFKINS

KENT   *Makes 10-12*

Like many old recipes, Huffkins, an East Kent tea cake, are now rarely made commercially, although I do know of one baker in Sandwich, Kent who when I last heard was making them for his shop. Copies of the recipe however, do most certainly exist and are well worth making.

Not unlike a Cornish Split in texture, Huffkins are thick flat cakes, always oval and characterised by a hole in the middle.

Spread thickly with butter and jam they are quite delicious but they can also be served hot, filled in the centre with such fruits as Kentish apples, plums or cherries and served as a pudding.

675 g/1lb 8 oz plain flour	1 teaspoon sugar
1 teaspoon salt	375 ml/^{3}/4 pint tepid milk
20 g/^{3}/4 oz fresh yeast	40 g/1 ^{1}/2 oz lard

Preheat the oven to 220°C/425°F/Gas Mark 7.

Sift the flour and salt into a bowl.

Cream the yeast and sugar adding the tepid milk, stir well. Make a well in the centre of the flour and add the yeast mixture stirring to form dough.

Knead lightly until soft and smooth. Return to the bowl and cover, leaving in a warm place until it has doubled in size. Turn onto a floured surface, knead in the lard and continue kneading until smooth.

Divide the dough into 10 to 12 pieces, rolling each into an oval about 2.5 cm/1 inch thick and make a hole in the centre. Transfer to a greased baking sheet and leave to rise for a further 30 minutes. Bake in the centre of the oven for 20 minutes or until golden brown.

Transfer to a rack and cover with a tea towel until cool. The steam will ensure they do not become too crusty.

WELSH CAKES/*Pice ar y maen*

WALES   *Makes 10-12*

Best cooked on a griddle, these excellent little cakes should be eaten whilst warm. Certainly when I ate one which had become cold it was rather dry and brittle, which did not do it justice, as fresh from the griddle, sprinkled with caster sugar, they are very more-ish.

The following is a 'rich' version, which gives, I think, the best results.

225 g/8 oz self raising flour
3/4 teaspoon baking powder
Pinch of nutmeg
3/4 teaspoon salt
115 g/4 oz butter
75 g/3 oz caster sugar

75 g/3 oz currants
1 beaten egg
A little milk to mix

Topping
Sugar for dredging

Sift the flour, baking powder, nutmeg and salt into a bowl. Rub in the butter to a breadcrumb texture and add the sugar and currants, stirring with a pallet knife. Add the egg and enough milk to form a stiff dough. Roll out on a lightly floured board to about 5 mm/1/4 inch thick and cut into 5 cm/2 inch rounds, using a cutter.

Cook on a hot greased griddle for about 4 to 5 minutes each side until golden brown. Lift onto a wire rack and dredge with caster sugar. Serve warm.

GOOSNARGH CAKES

LANCASHIRE   *Makes about 12*

Goosnargh, a village near Preston, lends its name to these caraway and coriander flavoured cakes, which were made in never-ending quantities for the Easter and Whitsun holidays. Traditionally eaten with ale, Goosnargh Cakes, with their very high butter content, spicy flavour and topping of dredged sugar, closely resemble shortbread.

Although no longer made in vast amounts, they can still be bought from several bakers in the area.

450 g/1lb plain flour
1 teaspoon coriander
350 g/12 oz butter

75 g/3 oz caster sugar
1/2 teaspoon caraway seeds

Preheat the oven to 150°C/300°F/Gas Mark 2.

Sift the flour and coriander into a bowl. Rub in the butter, working it with your fingertips until a soft dough is formed.

Roll out dough to 5 mm/1/4 inch thick and cut into 7.5 cm/3 inch rounds. Sprinkle the tops with sugar and caraway seeds.

Lift onto a greased baking tray and cook in the centre of the oven for 30 to 40 minutes until firm but still pale. The cakes should not brown.

Lift carefully from the baking sheet and leave to cool on a wire rack.

YORKSHIRE CURD CAKES
OR CHISSICKS

Makes 24

A classic Yorkshire recipe, these little cakes are enjoyed just as much today as in the past. They are characterised by the inclusion of currants and citrus peel but fortunately, we no longer have to make the curd cheese as it can be readily bought from any good supermarket.

450 g/1lb Shortcrust Pastry (see page 21)
450 g/1lb fresh curd cheese
115 g/4 oz caster sugar
2 large eggs, lightly beaten
50 g/2 oz melted butter

Grated rind of 1 small lemon
50 g/2 oz currants
1 tablespoon brandy (optional)
1/2 teaspoon of mace or nutmeg

Preheat the oven to 180°C/350°F/Gas Mark 4.

Roll the pastry thinly and cut into 7.5 cm/3 inch circles using a cutter. Place them into two lightly greased bun tins, each with 12 sections, pressing in gently. Set aside.

Put the curd cheese and caster sugar into a bowl and beat together until light and smooth. Add all the rest of the ingredients and stir thoroughly until well mixed together.

Spoon the mixture equally between the pastry bases and bake in the oven for 15 to 20 minutes or until the cheesecakes are lightly browned and set. Allow to cool for 5 minutes before removing carefully from the tins, using a pallet knife and gently place them on a wire rack to cool.

SHREWSBURY CAKES

SHROPSHIRE   *Makes about 24 cakes*

It was in 1760 that Thomas Plimmer, perhaps the most famous baker of Shrewsbury Cakes, opened his shop in Shrewsbury, although mention is made of them in several manuscripts and books dating back as far as 1602. Mrs Raffald's wonderful book *The Experienced English Housekeeper*, 1769, makes mention of two recipes for Shrewsbury Cakes, so that their popularity had spread widely amongst cooks of standing, was without doubt.

Plimmer was however, adamant in his claim to owning the original recipe, which he said had been acquired from one James Palin, the owner of a shop in Castle Street, Shrewsbury, where they were baked and sold.

What is without doubt is that Shrewsbury Cakes do not at present seem to be made commercially, perhaps because they are light and delicate and rather easily broken, but they are well worth trying to bake at home and should not be confused with Shrewsbury Biscuits, which are entirely different, and not nearly as nice.

The following recipe comes from a little book dated 1895, which I found recently in a junk shop and proclaimed, I am sure quite justifiably, to 'teach advanced students the art of cooking'. It is an altogether charming book and contained a thoroughly delicious version of the Shrewsbury Cake recipe, to which I have added only rosewater, as it appears in so many of the recipes and does I think add a little extra something to the finished cakes.

115 g/4 oz butter	1 egg
Zest of one lemon	2 teaspoons rosewater
115 g/4 oz caster sugar	225 g/8 oz plain flour

Preheat the oven to 150°C/300°F/Gas Mark 2.

Cream the butter thoroughly, adding the lemon zest. Add the caster sugar, and cream the mixture again. Beat in the egg and rosewater a little at a time.

Mix in the flour a tablespoon at a time, until a soft dough is formed. Wrap in cling film and place in the refrigerator for an hour or so.

Lightly flour a board with as little flour as possible, rolling the dough to approximately 5 mm/1/4 inch thick, cut into rounds and place on a baking tray, lined with greaseproof paper.

Bake in the oven until pale golden brown. Approximately 10 minutes.

Using a spatula, lift carefully onto a wire rack and leave to cool.

CORNISH AND DEVONSHIRE SPLITS

Makes approximately 8

The name Split derives from the manner in which these plain sweetened yeast buns are traditionally served. Split in half across the top, they are filled with raspberry or strawberry jam and clotted cream. Slightly less enticing with molasses and clotted cream, as an alternative traditional filling, they are known as 'thunder and lightning'. There is really little difference between Cornish Splits and Devonshire Splits, both originate from the recipe for Chudleighs. Chudleighs or Farthing Cakes are made from exactly the same ingredients, the difference being that the dough is divided into more portions, each bun being much smaller than the Cornish Split version, i.e. about 10 cm/4 inches. Even tinier are the Farthing Cakes which are about $5/8$ cm/$2/3$ inch. Splits are excellent served warm, filled, straight from the oven.

450 g/1lb plain flour	2 teaspoons caster sugar
$1/2$ tsp salt	25 g/1 oz butter
25 g/1 oz fresh yeast	300 ml/$1/2$ pint tepid milk

Preheat the oven to 200°C/400°F/Gas Mark 6.

Sieve the flour and salt into a warm bowl. Cream the yeast with the sugar.

Over a very low heat dissolve the butter gently in a small saucepan together with milk. When cool pour onto the yeast and sugar and stir thoroughly then pour into centre of flour and mix to a dough.

Knead for 5 minutes and then put into a lightly oiled bowl, cover and leave to rise in a warm place, for one hour.

When doubled in size, cut into about 8 pieces and knead gently into balls. Grease and flour a large baking sheet, placing the dough balls evenly on the tray. Leave to rise for a further 10 minutes. Brush with milk and bake in the oven for 20 minutes or until golden brown (they will sound hollow when tapped), leave to cool slightly on a wire rack. Then fill with jam and cream.

FLEAD CAKES

KENT   *Makes about 12-15*

Flead, or fleed, is the name given to the fat inside a pig which is rarely, if ever, available now. In fact it is doubtful if Flead Cakes are made any longer, probably because so few people keep pigs to kill at home, as was once common.

Very similar to Lardy Cake, Eliza Acton's *Modern Cookery for Private Families*, 1845, conjures up a delightful picture of flead cake making in the early 19th century. 'Having scraped the particles of flead from the membrane, add them to the flour and beat with a rolling pin, until blended with the flour'. No doubt an excellent way of releasing pent up anger! The resulting mix could either be used to make (we are assured) an excellent pastry or with the addition of fruit and sugar, it could be baked into light round cakes. Mrs Beeton's *Modern Household Cookery*, 1856, gives a similar recipe, which she calls Scrap Cakes, the only difference being the addition of allspice. These she assures us are very wholesome for children, although I reserve judgement.

Flead incidentally, can also be gently melted down and used in liquid form or left to set in a bowl. Gladys Pickard remembers her father preparing it in this way each winter ready to add to the traditional jars of Christmas mincemeat made in her childhood home. Sadly I have not been able to bake this cake as I have been unable to obtain flead.

A rather standard Flead Cake recipe of the mid 19th century would have been as follows:

450 g/1 lb flour	**Enriched cakes with the addition of:**
1 teaspoon salt	50 g/2 oz butter
175 g/6 oz flead	50 g/2 oz sugar
	50 g/2 oz currants

Preheat the oven to 180°C/350°F/Gas Mark 4.

Scrape the flead from the skin and add the particles of fat to the sifted flour and salt. Rub in very thoroughly to break up the globules of fat and form dough. Add the butter and rub it into the mixture together with the sugar and currants.

Knead the dough gently but thoroughly.

Cut into rounds of approximately 7.5 cm/3 inches diameter, placing them on a greased baking sheet. Bake in the centre of a medium oven for about 25 minutes or until golden brown.

Remove from the baking tray and pile straight onto a serving plate. Best eaten warm.

JERSEY CAKES

Like a lot of regional cakes the Jersey Cakes or Jersey Wonders as they were also named are a very old recipe, which continues to be baked and sold to this day. Traditionally fried, they are light and really delicious, the twisted shape giving them their particular character.

225 g/8 oz plain flour	2 large eggs
1 teaspoon baking powder	White vegetable fat or lard
75 g/3 oz butter	
75 g/3 oz caster sugar	**Topping**
1/4 teaspoon grated nutmeg	A little extra caster sugar

Sift the flour and baking powder into a bowl and lightly rub in the butter until it resembles fine breadcrumbs. Stir in the sugar and nutmeg and add the lightly beaten eggs. Using your hands, form the mixture into a ball and then lift onto a lightly floured surface.

Roll out to about 5 mm/1/4 inch thickness and cut into oblongs 4 x 7.5cm/1 1/2 x 3 inch, twisting them gently.

Heat enough vegetable fat or lard to form a depth of 5 cm/2 inches in the bottom of a medium sized pan until it is hot and gently drop in one or two Jersey Cakes at a time, cooking for about 5 minutes or until golden brown. Lift out with a draining spoon and place onto a sheet of greaseproof, dredging the cakes with caster sugar.

Leave until cool before eating. Best eaten on the day of making.

GOD'S KITCHELS

SUFFOLK   *Makes 9*

Not being able to find the word 'kitchel' in the dictionary was not a good start, so you can imagine my delight when the reference library in Bury St Edmunds cheerfully confirmed its existence.

And so I discovered that these small puff pastry squares filled with fruit and ground almonds, were baked during the twelve days of Christmas, 25th December to 6th January, when godchildren visited their godparents.

A charming saying in Suffolk was 'Ask me a blessing and I will give you a Kitchel'.

This recipe is well worth trying, they are really delicious.

75 g/3 oz butter	1 teaspoon mixed spice
275 g/10 oz currants	115 g/4 oz ground almonds
115 g/4 oz chopped glace peel	450 g/1 lb Puff Pastry (see page 20)

Preheat the oven to 200°C/400°F/Gas Mark 6.

Melt the butter over a low heat adding the currants, peel and spice together with the ground almonds and stir thoroughly. Set the mixture aside.

Divide the puff pastry into half, rolling each into two evenly sized oblongs and lift one carefully onto a greased baking sheet. Spread the pastry base with the filling mixture, leaving a small border at the edges, which you should moisten with a little water before lifting the second sheet of pastry over the top and sealing the edges.

Mark the pastry lightly into squares with a sharp knife.

Bake in the oven for 30 minutes or until puffed and golden.

Remove from the oven and allow to cool slightly before dividing into the outlined squares. Finish by sprinkling with a little caster sugar.

SUFFOLK CAKES

SUFFOLK   *Makes 12-15*

Mrs Anstey was a well-known cook in Suffolk during the 19th century and although it is by no means certain that the recipe originated from her private cookery notes, as it does appear elsewhere, there is every possibility that with her flair for devising delicious dishes, Suffolk Cakes were at least frequently on the menu.

115 g/4 oz butter	Zest of an orange or lemon
4 eggs	115 g/4 oz self-raising flour
225 g/8 oz caster sugar	

Preheat the oven to 200°C/400°F/Gas Mark 6.

Line a bun tin with greaseproof paper cases.

Warm the butter gently over a low heat until just melted.

Separate the eggs and whisk the egg whites stiffly, until peaks will form. In a separate bowl beat the sugar into the egg yolks together with the orange or lemon zest and using a large metal spoon, gently fold in the egg whites.

Stir the melted butter and sifted flour into the egg mixture and working quickly divide the mixture equally into the paper cases.

Bake in the oven for 10 to 15 minutes or until golden brown.

Remove and cool on a wire rack. As the cakes cool their tops will flatten to give the characteristic Suffolk Cake shape.

NELSON SLICES

NORFOLK   *Makes 6-8*

Admiral Lord Nelson was born in Norfolk, in the little village of Burnham Thorpe, a village I so enjoy visiting whenever I stay on the lovely windswept Norfolk coast.

At first reading, this recipe may not seem like a cake but it was always eaten as such, served cold and traditionally topped with a liberal dusting of icing sugar.

10 slices of thick white bread	Zest of I lemon
300 ml/¹/2 pint milk	2 tablespoons orange marmalade
115 g/4 oz raisins	2 eggs, lightly beaten
115 g/4 oz currants	I tablespoon rum
50 g/2 oz chopped glace peel	115 g/4 oz butter
115 g/4 oz soft brown sugar	
¹/2 teaspoon nutmeg	**Topping**
¹/2 teaspoon cinnamon	Icing sugar, to sprinkle

Preheat the oven to 180°C/350°F/Gas Mark 4.

Break the bread into pieces and place in a large bowl, pouring over the milk. Set aside to soak for at least I hour.

Mix the bread with a fork, until it forms a creamy mass and then stir in the dried fruits, peel, sugar, spices, lemon zest, marmalade, eggs and rum. Finally melt the butter in a small saucepan and add half to the mixture. Don't worry if it all looks a little unappetising.

Grease a baking dish, approximately 18 cm/7 inch x 28 cm/11 inch and spoon the cake mixture in, spreading evenly over the whole dish. Finally, pour the remaining butter over the top.

Place in the centre of the oven until the top is brown and crispy and the cake is well risen, this will take about 30 minutes.

Leave the cake in the dish to become cold, before sprinkling the top liberally with icing sugar and cutting the cake into squares.

Note: this cake can be served hot from the oven, with a little cream or custard.

TEA CAKES

LANCASHIRE

Makes about 14

Lancashire Tea Cakes vary a great deal from the Yorkshire Tea Cakes, in that they do not contain yeast; they are raised with baking powder. Traditionally made with lard, butter may be used if preferred.

450 g/1 lb strong plain flour
1 teaspoon baking powder
175 g/6 oz lard or butter
175 g/6 oz soft brown sugar
75 g/3 oz currants

75 g/3 oz raisins
50 g/2 oz chopped mixed peel
Zest of one large lemon
2 eggs lightly beaten

Preheat the oven to 190°C/375°F/Gas Mark 5.

Sift the flour and baking powder into a large bowl, rub in the lard or butter and stir in the sugar, vine fruits and peel together with the lemon zest. Stir in the lightly beaten eggs to form a soft dough.

Knead gently until smooth and then shape into 14 balls and place onto two lightly greased and floured baking sheets, allowing space between the cakes for them to expand.

Bake in the oven for approximately 25 minutes, or until the cakes are well-risen and golden brown.

Transfer them to a wire rack to cool. Best served slightly warm.

TEA CAKES

Made from sweetened milk dough, tea cakes are very much associated with Yorkshire high teas, and are still very popular and much eaten today. An old recipe, which was originally often made using barm, a raising agent made from a hop and potato mixture, (see the section on baking powder, yeasts etc, page 14).

The addition of currants and peel, enriches the mixture, which should be divided into generous rounds of about 10 cm to 13 cm/4 to 5 inches across and brushed with beaten egg and milk just before they have finished cooking, giving them their characteristic shiny glaze.

Tea cakes are best served thickly spread with butter.

450 g/1lb strong plain flour	1 egg
1 teaspoon salt	115 g/4 oz currants
50 g/2 oz lard	25 g/1 oz candied peel
25 g/1 oz fresh yeast	
Scant 300 ml/¹/2 pint tepid milk	**Glaze**
50 g/2 oz caster sugar	1 beaten egg and a little milk

Preheat the oven to 200°C/400°F/Gas Mark 6.

Sift the flour and salt into a large mixing bowl and rub in the lard. Dissolve the yeast in a little of the tepid milk, together with a teaspoon of sugar and set aside for 20 minutes.

Add the yeast mixture and beaten egg to the flour; kneading until smooth, this will take about 5 minutes. Add the currants and peel, knead again lightly.

Cover and put in a warm place until doubled in size. Knead again and divide into 10 cm/4 inch rounds, placing them on a greased baking sheet and pricking them with a fork. Leave to double in size.

Bake in the oven for around 20 minutes, then remove and brush the top with a little beaten egg and milk and return to the oven to glaze.

Cool on a wire rack. Best eaten on the day of baking.

WHETSTONE CAKES

LEICESTERSHIRE   *Makes about 12 squares*

Rather like the Biddenden Maids Cakes, the Whetstone Cakes are biscuit-like in texture, indeed they can be very crisp.

Like so many of the cakes of the 18th century, they contained caraway seed which gave them the strong spicy flavour so popular during that period.

I have been unable to find any being made in our home county at the present time and the village of Whetstone does not record them but perhaps printing this recipe will begin a revival, although I must warn you that they are rather hard, so do not over bake. However the result was very pleasing and worth trying if you enjoy the flavour of caraway and are looking for something a little different.

275 g/10 oz plain flour
275 g/10 oz pale soft brown sugar

1 teaspoon caraway seeds
2 large eggs

Preheat the oven to 160°C/325°F/Gas Mark 3.

In a medium sized bowl, sift the flour and add the sugar and caraway seeds, stirring thoroughly.

Beat the eggs in a small jug and pour into the mixture, stirring until a soft dough is formed.

Roll the dough out on a lightly floured surface, and cut into squares approximately 7.5 cm/3 inches x 7.5 cm/3 inches. Using a spatula transfer squares carefully onto a greased and lightly floured baking tray and place in the centre of the oven, baking for about 10 to 15 minutes or until very pale brown.

Remove the tray from the oven and allow cakes to rest for about 5 minutes before carefully lifting onto a wire cooling rack.

PEMBROKESHIRE BUNS

WALES

Currant fruit buns which were popular throughout Wales, seem in particular to be connected with New Year Celebrations in the lovely county of Pembrokeshire and so whilst very similar to Welsh Buns, these became known as Pembrokeshire Buns.

450 g/1 lb plain flour
25 g/1 oz butter or lard
25 g/1 oz caster sugar
50 g/2 oz currants

25 g/1 oz fresh yeast
1 teaspoon caster sugar
300ml/^{1}/2 pint tepid milk

Preheat the oven to 200°C/400°F/Gas Mark 6.

Sift the flour into a large bowl and rub in the butter or lard. Stir in the caster sugar and currants.

In a small bowl cream the yeast with the teaspoon of caster sugar and add the tepid milk, stirring well. Set aside in a warm place for 10 minutes to become frothy.

Stir the yeast mixture into the flour until a soft dough is formed. Turn onto a lightly floured surface and knead gently until it becomes soft and springy, about 5 minutes.

Divide into 12 evenly sized pieces and place onto two greased baking sheets, setting aside in a warm place to double in size. About 30 minutes.

Bake in the oven for 15 minutes or until golden and well risen.

Remove from the oven and transfer the buns onto a wire cooling rack.

Serve split with butter and jam or honey.

LONDON BUNS

Makes 12

The somewhat shrouded history of the London Bun had a shred of light thrown on it by Elizabeth David who believed it could have been the name given to the one million Bath Buns sold at the Great Exhibition in London 1851. Certainly I can find no mention of them earlier, although Bath Buns with a similar recipe go back further.

Mrs Elizabeth Raffald in her famous cookery book of 1890 gives a recipe for Bath Buns, which have a strong resemblance to the London Bun recipes found in more modern books, complete with caraway seeds.

However London Buns are rarely, if ever baked nowadays, due possibly to the dwindling enthusiasm for caraway seeds, which were once so very popular and appeared so often in old cake recipes. Interestingly, several years ago I came across an almost identical recipe for London Buns but without caraway seeds, in an American cookery book.

Recently, a friend lent me a delightful handwritten cookery book of 1923, which had belonged to his mother and to my delight I came across a recipe for London Buns, but without the caraway seeds of the very old recipes, rather confirming my thoughts that the Buns changed as the liking for this spice dwindled.

450 g/1 lb strong plain flour	50 g/2 oz currants
1 teaspoon salt	50 g/2 oz chopped candied peel
15 g/^{1}/2 oz fresh yeast	
75 g/3 oz caster sugar	**Topping**
100 ml/4 fl oz warm milk	1 egg, beaten
75 g/3 oz butter	1 teaspoon caraway seeds (optional)

Preheat the oven to 220°C/425°F/Gas Mark 7.

Sift the flour and salt into a large mixing bowl. Cream the yeast with the sugar and stir into the warm milk. Rub the butter into the flour and stir in the currants and candied peel. Pour on the milk and yeast, mixing well. Turn onto a floured surface and knead until the dough becomes smooth and elastic.

Place in a clean bowl, cover and leave in a warm place until doubled in size, then knead for a few minutes and divide into 12 evenly sized pieces. Roll into neat balls and place on a floured baking sheet, leaving for a further 30 minutes until well risen. Brush with the beaten egg and sprinkle with the caraway seeds. Bake in the oven for 15 to 20 minutes until risen and golden. Cool on a wire rack.

MAIDS OF HONOUR

SURREY   *Makes 12 tarts*

Whilst the story has many variations, the most agreeable is that these little tarts originated in Richmond, Surrey during the reign of Henry VIII, who lived in Richmond Palace. Henry was said to have been inspecting the palace kitchens when he came upon a cook trying out a new cake recipe. Tasting one, he liked it so much that he asked his 'Maids of Honour' to see that the cakes were added to the palace menu. Eventually, the secret recipe was passed to a baker in Richmond and finally to a shop in Kew where they can still be enjoyed either in the teashop or bought and taken home.

Whilst the recipe remains a closely guarded secret, the following will produce a very similar delicious little tart and was one of my grandmother's favourite recipes; the result is not dissimilar to an almond cheesecake.

225 g/8 oz Flaky Pastry (see page 30)	2 eggs
225 g/8 oz curd cheese, sieved	1 tablespoon brandy
75 g/3 oz butter	25 g/1 oz ground almonds
25 g/1 oz caster sugar	25 g/1 oz nibbed almonds

Preheat the oven to 220°C/425°F/Gas Mark 7.

Cream the sieved curd cheese and butter together with the sugar until light and smooth. Whisk the eggs, adding the brandy and stirring constantly, add to the curd mixture. Add the ground and nibbed almonds, stirring to ensure they are evenly folded in.

Roll the flaky pastry thinly and cut out 12 circles, placing them in a lightly greased bun tin, pressing the pastry down into each section. Half fill each pastry case with the curd mixture.

Bake in the centre of the oven for 15 to 20 minutes or until golden and firm when pressed lightly in the centre.

Remove and cool on a wire rack.

LLANDDAROG FAIR CAKES

WALES   ***Makes about 12***

Llanddarog was *en route* to the English markets and drovers enjoyed these little 'Fairing' Cakes, made with beer which were part of the tradition of many markets and fairs (see page 159). They often contained ginger, but these little cakes were topped with currants and sultanas instead.

175 g/6 oz self raising flour	2 tablespoons strong beer
75 g/3 oz caster sugar	A few currants and sultanas
115 g/4 oz butter	

Preheat the oven to 190°C/375°F/Gas Mark 5.

Mix flour and sugar together, rub in butter to resemble breadcrumbs. Add the beer and mix to a soft dough, adding a little extra beer if necessary. Roll out to 5 mm/¹/₄ inch thick on a floured surface and cut into squares of equal size.

Dot with currants and sultanas, place on a floured baking tray and cook in the centre of the oven until golden brown – about 15 minutes.

Lift carefully onto a wire rack and leave to cool.

IRISH FADGE CAKES   ***Makes 8***

Widely baked throughout Ireland, but in particular Northern Ireland, Fadge Cakes are traditionally made using mashed potato. I have seen a recipe, which did not use potato, but I do think that the unique character would be lost.

There may be people who consider it a mistake putting these into a cake book, but I must defend myself by saying that in every Irish cookery book, they seem to be in the cake section.

225 g/8 oz warm cooked potatoes	50 g/2 oz plain flour
¹/₂ teaspoon salt	25 g/1 oz pinhead oatmeal (optional)
25 g/1 oz butter	

In a medium bowl, mash the potatoes well, adding the salt and butter. Add the flour a little at a time, beating well to avoid lumps, finally adding the oatmeal, if liked.

Roll on a lightly floured board, into the 18 cm/7 inch circles about 1 cm/¹/₂ inch thick, marking each into 4 triangles.

Place on a lightly buttered griddle, which has been heated until the fat is just beginning to sputter and cook, browning on each side. Best served whilst warm.

ABERFFRAW CAKES/*Teisen 'Berffro*

WALES   ***Makes about 12***

Aberffraw, on the Isle of Anglesey, was once the home of Welsh princes and during the 6th century the home of the King of Gwynedd, the palace remaining standing until 1316, when it was demolished to help repair Caernarfon Castle. Another tale attached to this magical area was that a cave to the north of the village was said to contain treasure, having been the hiding place of King Arthur so I suppose this could have been where he canoodled with Guinevere.

Aberffraw Cakes are rich and buttery and are still being baked today in the small village overlooking the sea, tradition setting down that they would have been baked in scallop shells. I doubt that you will be able to obtain enough shells to continue the tradition, but the cakes will be no less delicious if you use a cutter instead.

175 g/6 oz butter
175 g/6 oz caster sugar
175 g/8 oz self raising flour

Topping
Caster sugar

Preheat the oven to 160°C/325°F/Gas Mark 3.

Cream together the butter and sugar until pale and creamy.

Sift the flour before adding slowly to the butter mix, stirring to form a soft dough.

On a lightly floured board, roll the dough out to about 1 cm/¹⁄₂ inch thick before cutting into 5 cm/2 inch rounds with a plain cutter.

Place the cakes on a lightly greased baking tray and place in the centre of the oven for 10 to 15 minutes or until golden brown.

When baked, lift them carefully onto a wire rack to cool and then sprinkle with caster sugar before serving.

When researching some of the very many excellent large regional cakes to be found throughout the British Isles, the biggest problem was tracing their ancestry. Often it was quite simple, but many times I found an interesting story, which has been impossible to back up in library reference books or old cookery books, and it becomes difficult to know quite what to believe. I have therefore tried always to have confirmation of any stories attached to a particular cake and have not included any information that I did not feel confident about, however much fun it sounded.

The number of recipes, which featured caraway seeds, a spice so widely used in the 16th and 17th centuries, that almost every bread or cake seemed to include a large quantity, simply amazed me. Nowadays caraway is much less popular, but I would still contend that used cautiously, it is a delightful, aromatic spice, which adds something a little different to a plain cake or teacake.

The idea of holiday makers from Lancashire packing a Rossendale Sad Cake into their luggage, when they went on holiday to Blackpool would seem rather unlikely in today's take-away consumer society, but it is nonetheless perfectly illustrative of the importance of simple well prepared food in every day life. Although I admit to finding the alternative name of 'Desolate Cakes' for these cakes, less than appealing for something taken on what is supposed to be a jolly holiday by the sea.

I have absolutely no doubt that among the recipes in this chapter you will find many which will appeal and hopefully enable compliments to be paid to the baker for their attempts to revive many of the lesser-known recipes. Some of the larger griddle cakes are seldom made today, although once so very popular. Sadly, the griddle is an uncommon item in the average household, which is a shame as they are great fun to cook on, and though we may not be using them over an open hearth, they can be used on the average oven top to bake cakes with evocative names such as Cornish Heavy Cake. Griddles have, however, remained rather more popular in the North and in Scotland where there are so many wonderful down-to-earth recipes.

So I hope that like me, you will find the following section will prove not only interesting but inspirational. Certainly my griddle, stored by the Aga in my kitchen, receives frequent employment.

LARGE
REGIONAL CAKES

BLACK BUN

SCOTLAND   *Serves 8-10*

One of my most happy memories of living in Scotland was Hogmanay, 31st December – 'First Footing' being an essential part of the festive celebrations. A tall dark stranger bearing a lump of coal, must be the first over the doorstep, in order to ensure good luck for the coming year and he in turn should be greeted with a dram of whisky and a slice of Black Bun. Formerly served at Twelfth Night, the cake became known as 'Scottish Christmas Bun' although this was eventually shortened to Black Bun.

It is a very rich dark fruitcake, encased in short crust pastry, and is really quite delicious. Stored in greaseproof paper and foil, until fully matured, it will keep well for up to five months.

350 g/12 oz Shortcrust Pastry (see page 21)	350 g/12 oz sultanas
	350 g/12 oz currants
Filling	115 g/4 oz chopped glace peel
225 g/8 oz plain flour	115 g/4 oz pale muscovado sugar
1 teaspoon bicarbonate soda	115 g/4 oz blanched chopped almonds
1 teaspoon mixed spice	5 tablespoons milk
1 teaspoon ground ginger	1 egg
1 teaspoon ground cinnamon	2 tablespoons whisky
1 teaspoon ground mace	
1 teaspoon baking powder	**Glaze**
115 g/4 oz raisins	1 beaten egg

Preheat the oven to 180°C/350°F/Gas Mark 4.

Grease a 20 cm/8 inch loose-bottomed round cake tin and rolling out two thirds of the pastry into a large circle, line the bottom and sides, carefully pressing it into the corners. Place the tin into the refrigerator, together with the remaining pastry wrapped in cling film, ready to use for the lid, while you make the filling.

Sift the flour, bicarbonate of soda, spices and baking powder into a bowl and add the fruit, sugar and chopped nuts, stirring thoroughly.

Pour in the milk, add the lightly beaten egg and finally the whisky. Then using a pallet knife stir the mixture until it forms a pliable dough.

Spoon the mixture into the lined pastry case, pressing down carefully with your fingers, to ensure there are no gaps in the corners, finally smoothing the top. Roll the remaining pastry into a circle of approximately 23 cm/8 inches, dampen the edges with water and place over the fruit, sealing together with finger and thumb, to produce a fluted edge.

Glaze the top of the pastry cake with the beaten egg and make two or three holes in the surface, using a skewer. Bake in the oven for 2¹/₂ to 3 hours, covering the top with brown paper if the cake begins to darken too quickly.

Remove from the oven and leave the cake for at least 1 hour before removing carefully from the tin and lifting onto a wire rack to become completely cold.

WHITSUN CAKE

LINCOLNSHIRE

Serves approximately 8-10 slices

Most festivals have their own speciality foods and Whitsun is no different. The Lincolnshire Whitsun Cake bears a strong similarity to the Plum Bread always so popular in this area of Eastern England, except that the fruit is layered in the centre.

15 g/¹/2 oz yeast	1 teaspoon ground mixed spice
1 teaspoon caster sugar	115 g/4 oz raisins
150 ml/¹/4 pint tepid milk	115 g/4 oz currants
450 g/1 lb strong wholemeal flour	50 g/2 oz chopped mixed peel
50 g/2 oz lard	1 egg
50 g/2 oz butter	
225 g/8 oz dark muscovado sugar	**Topping**
115 g/4 oz butter	A little milk or egg wash

Preheat the oven to 190°C/375°F/Gas Mark 5.

Cream the sugar and yeast together, add the tepid milk, stirring thoroughly and then set aside.

Rub the butter and lard into the flour to form fine breadcrumbs and then pour on the yeasted milk, beating with your hand until it forms a soft smooth dough. Cover with a clean cloth and set aside to double in size – about 1 hour.

Put all the remaining ingredients (except the egg) into a medium saucepan and place over a low heat until the butter and sugar has melted, stirring frequently. Set aside to cool and then beat in the egg thoroughly.

Grease a square 18 cm/7 inch cake tin and divide the dough into three sections, rolling each into 18 cm/7 inch squares. Place one into the bottom of the cake tin.

Spoon half the fruit mixture on to the top of the dough base, leaving a gap of 1 cm/¹/2 inch around the edges. Cover with a second square of dough and spoon the remaining fruit on top, finishing by placing the third dough square on top.

Press the edges down as firmly as possible forming a fluted pattern around the edge. Brush the top with the milk or egg wash and place in the oven for 35-40 minutes or until golden and well risen.

Allow to cool in the tin for 20 minutes before running a sharp knife around the edge and turning the cake onto a wire rack to cool.

The cake will keep well for several days wrapped in foil.

PLATE CAKE/*Teisen Lap*

Serves 6-8

It is difficult to pick up a Welsh cookery book without finding a recipe for this most famous of Welsh cakes and probably even harder to find a Welsh kitchen where one has not been baked.

A lightly fruited moist cake traditionally baked on an enamel plate, or very shallow dish, 'lap' being Welsh for plate.

225 g/8 oz self raising flour	50 g/2 oz currants
1/2 level teaspoon nutmeg	115 g/4 oz soft brown sugar
115 g/4 oz butter	2 eggs, lightly beaten
50 g/2 oz raisins	150 ml/1/4 pint single cream or milk

Preheat the oven to 180°C/350°F/Gas Mark 4.

Sieve the flour and nutmeg into a bowl; rub in the butter to breadcrumb consistency.

Add the fruit and sugar stirring well with a pallet knife. Pour in the eggs and cream or milk, mixing to form a soft dough.

Grease a 18 cm/7 inch enamel plate or shallow dish and lift the dough into the middle, pressing it to the outer edges. Bake in the oven for approximately 30 minutes or until pale golden brown and firm to touch. Cover the top if the cake begins to brown too much, reducing the oven temperature to 100°C/212°F/Gas Mark 3.

Best eaten the same day and served whilst slightly warm.

FOUR O'CLOCK CAKE

SUFFOLK   ***Serves 8***

Traditionally baked for farm workers to eat during their four o'clock tea break, I have found this recipe baked as both an individual cake or, as in the following recipe, a cake to spread with butter. Originally made with lard and with the simple addition of currants, the recipe gradually came to include butter rather than all lard and a wider variety of vine fruits. But the spice used was always quite dominant and gave the cake an aroma which was doubtless welcome and appetising for hungry workers during the long afternoons.

900 g/2 lb plain flour	175g/6 oz butter or lard
$^1/_2$ teaspoon salt	175 g/6 oz currants
2 teaspoons mixed spice	175 g/6 oz sultanas or raisins
100 g/4 oz soft pale brown sugar	2 eggs, lightly beaten
25 g/1 oz fresh yeast	
1 teaspoon caster sugar	**Topping**
300 ml/$^1/_2$ pint tepid milk	Caster sugar

Preheat the oven to 200°C/400°F/Gas Mark 6.

Sift the flour, salt and spice into a large bowl and stir in the sugar.

In a separate small bowl cream the yeast and teaspoon of caster sugar, adding the tepid milk. Stir and set aside for 10 minutes for a light froth to form.

Add the butter or lard to the flour mixture, rubbing it in thoroughly until it resembles fine breadcrumbs.

Stir in the currants, sultanas or raisins and then the two lightly beaten eggs. Finally pour in the yeast mixture stirring until a dough is formed. Then with your hands knead the cake mix until a ball forms and lift it onto a lightly floured surface.

Knead thoroughly and then return to a clean bowl, cover with a cloth and leave in a warm place to double in size. About 30 to 40 minutes.

Meanwhile grease a 900 g/2 lb loaf tin.

When the dough is risen, knead again and place in the loaf tin, setting it aside to rise for a further 30 minutes, by which time the dough will have reached the top of the tin. Brush a little water over the top of the cake and lightly dredge with a little caster sugar. Bake in the oven for 45 minutes or until the cake is well risen and golden brown.

Remove from the oven and turn onto a wire rack to cool.

Serve sliced and buttered – preferably at 4 o'clock in the afternoon with a steaming mug of tea.

IRISH WHISKEY CAKE

IRELAND   *Serves 10*

A familiar sight at teatime in Ireland, Whiskey Cake, sometimes drizzled on top with a little orange or lemon icing, was traditional shooting party fayre during country weekends. On a recent trip to Connemara I found and tasted plenty of Whiskey Cakes, so they are clearly still great favourites in Ireland.

As always with 'traditional' cakes, several versions of the recipe exist, sometimes using orange rather than lemon, often leaving the top unadorned, but this light cake only ever contains sultanas, never peel or currants, sultanas combining very well with the whiskey.

The following recipe is an excellent variation.

225 g/8 oz sultanas	**Topping**
3 tablespoons Irish whiskey	Juice of large lemon
Grated rind of 1 large lemon	225 g/8 oz icing sugar
175 g/6 oz butter	
175 g/6 oz pale brown sugar	
225 g/8 oz self raising flour	
3 eggs, lightly beaten	

Preheat the oven to 180°C/350°F/Gas Mark 4.

Put the sultanas into a small bowl, add finely grated rind of the lemon stirring well and reserving the lemon for juicing. Spoon over the whiskey and stir again. Cover and leave to stand overnight.

Next day cream the butter and sugar until light and fluffy, add the eggs and flour alternately, beating thoroughly between each addition.

Fold the whiskey fruit into the mixture gently, using a metal spoon.

Spoon the cake mixture into a 18 cm/7 inch greased and lined round cake tin and bake in the oven for approximately 1 hour or until the cake is well-risen, golden brown and firm to the touch.

Cool in the tin for 20 minutes before turning onto a wire rack.

When cold, juice the lemon and mix the lemon juice with enough icing sugar to form a thick pouring consistency and drizzle it gently over the top of the cake. Leave to set before serving.

BARMBRACK

IRELAND   *Makes 2 loaves, each serves 6-8*

This most famous of Irish cakes, derives its name 'barm' from bairm or beorma meaning ale yeast and 'brack' meaning speckled or spotted. Nobody would argue that this fruited tea cake lives up to its name perfectly.

Several varieties emerged with bakers often having their favourite recipe, and the connection with Halloween when 'charms' may be added to the mixture, is without doubt a delightful legend.

Widely available through Ireland, Barmbrack is eaten sliced and buttered and may be baked either in a loaf tin or formed into a round and baked on a baking tray.

25 g/1 oz fresh yeast	150 g/6 oz sultanas
1 teaspoon caster sugar	150 g/6 oz currants
300 ml/^{1}/2 pint tepid milk	50 g/2 oz chopped mixed peel
450 g/1 lb strong white flour	1 egg, lightly beaten
^{1}/2 teaspoon ground cinnamon	
^{1}/2 teaspoon mixed spice	**Glaze**
Pinch salt	50 g/2 oz sugar
50 g/2 oz butter	2 tablespoons water
50 g/2 oz sugar	

Preheat the oven to 180°C/350°F/Gas Mark 4.

In a small bowl, cream the yeast with the teaspoon of caster sugar, add the tepid milk and stir thoroughly. Set aside.

Sift the flour, spices and salt into a bowl and rub in the butter. Stir in the fruits and making a well in the centre, pour in the yeast mixture and the egg, stirring with a pallet knife.

On a lightly floured board, knead the dough thoroughly until light and springy and then place in a clean bowl, cover with a clean dry cloth and set in a warm place for 1 hour. Knead again for a short time and then divide into two, placing each piece of dough in a greased 900 g/2 lb loaf tin and leave uncovered in a warm place to double in size.

Bake in the oven for 50-60 minutes or until golden brown and a skewer inserted into the centre comes out cleanly.

Meanwhile, in a small saucepan, boil together the sugar and water for 2 minutes and when the cakes are removed from the oven brush lightly with the glaze.

Turn out and cool on a wire rack.

HUISH CAKE

WALES Serves 6-8

Made with ground rice, the history of this cake is unclear, but it was certainly considered a treat eaten for Sunday tea, with its rich buttery colour and flavour enhanced by lemon zest.

Another popular alternative was to add a little caraway seed, just before baking. I read recently that originally the cake had been served as a baby's Christening cake, but I have been unsuccessful in confirming this.

The cake remains popular in Wales, although it is rarely made with caraway seeds, relying on lemon zest to add a more delicate flavour.

115 g/4 oz butter	175 g/6 oz self raising flour
175 g/6 oz caster sugar	115 g/4 oz ground rice
Zest of one large lemon	2 tablespoons milk
4 egg yolks	

Preheat the oven to 180°C/350°F/Gas Mark 4.

Cream the butter and sugar until pale and fluffy, adding the lemon zest. Beat in the egg yolks, one at a time, adding a little flour if they start to curdle.

Stir in the remaining flour and ground rice, together with the milk.

Spoon into a greased and lined 15 cm/6 inch cake tin and bake in the oven for 50 to 60 minutes or until it is well risen, golden brown and a skewer inserted into the centre comes out cleanly.

Remove from the oven and allow to cool in the tin for 20 minutes before turning carefully onto a wire cooling rack.

NORFOLK SPONGE CAKE

NORFOLK   *Serves approximately 10*

Whilst I have seen this cake recorded as a Norfolk Sponge Cake, I have also found the recipe dating back many years, set down as simply an alternative sponge cake.

However the recipe does make an excellent sponge, being particularly suitable as a base for fruit and cream and is ideal for making a flan case.

275 g/10 oz granulated sugar
300 ml/¹/₂ pint water
6 egg yolks

4 egg whites
Zest of one orange
225 g/8 oz plain flour

Preheat the oven to 180°C/350°F/Gas Mark 4.

In a medium sized saucepan, dissolve the sugar in the water, bringing to the boil. Boil for 6 minutes or until the thread stage is reached – if you prefer to use a jam thermometer the temperature should be 110°C/215°F. Skim and leave to cool slightly.

Put the egg whites and yolks into a bowl and whisking continuously, add the sugar syrup in a slow steady stream. The mixture will eventually thicken, taking about ten minutes to reach this stage. Very gently, using a large metal spoon, fold in the sifted flour and zest of orange. Take care to ensure that the mixture remains lump free.

Pour the cake mix into a greased and lined 18 cm/7 inch cake tin and bake in the oven for 1¹/₄ hours or until well risen and the sponge has shrunk away slightly from the edge of the tin. The sponge will feel firm when lightly pressed.

Turn onto a wire rack to cool.

This cake is best eaten within a day of baking. Use as required, either split in half and sandwich with jam and cream or topped with fruit.

OXFORD SPICED FRUIT CAKE   *Serves 8-10*

Despite coming across this cake in a modern cookery book, I have failed entirely to establish its existence and even the most helpful of reference library staff in Oxford were unable to find any recipes or even a mention of such a cake, the nearest being an Oxford Plum Cake.

However, one of the many idiosyncrasies in life is illustrated by the fact that I came across the Oxford Spiced Fruit Cake, many, many times in bakeries and on supermarket cake shelves in Ireland. So we can smile again knowing that they do at least exist, if not in Oxford.

A dark, moist, lightly fruited cake, the following recipe is based on a cake bought in Ireland and a helpful baker.

150 g/5 oz butter	Zest of 1 lemon
150 g/5 oz dark brown sugar	A little milk, if necessary
250 g/9 oz self raising flour	115 g/4 oz raisins
1 teaspoon mixed spice	50 g/2 oz currants
1/4 teaspoon salt	50 g/2 oz sultanas
2 eggs, beaten lightly	50 g/2 oz chopped mixed peel
2 tablespoons black treacle	

Preheat the oven to 160°C/325°F/Gas Mark 3.

Cream the butter and sugar. Sift the flour, spice and salt and add alternately with the beaten egg to the butter mixture, beating until smooth. Stir in the black treacle and lemon zest. Add a little milk if necessary to give a dropping consistency.

Stir in the fruit and peel and spoon the mixture into a greased and lined 18 cm/7 inch cake tin and bake in the oven for approximately 1 1/2 hours. Cover the top with brown paper if the cake begins to darken too quickly.

When the cake is well-risen and firm to touch, a skewer inserted into the centre should come out cleanly.

Allow to cool before turning onto a wire rack.

GRASMERE CAKE

CUMBRIA   *Serves 6-8*

Several very good fruit cake recipes originated from this area, all slightly different, often with unusual ingredients, the egg-less Grasmere fruit cake for example being made with soured milk or buttermilk.

Baked in a loaf tin, the Grasmere Cake is an excellent, easy to make, weekend cake.

450 g/1 lb plain wholemeal flour
1 level teaspoon mixed spice
225 g/8 oz butter
225 g/8 oz soft brown sugar

350 g/12 oz sultanas
1 1/2 level teaspoons bicarbonate soda
450 ml/3/4 pint soured milk or buttermilk

Preheat the oven to 160°C/325°F/Gas Mark 3.

Sift the flour and spice into a large bowl and rub in the butter until it resembles fine breadcrumbs.

Stir in the other dry ingredients and mix with enough soured milk or buttermilk to form a dropping consistency.

Cover the bowl with greaseproof paper, tucking in the edges and leave over night in a cool place.

Spoon the mixture into a greased and lined 900 g/2 lb loaf tin and bake in the oven for 1 1/2 to 2 hours or until the cake feels firm to touch when pressed.

Allow to cool in the tin before turning onto a wire rack to become cold.

Can be served sliced and buttered if liked.

DUNDEE CAKE

SCOTLAND   *Serves 8-10*

This cake has great sentimental value for me. When I was a child, my Granny Bristow used to bake a Dundee Cake as a 'special occasion treat' and it was the first cake I baked when I had progressed from licking the bowl and stirring the mixture. It is little wonder that I feel great affection for these delicious cakes.

The history of this famous Scottish fruit cake is a little hazy, even in Dundee. It does seem however, to be linked to Keiller's Marmalade Factory, who it is said, devised the recipe in the 18th century as a way of using some of their surplus orange peel.

The illustrious Scottish cook, Katie Stewart believes however, that the cake is even older, dating from the 17th century, when bakers created a cake for Mary Queen of Scots, who it is said disliked cherries, hence the almond-topped Dundee Cake we know today.

What is beyond dispute however is that a Dundee Cake, which should never contain cherries, but is made with the zest of orange and glace orange peel, is an absolutely delicious, light fruit cake which would grace the tea table in any home.

150 g/6 oz softened butter	115 g/4 oz raisins
150 g/6 oz pale muscovado sugar	50 g/2 oz currants
150 g/6 oz plain flour	50 g/2 oz chopped candied orange peel
1 teaspoon baking powder	Grated zest of 1 orange
1 teaspoon mixed spice (optional)	1 tablespoon of brandy or sherry (optional)
4 large eggs	
50 g/2 oz ground almonds	**Topping**
175 g/6 oz sultanas	18-20 whole blanched almonds

Preheat the oven to 160°C/325°F/Gas Mark 2.

Cream the butter and sugar together until light and fluffy.

Sift together the flour, baking powder and spice. Beat the eggs in a jug and add the eggs and flour mixture alternately to the creamed butter and sugar, mixing slowly.

Stir in the ground almonds, fruit, peel and zest, using a large metal spoon. Finally add the brandy or sherry. The mixture will be a soft consistency.

You will need an 18 cm/7 inch round cake tin greased and lined. Spoon the cake mix into the prepared tin, smoothing the top and arrange the whole blanched almonds in neat circles.

Place onto the lower shelf of the oven, and bake for about 2 hours. Turn the oven down to 140°C/275°F/Gas Mark 1 for a further hour or until the cake is firm to touch and a skewer inserted into the centre comes out cleanly.

Leave to cool in the tin for one hour before carefully turning out onto a wire rack.

DRIPPING CAKE

LINCOLNSHIRE   *Serves approximately 12*

Like many country recipes, the actual history of the Dripping Cake is something we can only guess at. However, like other dripping cakes it is certainly a very old recipe, which has several variations, all of which are spicy, generously fruited and baked in a square tin.

Cut into squares or sliced and buttered, it would have been packed into workers lunch boxes or eaten with a hot mug of tea. No longer for the health conscious – it is despite that, rather good.

450 g/1 lb plain flour	50 g/2 oz currants
1 teaspoon mixed spice	75 g/3 oz chopped candied peel
1 level teaspoon bicarbonate soda	175 g/6 oz dripping
1/4 teaspoon salt	175 g/6 oz dark brown sugar
300 ml/1/2 pint milk	2 eggs, lightly beaten
175 g/6 oz raisins	

Preheat the oven to 180°C/350°F/Gas Mark 4.

Sift the flour, spice, bicarbonate of soda and salt into a bowl, making a well in the centre.

Warm the milk gently and add the fruits, peel, dripping and sugar, stir over a low heat until the dripping and sugar have melted. Remove from the heat and leave to cool slightly, before pouring into the flour and adding the lightly beaten eggs. Stir well until fully blended.

Pour immediately into an 20 cm/8 inch greased and lined square cake tin and bake in the centre of the oven for 1 hour, reducing the temperature to 160°C/325°F/Gas Mark 3 for a further 45 minutes or until well risen and firm to touch.

Allow to cool in its tin.

ROSSENDALE SAD CAKE

LANCASHIRE   *Serves 6-8*

The older inhabitants know the Rossendale area of Lancashire as 'sad cake land'. These traditional currant and pastry cakes, which were served buttered, were said to have been taken to Blackpool by the people of Rossendale for their summer holidays as part of their luggage.

A second version of the sad cake, with no sugar or currants, was baked in a flat tin and eaten covered in butter and syrup or jam. I understand that Sad Cakes were also sometimes called Desolate Cakes, all in all not a very cheery teatime subject.

The following recipe is the rather more interesting currant version, but although I have used butter, it is important to note that the original recipes would have used suet or lard, which you may of course substitute for the butter if you wish to be more authentic.

450 g/1 lb plain flour
1/4 teaspoon salt
225 g/8 oz butter, or lard or suet
50 g/2 oz caster sugar

50 g/2 oz currants
A little water to mix

Preheat the oven to 200°C/400°F/Gas Mark 6.

Sift the flour and salt into a bowl and rub in the fat to form a breadcrumb texture. Using a pallet knife, stir in the sugar and currants, together with enough water to form soft dough.

Roll into a large round, and place on a greased baking tray. Bake in the oven. When risen and golden brown, about 20 to 25 minutes, remove and allow to cool a little on a wire rack.

Serve slightly warm with unsalted butter.

MADEIRA CAKE

AVON AND SOMERSET   *Serves 8*

Madeira Cake is a simple light textured cake, enhanced by the addition of a little grated lemon peel.

Originally devised in the 19th century as an accompaniment to fortified sweet white wine, it is believed to have originated in Bristol, historically an important centre for wine to which names such as Bristol Cream and Bristol Milk testify.

Perfect for afternoon tea on warm summer days, it is perhaps best eaten accompanied by a glass of the Madeira wine from which it takes its name.

175 g/6 oz butter
175 g/6 oz caster sugar
285 g/10 oz self-raising flour
4 large eggs, beaten
Finely grated rind of one small lemon

Topping
3 thin slices of lemon peel

Preheat the oven to 180°C/350°F/Gas Mark 4.

Cream butter and sugar together in a bowl, until fluffy. Add the flour and eggs gradually, beating well after each addition. Then fold in the grated lemon rind.

Spoon into a prepared 18 cm/7 inch round greased and lined cake tin and smooth the top. Place in the centre of the oven for 30 minutes, gently remove from the oven and working quickly, lay the citrus slices on top of the cake (I find the easiest kitchen tool to use is a potato peeler, which gives nice thin slices of the lemon rind) and return it to the oven. Bake for a further 30 minutes, checking occasionally until the cake is golden brown, well risen and firm when gently pressed on the top.

Remove from the oven and leave to cool in the tin for 10 minutes before turning out gently to cool on a wire rack.

CIDER CAKE

HEREFORDSHIRE   *Serves 8-10*

Like the Apple Cake of the West Country, Cider Cakes are most closely connected with the apple orchards of the South West and Herefordshire. During the 12th century, cider making, originally from France, was introduced into England. But it was not until the 17th century when John Viscount Scudamore increased production by improving the quality of apple tree stock and developed new varieties of cider apples, that cider-making became prolific.

The use of this most adaptable of alcoholic drinks includes meat dishes, puddings and cakes.

Like the cider apple itself, there are many varieties of cakes, including a Madeira type, which has no fruit but a little apple brandy added to the cider. However, my favourites are those with fruit, which has been steeped overnight in cider, giving a really moist aromatic finish to the cake.

225 g/8 oz sultanas	225 g/8 oz plain flour
50 g/2 oz chopped glace peel	1 teaspoon baking powder
150 ml/¼ pint cider	1 teaspoon mixed spice
175 g/6 oz butter	2 large eggs, lightly beaten
175 g/6 oz pale muscovado sugar	

Preheat the oven to 180°C/350°F/Gas Mark 4.

Place the sultanas and peel into a small bowl and pour over the cider, stirring well. Cover and leave overnight.

Cream the butter and sugar until light and fluffy. Sift the flour, baking powder and spice and together with the beaten eggs adding a little at a time, stir briskly until the mixture is smooth and evenly mixed.

Gently fold in the fruit with a metal spoon and turn into a greased and lined 18 cm/ 7 inch round cake tin.

Bake in the oven for 1 hour or until the cake is well risen and a skewer inserted into the centre, comes out cleanly.

Cool in the tin for 15 minutes, then turn carefully onto a wire rack to cool.

SODA CAKE

ISLE OF MAN   **Serves 6-8**

The first thing I noticed about this recipe was the close resemblance to the Welsh Bara Planc, or Bakestone Bread.

On the Isle of Man, like a lot of ancient recipes baked in rural cottages, the soda cake would have been cooked on a griddle, the most common method of cooking, placed on an iron tripod, called a 'croue', by an open fire. The fire would have been fed with gorse, which whilst providing adequate heat, had the benefit of being a smokeless fuel.

The simple ingredients belie the skill which would have been required to bake the perfect Soda Cake. Great care must be taken not to burn the cake, whilst ensuring that it is cooked right through to the middle, so a steady heat from the fire would have been essential.

Nowadays, it is of course possible to use a griddle on the hot plate of a cooker, which ensures greater control.

450 g/1 lb strong white flour	$^1/_2$ teaspoon cream of tartar
Good pinch salt	300 ml/$^1/_2$ pint buttermilk
1 teaspoon bicarbonate soda	50 g/2 oz sultanas (optional)

Sift the flour and salt into a bowl, making a well in the centre.

Add the buttermilk to the bicarbonate of soda and cream of tartar, stirring well.

Pour liquid into the well in the flour, stirring with a pallet knife until a soft dough is formed. Turn onto a floured board and knead gently until smooth. Add the sultanas if desired.

Shape into a ball and roll out to a 5 cm/2 inch thick round.

Grease the griddle and set to a medium heat, place the soda cake onto the griddle and bake until brown, turning over carefully using a spatula, to cook the other side. Practice will be needed to make the perfect Soda Cake but it is well worth the trial and error for the sense of satisfaction which will be felt.

If preferred the Soda Cake may be baked on a greased baking sheet and put into a preheated oven to 180°C/350°F/Gas Mark 6 for approximately 30 minutes. Remove and allow to cool on a wire rack.

Soda cakes should be split and buttered before serving. They are excellent served with jam or honey.

SODA CAKE

SOMERSET *Serves 8–10*

A rather plain 'week day' cake of which there are several versions, including currants and almonds, or my personal favourite, cherries. But to be fair my husband Malcolm thinks this cake makes a great change from the rich sponges and fruit cakes so often baked.

Traditionally made with lard or dripping, they are vastly improved by using butter instead.

115 g/4 oz butter, lard or dripping	2 large eggs, beaten
175 g/6 oz caster sugar	450 g/1 lb plain flour
1 teaspoon bicarbonate soda	115 g/4 oz glace cherries
150 ml/¼ pint milk	75 g/3 oz chopped mixed peel

Preheat the oven to 160°C/325°F/Gas Mark 3.

Cream the butter and sugar until light and fluffy. Dissolve the bicarbonate of soda in the milk and beaten eggs, and working quickly stir together with the flour into the butter mixture. Add the halved, washed and dried cherries and the mixed peel, folding in gently with a metal spoon.

Pour into a greased and lined 18 cm/7 inch cake tin and bake in the oven for 1½ hours or until well risen, and the top when lightly pressed, feels firm to touch.

Remove from the oven and allow to cool in the tin for 20 minutes before turning onto a wire rack.

SODA CAKE/*Teisen Soda Gymreig*

WALES   ***Serves 8***

Always simple cakes, soda cakes are traditional country cakes, which like the Isle of Man Cake and the Somerset Soda Cake are made with bicarbonate of soda as the raising agent.

225 g/8 oz plain flour	175 g/6 oz sultanas
1/2 teaspoon cinnamon	150 ml/1/4 pint milk
1/2 teaspoon nutmeg	1 egg, lightly beaten
115 g/4 oz butter	1 level teaspoon bicarbonate soda
115 g/4 oz caster sugar	

Preheat the oven to 180°C/350°F/Gas Mark 4.

Sift the flour and spices into a large bowl and rub in the butter until it forms the texture of fine breadcrumbs. Stir in the sugar and sultanas.

Lightly beat the egg into the milk and add the bicarbonate of soda. Working quickly, stir the liquid into the dry ingredients to form a soft mixture. Spoon immediately into a greased and lined 18 cm/7 inch cake tin and put into the centre of the oven. Bake until well risen and golden brown, turning down the heat slightly if the cake begins to brown too much. When the cake is firm and a skewer inserted into the centre comes out cleanly, about 1 hour, remove from the oven and allow to cool for 30 minutes before removing gently from the tin and leaving to become completely cold on a cooling rack.

Best eaten within 2 days of baking.

PITCAITHLY BANNOCK

SCOTLAND   *Approximately 16 portions*

'Bannock' is a Scottish word describing a variety of large cakes all of which are circular in shape.

The Pitcaithly Bannock most closely resembles a thick round shortbread baked with almonds and glace peel and is a thoroughly delicious cake, well worth making.

175 g/6 oz butter	50 g/2 oz ground rice
115 g/4 oz caster sugar	50 g/2 oz flaked almonds
225 g/8 oz plain flour	25 g/1 oz chopped mixed peel

Preheat the oven to 160°C/325°F/Gas Mark 3.

Cream the butter and sugar together and slowly add the flour and ground rice, mixing together until a dough is formed. Add the almonds and peel, kneading gently. Roll into a ball.

Grease two baking trays and divide the dough evenly, forming two large circles, at least 2$^{1}/_{2}$ cm/1 inch thick. Prick the top gently with a fork and bake in the oven for about 20 to 25 minutes or until pale golden brown.

Allow to cool before lifting carefully with a spatula onto a wire rack.

CHOCOLATE CAKE

Serves 10

Once you have read through the ingredients you will quickly realise that this is not 'just another chocolate cake'. It is so Irish as to be a recipe which must be eaten to be believed, but it really does work.

Firstly the filling has Irish whiskey liqueur and secondly the cake itself is made with mashed potato as one of the many ingredients. It is moist and delicious.

225 g/8 oz self raising flour	**Filling**
50 g/2 oz cocoa powder	115 g/4 oz dark chocolate
50 g/2 oz dark chocolate	150 ml/¼ pint double cream
175 g/6 oz butter	115 g/4 oz icing sugar
175 g/6 oz soft pale brown sugar	3 tablespoons liqueur
115 g/4 oz cooked mashed potato	
3 eggs, lightly beaten	

Preheat the oven to 180°C/350°F/Gas Mark 4.

Sift the flour and cocoa into a bowl.

Break the dark chocolate into a heatproof bowl and place over a small saucepan of very hot water, stirring gently until the chocolate has melted.

Cream the butter and sugar until light and fluffy and gradually beat in the melted chocolate and mashed potato, finally adding the eggs and flour a little at a time, beating gently until smooth.

Divide the mixture evenly between two 20 cm/8 inch greased sandwich cake tins, smoothing the tops gently.

Place in the oven and bake for about 30 minutes or until well risen and firm to touch. Do not overcook.

Remove from the oven and when cool enough to handle gently turn onto a wire rack to become cold.

Meanwhile in a separate bowl prepare the filling by breaking the chocolate into a bowl, place over a pan of very hot water and stir until the chocolate has melted. Remove the bowl from the heat, allow the chocolate to cool and then using a wooden spoon beat in the other ingredients until the mixture becomes smooth.

Sandwich the two cakes together and spoon the remaining mixture over the cake, smoothing gently.

Leave to set before transferring to a serving plate.

DOVER CAKE

Serves 6-8

A plain but aromatic cake, which is particularly good if served sliced and buttered. Sadly despite its name, I have been unable to find any historical facts about this cake with its Kentish connection.

115 g/4 oz butter	1 tablespoon brandy
225 g/8 oz caster sugar	225 g/8 oz plain flour
2 eggs, lightly beaten	1/2 teaspoon nutmeg
150 ml/1/4 pint milk	1/2 teaspoon cinnamon
1/2 teaspoon vanilla extract	1/2 teaspoon baking powder

Preheat the oven to 160°C/325°F/Gas Mark 3.

Cream the butter and sugar until light and fluffy. Add the eggs, milk, vanilla extract and brandy, and beat gently. Sift the flour and spices and add to the mixture, stirring well.

Pour into a greased and lined 15 cm/6 inch cake tin and bake in the oven for 1 1/2 hours or until a skewer inserted into the centre comes out cleanly.

Allow to cool in the tin for 30 minutes before turning carefully onto a wire rack.

PEPPER CAKE

In 1180 a Pepperer's Guild was founded in London but it was not until the 18th century when spices, molasses and rum were widely imported from the West Indies that spices were often exchanged for wool from the areas of Westmorland, and Yorkshire in particular. This together with the use of coal or wood stoves becoming more commonplace, meant that any one who could afford the spices and wanted to add them to their culinary delights, could now do so.

In Westmorland a rich fruitcake made with vine fruits, lemon, cloves and ginger became famous for the addition of a little aromatic ground black pepper. An unusual recipe with its spicy fruitiness, this cake is much pleasanter than might be imagined.

In some areas this cake seems to be long connected with carol singers who were traditionally offered slices at Christmas time.

225 g/8 oz plain flour	115 g/4 oz soft brown sugar
1/2 teaspoon baking powder	115 g/4 oz butter
1/4 teaspoon ground cloves	75 g/3 oz currants
1/2 teaspoon ground ginger	75 g/3 oz raisins
1/2 teaspoon black pepper	25 g/1 oz candied lemon peel
225 g/8 oz black treacle	1 large egg, lightly beaten

Preheat the oven to 160°C/325°F/Gas Mark 3.

Sift the flour, baking powder and spices into a bowl, make a well in the centre and set aside.

In a medium saucepan melt the black treacle, sugar, and butter over a very low heat and allow to cool slightly.

Add the fruits to the flour mixture and stir well. Pour in the cooled treacle mixture, together with the beaten egg and mix vigorously with a wooden spoon to ensure it is lump free.

Pour the cake mixture into a greased and lined 18 cm/7 inch cake tin and bake in the centre of the oven for 1 3/4 hours or until the cake is pale brown and firm to touch, allow a little longer if necessary, covering the top with brown paper if the cake begins to brown too quickly. A skewer inserted into the centre will come out cleanly when the cake is cooked.

Allow to cool in the tin for 30 minutes before turning onto a wire rack to cool.

SPOTTED DICK OR SPOTTED DOG CAKE

IRELAND   *Serves 6-8*

Sometimes called 'Fruit Cake in a Pot' or 'Spotted Dog' this simple, inexpensive cake was made in many cottages in Ireland for a Sunday treat.

I had the good fortune to see this cake being baked by the side of a peat fire in County Clare at a working museum. The ashes on the lid of the iron pot oven called a 'bastible' were scraped away and the lid lifted so that I could peep inside at the browning cake. I was assured that after lining the pot oven with greased paper, the cake nestled in the centre, baked extremely well. Certainly the resulting fruit cake, made with the traditional deep cross cut onto the top, served buttered, was excellent, the lid on the pot oven keeping it moist.

Closely resembling a lidded casserole dish, a pot oven is a traditional cooking utensil used to bake a variety of meals. Placed on a trivet close to a good peat fire, or hung on a hook above, then covered with ashes, they make an excellent 'oven'.

Cakes or breads baked in this way have the advantage of remaining soft crusted. For a similar effect, it is possible to use an iron-lidded casserole to bake the cake in an ordinary oven.

Whilst still very popular as an Irish teatime cake, they are now more commonly baked on a baking sheet, although it is important to cover the cake with a clean cloth when it is removed from the oven, to ensure a soft textured crust.

450 g/1 lb self raising flour	175 g/6 oz sultanas
50 g/2 oz sugar	1 large egg, lightly beaten
Good pinch salt	250 ml/9 fl oz milk or buttermilk
1/2 teaspoon mixed spice	

Preheat the oven to 200°C/400°F/Gas Mark 6.

Place all the dry ingredients into a large bowl, stir and then make a well in the centre.

Pour in the egg and most of the milk, mixing with a pallet knife to form a soft dough. Add the remaining milk if necessary.

Knead gently on a lightly floured surface and form into a round, about 5 cm/2 inches deep. Cut a large cross on the top and place onto a greased and lightly floured baking tray.

Place in the oven, baking for 35 to 45 minutes. When well risen and golden brown, tap the cake on the bottom, if cooked it will sound hollow.

Transfer onto a clean cloth on a wire rack, wrapping the cloth around the cake to trap the steam.

Best eaten the same day, sliced and buttered.

LEMON CAKE

Serves 6-8

The history of this cake is unclear, but it crops up consistently in bakery shops and old Irish cookery books and is often associated with weekend shooting, fishing or hunting parties. Its sharp distinctive flavour awakens a jaded palate and it makes an excellent pudding served with cream, but I admit to liking it best, sliced and eaten with a cup of tea at teatime.

175 g/6 oz butter	Grated zest of one large lemon
175 g/6 oz caster sugar	2 extra tablespoons caster sugar
3 large eggs	Juice of one large lemon
175 g/6 oz self raising flour	

Preheat the oven to 180°C/350°F/Gas Mark 4.

Cream the butter and sugar together and add the eggs and flour alternately, a tablespoon at a time, beating in gently. Finally add the lemon zest (reserving the remainder of the lemon) and pour the cake mixture into a greased and lined 900 g/ 2 lb loaf tin.

Bake in the centre of the oven for approximately 50 to 60 minutes, until golden brown and firm to touch. A skewer inserted into the centre of the cake should come out clean.

Meanwhile strain the juice of the lemon and add it to the 2 tablespoons of caster sugar in a small saucepan. Boil the mixture together for 2 minutes until the sugar is dissolved.

Remove the cake from the oven and leaving it in the tin, prick the surface lightly with a fine skewer.

Pour the lemon syrup over the cake, leaving it to become cold before turning onto a plate to serve.

TURF CAKE

YORKSHIRE   *Serves 6-8*

The odd thing about this recipe is that there really isn't one. Traditionally, the farmer's wife would simply gather all the left overs from baking day, such as bread dough, pastry and cake mixture, together with any spare vine fruits or grated citrus rind. After kneading them gently to form a 'round cake', she would line an iron pot oven or bastible with greased paper and press in the Turf Cake sealing with a close fitting lid.

Farmers who often spent whole days or nights on the moors when tending lambing flocks, would then cook the 'cake' over a fire built from turf or 'turves' covered with more turf, to keep in the heat. Hence Turf or Turve Cake.

I have found recipes suggesting the cakes were sometimes baked on a griddle over a turf or peat fire. However, I suspect this would have been inside a cottage rather than on the moors, as it would have proved very much simpler to transport the cake in an iron pot oven. The resulting cake would also require less watching whilst the farmer was tending his sheep and would be better protected from the elements.

The nearest recipe is one for Yorkshire Fat Rascals, which are believed to have originated from the Turf Cake, and certainly, this gives us a more identifiable set of ingredients. Also there are great similarities with the Oven Bottom Cake, which also used left over bits and pieces from baking day. The traditional baking day was characterised by the food requiring the hottest temperature being baked first, probably bread, followed by pies and cakes as the oven lost its heat.

225 g/8 oz plain flour	50 g/2 oz sultanas
1 teaspoon baking powder	50 g/2 oz currants
¹/2 teaspoon mixed spice	25 g/1 oz grated lemon rind
75 g/3 oz butter or lard	25 g/1 oz grated orange rind
50 g/2 oz pale brown sugar	5-6 tablespoons milk or buttermilk

Preheat the oven to 220°C/425°F/Gas Mark 7.

Sift the flour, baking powder and mixed spice into a bowl. Using your fingertips, rub in the butter or lard until the mixture forms a fine breadcrumbs texture. Then add the sugar, sultanas, currants and citrus rinds, stirring in well. Finally using a pallet knife, stir in the milk to form a stiff dough.

Turn onto a lightly floured surface and gently knead before forming into a round and lifting carefully into the greased and lined iron pot oven or casserole. Place a sheet of greaseproof paper over the top of the cake and put on the lid.

Place the iron pot or casserole into the oven and bake for about 25 to 30 minutes or until well risen and golden brown. Remove the lid and leave the cake to cool slightly in the pot before lifting carefully onto a wire rack and cutting or breaking into bite-sized portions.

BALMORAL CAKE

SCOTLAND   *Serves 6*

Despite our best endeavours and help from Scottish reference libraries, the history of the Balmoral Cake has eluded me (and the libraries). That it exists is beyond doubt however, even being baked in a special cylindrical tin named a Balmoral Tin.

Although tenuous, the connection with Queen Victoria is highly likely as she was noted for enjoying Scottish teatime baking such as the Balmoral Shortbread and Balmoral Tartlets. It is not unreasonable therefore to imagine a link between this uniquely shaped sponge cake and the Royal tea table.

The following recipe came from a cookery book, long out of print – even the publishers were untraceable, adding to the mystery.

4 large eggs	115 g/4 oz self raising flour
115 g/4 oz caster sugar	1 tablespoon caster sugar

Preheat the oven to 160°C/325°F/Gas Mark 3.

Place the eggs and sugar in a large bowl over a saucepan of hot water and whisk until pale and creamy. About 10 to 15 minutes.

Sift the flour and using a metal spoon and a figure of 8 movement, fold in the flour a little at a time.

Grease and dust the Balmoral cake tin with the tablespoon of caster sugar and pour in the mixture. Bake in the oven until well risen and firm to touch. When cool enough to handle turn out of the tin onto a wire rack to get cold.

Best eaten on the day of baking.

LARDY CAKE

History does not date lardy cakes but it is a very ancient recipe, probably medieval, and many of the ingredients would today be frowned upon as incredibly unhealthy, the main characteristic being that they are made using pork lard.

There are many variations of the Lardy Cake, counties such as Oxfordshire, Kent and Gloucestershire have their own recipes with differing fruits and spices. They are usually baked as square cakes, but they are sometimes baked as buns. However, one thing is beyond dispute, when making this recipe it is not possible to substitute the pork lard for butter as it just won't taste or look like a lardy cake.

450 g/1 lb bread dough (see page 21)	25 g/1 oz mixed peel
150 g/5 oz pork lard	1/2 teaspoon mixed spice
150 g/5 oz pale brown sugar	1/2 teaspoon salt
50 g/2 oz currants	

Preheat the oven to 200°C/400°F/Gas Mark 6.

Allow the bread dough to rise once, and then roll into an oblong on a well-floured board. Dot two thirds with half the lard and sprinkle with half the fruit. Fold into three, bringing the plain third over to the centre first and the remaining third over the top, pressing the edges together with a rolling pin. Give the dough a half turn and roll into an oblong again, repeating the process. Leave for 30 minutes in a warm place.

Carefully lift the folded dough onto a large greased baking sheet and bake in the oven for about 35 minutes until golden brown.

Remove from the baking sheet immediately and place on a plate. Serve hot spread with butter.

DOUGH CAKE

LINCOLNSHIRE   *Serves 10-12*

Sir Kenelm Digby's recipes of 1669 were well documented including this original method for a Dough Cake, which has changed little to the present day.

It should not be confused with the famous Lincolnshire Plum Loaf; though similar, the Dough Cake is very much more highly spiced, and contains almonds which give an interesting flavour and moist texture.

450 g/1 lb bread dough (see page 21)
75g /3 oz sultanas
75 g/3 oz raisins
75 g/3 oz currants
50 g/2 oz chopped glace peel
1 teaspoon mixed spice
1/2 teaspoon ground mace

75 g/3 oz caster sugar
50 g/2 oz ground almonds
50 g/2 oz butter, diced
2 eggs, lightly beaten

Topping
A little caster sugar

Preheat the oven to 200°C/400°F/Gas Mark 6.

Put the dough into a large warmed bowl, add all the other ingredients and mix in thoroughly.

Turn the mixture onto a floured surface and knead for 10 minutes.

Place in a greased 18 cm/7 inch cake tin and leave to rise for 30 minutes.

Brush the top of the cake with a little water and sprinkle with the extra sugar and bake in the centre of the oven for 30 to 35 minutes until well risen and golden brown.

Allow to cool in the tin for 10 minutes before turning onto a wire rack and leaving to become cold.

APPLE CAKE

IRELAND   *Serves 6-8*

This cake simply had to be included, not only is it completely different to the apple cakes of Dorset, Somerset and Devon, which are enjoyable in their own right, but it is absolutely delicious.

Baked with apple slices sandwiched in the centre, it also makes an excellent pudding served with cream.

An iron pot oven, placed close to an open fire and topped with burning coals would have been used to bake the apple cake in Irish cottage hearths, but if you use a deep flan dish and place the cake in the centre of an oven, your efforts will be rewarded with a very good modern day version.

225 g/8 oz self raising flour
115 g/4 oz butter
1 egg, lightly beaten
115 g/4 oz caster sugar
75 ml/3 fl oz milk

Filling
2 cooking apples, peeled and sliced

$^1/_2$ teaspoon cinnamon
50 g/2 oz soft brown sugar

Topping
A little beaten egg
1 level tablespoon caster sugar

Preheat the oven to 180°C/350°F/Gas Mark 4.

Place the flour and butter in a large bowl and rub in to form a breadcrumb texture.

Add the beaten egg, sugar and milk and mix with a pallet knife to form a soft dough. Turn onto a floured board and cut the dough in half. Place one half into a deep flan dish, pressing down with floured fingers to cover the surface of the dish.

Spread the apple slices evenly over the base and sprinkle with cinnamon and the soft brown sugar.

Carefully roll the second half of the dough into a circle roughly the same size as the dish, place on top of the apples, pressing the edges together and cutting several slits in the top of the cake.

Brush with a little of the beaten egg and sprinkle with the tablespoon of caster sugar. Bake in the oven for 35 minutes until well risen and golden brown.

POTATO APPLE CAKE

Serves 6-8

I do have to admit that I find potato an unlikely addition for cakes, but on the other hand potato flour is often used in Europe so why should it be any different here? Certainly, once I began looking into the use of potato in cakes I realised that whilst not common, it was an ingredient that was used and after all it is not that much different to adding carrots, which are now so acceptable. This Potato Apple Cake is excellent and well worth experimenting to quell such prejudices.

225 g/8 oz self raising flour	115 g/4 oz cooked and mashed potato
1/2 teaspoon mixed spice	2 large cooking apples
150 g/5 oz butter	2 eggs, lightly beaten
115 g/4 oz soft brown sugar	Little milk if necessary

Preheat the oven to 180°C/350°F/Gas Mark 4.

Sift the flour and spice into a bowl and rub in the butter until it forms the texture of fine breadcrumbs.

Stir in the sugar and the potatoes.

Peel and core the apples and dice them into small pieces, stir into the flour mixture, finally adding the eggs and mixing to a soft dough. Add a little milk if necessary.

Spoon into a greased and lined 900 g/2 lb loaf tin and bake in the centre of the oven for approximately 1 1/4 hours or until well risen and a skewer inserted into the centre comes out cleanly.

Remove from the oven and turn out gently onto a wire rack to cool.

APPLE CAKE

SOMERSET AND DEVON

Serves 8-10

A West Country Apple Cake is simplicity itself, each county seeming to have its own variation; indeed each baker or housewife seems to have their favourite addition such as spices or almonds. The older recipes used lard for this fairly basic cake, but personally I think it is vastly improved if made with butter and I doubt if in this rather more health conscious age it is still made with lard in many homes. White vegetable fat would be a good substitute if you wanted to remain true to the original recipe. My favourite version includes a little cinnamon and some sultanas.

A cake enhanced by apples, an ingredient which was so prolific in the autumn and winter months, made an apple cake inexpensive and seasonal.

225 g/8 oz softened butter
275 g/10 oz soft pale brown sugar
350 g/12 oz wholemeal plain flour
2 level teaspoons baking powder
1 teaspoon ground cinnamon
4 large eggs, lightly beaten

450 g/1 lb apples, peeled and chopped
50 g/2 oz sultanas
A little milk

Topping
2 tablespoons clear honey

Preheat the oven to 170°C/325°F/Gas Mark 3.

Cream the butter and sugar until light and fluffy. Sift the flour, baking powder and spices into a bowl and add to the butter a little at a time, together with the eggs, mixing until thoroughly incorporated.

Fold in the chopped apples and sultanas, adding a little milk if necessary to give a soft dropping consistency.

Grease and line a 18 cm/7 inch round cake tin and fill with the cake mixture. Place in the centre of the oven and bake until the cake is well risen and springs back when lightly pressed on the top, approximately 1¼ to 1½ hours. Leave to cool for 10 minutes, before removing from the tin and whilst still warm, pour a little warmed honey over the top of the cake.

Eaten whilst warm, it makes a very good pudding, served with cream. Or leave to cool completely. Best eaten within 2 days of making.

APPLE CAKE

DORSET   *Serves 7-8*

An excellent recipe which does not include any spices, so there is nothing to detract from the flavour of apples.

Simple honest fare, it is also straightforward and easy to bake.

115 g/4 oz butter	115 g/4 oz soft pale brown sugar
115 g/4 oz wholemeal flour	225 g/8 oz eating apples
115 g/4 oz plain white flour	50 g/2 oz sultanas (optional)
1 generous teaspoon baking powder	1 large egg, lightly beaten

Preheat the oven to 180°C/350°F/Gas Mark 4.

Rub the butter into the sifted flours and baking powder. Stir in the sugar.

Peel, remove the core and dice the apples quite finely, stirring them into the mixture. Finally stir in the sultanas, if using, and the egg.

The mixture will form a dough.

Form the cake into a round and bake on a greased baking sheet in the centre of the oven for about 25 minutes or until well risen and golden brown.

Place on a wire cooling rack to cool. The cake is delicious served sliced and buttered.

APPLE CAKE/*Teisen Fala*

WALES   ***Serves 8***

Not famous for their apples, it would be something of a surprise however, if the Welsh did not have their own apple cake and this recipe is so good that it should not be left out of the book.

Enjoyable eaten whilst still warm, as with all apple cakes they do not have a long shelf life, but that matters little as it will probably be devoured quickly anyway.

275 g/10 oz plain flour
1/2 teaspoon cinnamon
1/2 teaspoon baking powder
150 g/5 oz butter

150 g/5 oz soft brown sugar
275 g/10 oz eating apples
A little milk to mix

Preheat the oven to 180°C/350°F/Gas Mark 4.

Sift the flour, cinnamon and baking powder into a bowl and rub in the butter to form a fine breadcrumb texture.

Peel the apples, removing the core section and cut into small pieces. Stir the apple and sugar into the flour mixture and add enough milk to form a stiff dough.

Grease a large baking sheet and after forming the cake mix into a large round, transfer it onto the prepared sheet.

Bake in the oven for about 35 minutes or until golden brown.

Slide the cake gently onto a serving plate and leave to cool slightly before cutting. This cake may be served as a pudding, with custard or cream if liked. Or cut into sections and eaten for afternoon tea.

WILFA APPLE CAKE

YORKSHIRE   *Serves about 16*

A pastry-based cake, baked in honour of St Wilfred's Day in early August, the Wilfa Apple Cake is unusual in that it contains not only apples but Wensleydale Cheese, a delicious combination.

When the cake is cold it should be cut into squares or fingers and served, much as it would have been traditionally when it was baked to celebrate the return of St Wilfred after a long trip away from his home country.

450 g/1 lb Shortcrust Pastry (see page 21)	115 g/4 oz Wensleydale cheese
700 g/1 1/2 lb cooking apples	1 egg, lightly beaten
115 g/4 oz caster sugar	

Preheat the oven to 180°C/350°F/Gas Mark 4.

Make the short crust pastry, wrap in film and place in the refrigerator.

Peel, core and slice the apples and place in a bowl of cold water.

Roll out half of the short crust pastry into an oblong on a lightly floured board and place on a lightly greased Swiss roll tin, approximately 17.5 x 27.5 cm/7 x 11 inches. Dry the apples on kitchen roll and spread the slices evenly over the pastry base, topping with the sugar. Grate the cheese evenly over the top of the filling and finally roll the remaining portion of pastry to an oblong and lay over the top, sealing the edges well.

Brush the top with the beaten egg and place in the oven for about 30 minutes, until the pastry is cooked and golden.

Remove from the oven and allow to become completely cold, in the tin, before cutting into portions.

HEAVY CAKE

CORNWALL   *Serves approximately 9*

It is not clear how often this very old Cornish cake recipe is baked nowadays, although I have heard of at least one baker who is trying to preserve the tradition. Possibly due to its unappetising name it became rather unfashionable, but it is quite possible judging from the stories I have traced, that this old fashioned lacklustre cake was originally baked on a griddle over cottage fires and would have been considered a great treat. In fact I rather like the plain, fruited, griddle cakes simply for their earthy charm and everyday teatime appeal. There are several variations of this cake but I do feel that it is greatly improved by the addition of two lightly beaten eggs, not always included in older recipes.

Despite its 'heavy' ingredients – flour, beef dripping, butter or cream, currants, a little sugar and citrus peel – the Heavy Cake is actually quite light in texture, and rolled into a square and marked into portions before baking, it is best eaten fresh from the oven.

One popular story about how the 'Heavy Cake' got its name, is that it was baked by the wives of fishermen in Cornwall, whose cries whilst hauling in their nets from the sea was 'hevva' meaning 'Heave Ho' and when their wives heard this knowing that the fishermen would soon be home for their tea, they set the prepared cake onto the griddle to bake. Hence Hevva Cake, which eventually became known as Heavy Cake.

450 g/1 lb plain flour	25 g/1 oz sugar
75 g/3 oz butter or cream	25 g/1 oz mixed peel
75 g/3 oz beef dripping	2 eggs, lightly beaten
225 g/8 oz currants	A little water, if necessary

Preheat the oven to 200°C/400°F/Gas Mark 6.

Sift the flour into a bowl and roughly mix in the butter or cream together with the beef dripping. Stir in the currants, sugar and peel, adding the eggs and enough water to form a stiff dough.

Roll out into an oblong on a lightly floured board and then fold into a 'Swiss Roll' shape. Lift carefully onto a greased baking tray and roll out into a square approximately 1 cm/½ inch deep, marking the surface with a sharp knife into equal sized square portions.

Bake in the oven for 25 minutes or until well risen and golden brown.

Leave for 10 minutes and then cut or pull the cake into portions, transferring them onto a wire rack to cool.

HONEY CAKE

NORFOLK   *Serves 6-7*

Walsingham, in the north of Norfolk, is not only famous for its beautiful Abbey surrounded by snowdrops in spring, and for the story of the vision of the Virgin Mary, which still draws pilgrims to the shrine in the village but also the colonies of bees in the area provide visitors with jars of their creamy, sweet honey to buy and take home. Walsingham it seems is famous for a good many things.

Traditionally then this recipe for Honey Cake would have been baked with just such honey, but of course, you can use a jar of your local honey, unless you are lucky enough to be visiting Walsingham.

450 g/1 lb plain flour	225 g/8 oz dark muscovado sugar
1 teaspoon bicarbonate soda	125 g/5 oz clear honey
1 teaspoon cinnamon	150 ml/1/4 pint milk
1 teaspoon ground ginger	2 eggs
1/2 teaspoon mixed spice	
50 g/2 oz raisins	**Topping**
50 g/2 oz sultanas	4 tablespoons warmed honey
50 g/2 oz chopped mixed peel	50 g/2 oz flaked almonds
225 g/8 oz butter	

Preheat the oven to 160°C/325°F/Gas Mark 3.

Sift together the flour, bicarbonate of soda and spices in a bowl and stir in the raisins, sultanas and mixed peel.

Cream the butter and sugar until light and fluffy.

Measure the honey into a small saucepan. I find the easiest way to do this is to place the saucepan on the scales and set them to zero before pouring in the required weight of honey. Warm the honey slightly before whisking in milk and eggs.

Finally incorporate all the ingredients together, beating with a wooden spoon to ensure that they are all thoroughly mixed.

Pour into a 18 cm/7 inch lined and greased cake tin. Place in the centre of the oven for about 1 1/4 hours or until well risen and firm to touch. If the cake starts to brown too quickly turn the oven down a little and cover the top of the cake with a piece of brown paper. A skewer inserted into the centre will come out cleanly when the cake is ready.

Meanwhile warm the honey for the topping in a small saucepan. As soon as the cake is baked remove from the oven and pierce all over with a thin skewer before pouring the honey over. Finally sprinkle with flaked almonds. Leave in the tin to cool for at least 30 minutes before turning out carefully onto a wire cooling rack. Remove the greaseproof paper when the cake is completely cold.

BARA BRITH

Serves 6-8

One of the first problems when looking at the history of this much loved Welsh cake was the number of different recipes. The older recipes were made with yeast, which was the traditional raising agent but more recently it is often made with self raising flour, giving it a lighter texture. What is constant however is the loaf shape, the use of brown sugar, vine fruits, candied peel and mixed spice.

An extremely popular cake in Wales – I think I can safely say that I saw one in every baker's shop I visited. It is very good to eat when freshly baked and in particular, buttered.

Recipe 1 – yeast based

10 g/^{1}/2 oz fresh yeast	115 g/4 oz butter
1 teaspoon caster sugar	75 g/3 oz currants
150 ml/^{1}/4 pint tepid milk	75 g/3 oz raisins
450 g/1 lb plain wholemeal flour	50 g/2 oz chopped glace peel
1 teaspoon mixed spice	75 g/3 oz soft brown sugar
^{1}/2 teaspoon salt	

Preheat the oven to 200°C/400°F/Gas Mark 6.

Cream the yeast and caster sugar and add the tepid milk, stirring. Sift the flour, spice and salt into a large bowl and rub in the butter. Stir in the fruit and sugar, followed by the yeast mixture. Stir with a pallet knife until the dough forms a ball.

Knead very gently on a lightly floured board until the dough is smooth, and then place in a clean bowl. Cover with a cloth, leaving in a warm place until doubled in size.

Knead lightly for a second time and then place the dough in a 900 g/2 lb loaf tin and leave in a warm place for a further 30 minutes to rise.

Bake in the centre of the oven for 1 hour, but if the top begins to darken too much, reduce the oven to 160°C/325°F/Gas Mark 3.

When the cake is cooked, turn onto a wire rack to cool.

Best eaten within 2 days of baking but excellent toasted if it becomes a little stale.

BARA BRITH

WALES   *Serves 6-8*

Recipe 2 – self raising flour

115 g/4 oz currants	350 g/12 oz self raising wholemeal flour
50 g/2 oz raisins	115 g/4 oz soft brown sugar
50 g/2 oz chopped mixed peel	1 large egg
400 ml/²/3 pint hot black tea	1 teaspoon mixed spice

Preheat the oven to 180°C/350°F/Gas Mark 4.

In a small bowl steep the dried fruit and peel in the hot tea and leave to stand overnight.

The next morning strain the fruit, setting aside the liquid.

Place all the remaining ingredients in a large bowl and add the fruit, stirring thoroughly. Add a little of the liquid, just enough to form a soft dough.

Spoon the mixture into a greased and lined 900 g/2 lb loaf tin and bake in the oven for approximately 45 minutes or until risen and firm to touch.

Turn onto a cooling rack and when cold serve sliced and buttered.

SAFFRON CAKE

DEVON AND CORNWALL

Makes 3 loaves, each serving 6-8

Reduce the quantities proportionately if you wish to make less

Production of saffron has gradually died out in England so most of the saffron we buy today is imported from Spain and although India grows large quantities of the spice, it is mainly for their own use.

In the spice section (see page 18) you will find some very interesting background reading about the growing of this spice and how it is linked to the making of saffron buns and cakes which developed mainly in Devon and Cornwall, where they continue to be baked to this day. The sunshine yellow cakes being aromatic, generously fruited and rather sweet make an excellent teatime addition, although I always think they are very suited to 'elevenses' with coffee.

1/2 teaspoon saffron	225 g/8 oz soft brown sugar
150 ml/1/4 pint boiling milk	1/2 teaspoon mixed spice
25 g/1 oz fresh yeast	1/2 teaspoon salt
1 1/2 teaspoons sugar	175 g/6 oz butter (or use half lard, half butter)
300 ml/1/2 pint tepid water	450 g/1 lb currants
900 g/2 lb plain flour	75 g/3 oz chopped mixed peel

Preheat the oven to 220°C/425°F/Gas Mark 7.

Pour the boiling milk over the saffron and leave to stand overnight.

Cream the yeast with the teaspoon of sugar adding the tepid water. Stir and set aside for 20 minutes until a light froth is formed.

Sift flour into a large warmed bowl adding the sugar, spices and salt. Rub in the butter.

Make a well in the middle of the flour mixture and pour in the yeast and saffron liquid. Using your hands, mix well until it forms very soft, smooth dough. Knead gently into a ball. Place the dough in a lightly oiled bowl and cover with a clean cloth. Leave in a warm place until it doubles in size.

On a lightly floured surface, knead the dough for 5 minutes before adding the fruit and peel kneading again until it is evenly distributed throughout the cake mixture.

Divide the dough into three, placing a third into each of the three well greased, 900 g/2 lb loaf tins. Leave in a warm place for the dough to prove and double in size. This will take about 30 minutes.

Bake in the oven for 30 to 40 minutes, until golden. Remove and turn out onto a wire rack to cool.

Note: Saffron cake will sink slightly in the middle and appear slightly moist when cut, do not worry this is normal and entirely as it should be.

YORKSHIRE CAKE

Serves 7-8

This delightful recipe came from Mrs Gertrude Latter's wonderful 1920's handwritten cookery book. I thoroughly enjoyed making it and despite the slightly unconventional appearance of the cake, it did work and tasted very good.

115 g/4 oz butter
115 g/4 oz caster sugar
2 eggs, lightly beaten
1 tablespoon milk
115 g/4 oz plain flour
1 teaspoon baking powder

115 g/4 oz ground rice
Pinch salt

Filling
Greengage jam

Preheat the oven to 180°C/350°F/Gas Mark 4.

Cream the butter and sugar until light and fluffy. Add the eggs and milk, beating constantly with a wooden spoon.

Sift the flour and baking powder. Add the flour, ground rice and salt to the cake mixture, beating until thoroughly incorporated and lump free.

Grease two oven-proof dinner plates and spoon half of the mixture into each plate, spreading it to a circle of about 15 cm/6 inch diameter. Bake in the centre of the oven for about 20 minutes or until risen and firm to touch.

Remove from the oven and leave to cool for five minutes before gently turning onto a wire rack and leaving to become cold.

Sandwich together with greengage jam and sprinkle a little caster sugar on top before serving.

SULTANA CAKE

SCOTLAND

It is certainly not unusual for there to be many variations of popular cake recipes and the Sultana Cake is no exception. During my time living in the glorious Highlands of Scotland, overlooking the Carse of Lecropt, I developed a love of the Scottish version of Sultana Cake, particularly if the sultanas had been steeped in whisky overnight prior to baking. Whilst the non-alcoholic version is just as delicious it is certainly not as aromatic.

A quick and easy cake to make and certainly inexpensive, it ought to be in everyone's repertoire of favourite weekend recipes.

175 g/6 oz golden sultanas
2 tablespoons whisky
175 g/6 oz butter
175 g/6 oz soft brown sugar

3 large eggs, lightly beaten
175 g/6 oz self raising flour
50 g/2 oz ground almonds

Preheat the oven to 160°C/325°F/Gas Mark 3.

Place the sultanas in a small bowl and spoon over the whisky, stirring well. Cover with film and set aside overnight to soak.

Cream the butter and sugar until light and fluffy and add the eggs and flour a little at a time, beating between each addition. Add the ground almonds and finally the sultanas, stirring gently but thoroughly.

Pile the mixture into a greased and lined 18 cm/7 inch cake tin and bake in the oven until well risen and the top feels firm when pressed lightly in the centre. A skewer inserted into the middle should come out cleanly. It should take about 1 1/2 hours but as all ovens vary, do not worry if it takes a little longer.

Leave the cake to cool in the tin before turning onto a wire rack.

PATAGONIAN BLACK CAKE/*Cacen Ddu*

PATAGONIA AND WALES   *Serves 10-12*

Your puzzlement is justified, but this cake does have its place in our book. Welsh families migrated to Patagonia in large numbers to work in the gold mines, however sheep farming being such a way of life there, it inevitably attracted the Welsh to alternative employment as the mines proved less lucrative than hoped. Even today there are settlements with strong Welsh roots, including Chapels, and although Welsh is no longer spoken in these communities (they speak Spanish), to remain in contact with their ancestors, their hymns are still sung in the Welsh language during the Sunday services. It is therefore hardly surprising that a South American cake found its way into Welsh cookbooks, probably brought home and treasured by families returning to their home land. It is delicious and rather unusual.

275 g/10 oz butter
275 g/10 oz dark muscovado sugar
450 g/1 lb plain flour
1 teaspoon baking powder
1 teaspoon cinnamon
2 teaspoons mixed spice
4 large eggs, lightly beaten
115 g/4 oz ground almonds
3 tablespoons black rum
1 teaspoon almond extract

225 g/8 oz currants
225 g/8 oz raisins
225 g/8 oz sultanas
115 g/4 oz chopped mixed peel
115 g/4 oz flaked almonds

Coating
225 g/8 oz icing sugar
A little boiling water

Preheat the oven to 150°C/300°F/Gas Mark 2.

Cream the butter and sugar together in a large bowl, until light and fluffy. In a separate bowl, sift the flour, baking powder and spices together and then stir them together with the beaten eggs into the creamed butter and sugar.

Stir in the ground almonds, the rum and the almond extract ensuring that it is well mixed and finally stir in the remaining ingredients.

Grease and line a 20 cm/8 inch cake tin and carefully spoon in the mixture, levelling the top.

Place in the centre of the oven and bake for 3$^{1}/_{2}$ to 4 hours or until the top is firm to touch and a skewer inserted into the centre comes out cleanly.

Cover with a clean cloth and leave to cool in the tin overnight.

When completely cold, remove from the tin and place on a wire rack, removing the greaseproof paper.

In a small bowl, sift the icing sugar and add enough water to form a smooth coating consistency. Finally spoon the icing over the cake, allowing the mix to run down the sides of the cake, giving it its traditional icing finish.

PORTER CAKE

IRELAND   *Serves 10*

Whilst holidaying in southern Ireland we had the good fortune to visit the Ennystyman Agricultural Show in County Clare, where we saw not only some wonderful Irish horses, living up to their reputation for being the best bloodstock in the world, but had the opportunity to view at first hand the cake section of the home baking competition. We were not disappointed, Porter Cake confirming its importance in Irish baking by competing for a Challenge Cup.

This lovely, dark, aromatic, Irish fruitcake can be easily made by substituting Guinness for porter, the dark stout-like ale brewed from black malt. I had great trouble buying a bottle of genuine porter, even from the best off-licences and probably the only real source today would be one of the many excellent speciality breweries.

A similar Porter Cake was made here in England, named after the dark smoky taverns and ale houses known as Porter Houses, where it was widely believed 'Porters' drank the dark ale.

I was shown how to make this very special cake, by Ethna and Maureen, two charming bakers who used the all-in-one melting method to produce dozens of these cakes each week for the tourists to enjoy, although I have used the creaming method when baking the following recipe, as I rather enjoy the more tactile approach to cake making.

115 g/4 oz butter	$1/2$ teaspoon mace
115 g/4 oz dark muscovado sugar	Zest of one orange
225 g/8 oz self raising flour	115 g/4 oz currants
2 large eggs, lightly beaten	115 g/4 oz sultanas
150 ml/$1/4$ pint Porter (or Guinness)	115 g/4 oz raisins
1 teaspoon mixed spice	50 g/2 oz chopped mixed glace peel

Preheat the oven to 170°C/325°F/Gas Mark 3.

Cream the butter and sugar together until light and fluffy. Sift flour and spices and add together with the egg, in alternative spoonfuls, to the creamed fat, beating until well incorporated and smooth. Pour the Porter into the mixture and beat well. Add fruits, peel and zest stirring thoroughly.

Spoon into a 18 cm/7 inch round, greased and lined cake tin and bake for 1 hour, reducing the temperature to 150°C/300°F/Gas Mark 2 for a further 30 to 40 minutes or until the cake feels firm when pressed gently in the centre or a skewer inserted into the cake comes out clean.

Cool in the tin. This cake improves with keeping and is best wrapped in greaseproof and foil for 4 to 5 days before eating.

GUINNESS CAKE

IRELAND   *Serves 10-12*

This robust, moist, dark fruitcake is absolutely mouth-watering, made with the traditional Irish stout – Guinness; it should be kept for at least a week before eating.

Not to be confused with a Porter cake, which is much paler in colour, there are, as with most time-honoured cakes, many variations but the main ingredients seem to have remained much the same throughout Ireland over the years, differences being small, such as the addition of cherries or nuts.

The following recipe uses the most traditional ingredients and method of preparation.

75 g/3 oz sultanas	115 g/4 oz butter
75 g/3 oz raisins	225 g/8 oz dark muscovado sugar
75 g/3 oz currants	3 large eggs
75 g/3 oz chopped mixed peel	350 g/12 oz self raising flour
150 ml/¼ pint Guinness	1 teaspoon mixed spice

Preheat the oven to 180°C/350°F/Gas Mark 4.

Place all the dried fruit and peel in a medium bowl, pour over the Guinness and stir. Leave overnight to steep.

Cream the butter and sugar together until light and fluffy and then beat in the eggs one at a time. Fold in the flour and spice using a metal spoon and when thoroughly combined, add the fruits, stir well and spoon the mixture into a greased and lined 18 cm/7 inch cake tin. Smooth the top and place the cake in the centre of the oven, reducing the temperature to 140°C/275°F/Gas 1 after 1 hour. Continue to bake for a further hour or until a skewer inserted into the top of the cake, comes out cleanly.

If the cake begins to brown too quickly, place a sheet of brown paper over the top of the tin.

When the cake is baked, allow it to cool completely in its tin before turning out and wrapping in clean greaseproof and foil and storing for 6 or 7 days to mature.

CUMBERLAND CURRANT CAKE   *Serves 8*

A very traditional but unusual cake with a layer of pastry on the top and bottom. It has many variations, some simply contain currants, butter and sugar but rather more elaborate versions are baked with apple and spices in addition to currants, sultanas, raisins, peel and a generous measure of rum.

The following excellent recipe is a 'moderate' version.

450 g/1 lb Shortcrust Pastry (see page 21)	$^1/_2$ teaspoon mixed spice
115 g/4 oz butter	2 tablespoons rum
115 g/4 oz pale brown sugar	
75 g/3 oz currants	**Glaze**
75 g/3 oz raisins	1 beaten egg white
75 g/3 oz sultanas	A little caster sugar
50 g/2 oz chopped mixed peel	

Preheat the oven to 200°C/400°F/Gas Mark 6.

Cut the pastry in half and roll one piece into an oblong 28 x 18 x 1 cm/11 x 7 x $^1/_2$ inch. Lift carefully, over a rolling pin, onto a greased and floured baking sheet, prick all over with a fork.

Cream together the butter and sugar until light and fluffy, add the fruit and peel, together with the spice and rum. Spread mixture evenly over the sheet of pastry, leaving 1 cm/$^1/_2$ inch free at the edges.

Roll the remaining pastry to the same size and lay over the top of the fruit, damp the edges and pinch them together using your thumb and forefinger.

Bake in the oven for 25 to 30 minutes or until golden brown.

Remove from the oven and brush with the beaten egg white, then sprinkle with the caster sugar and return to the oven for a few minutes until set and browned.

Cut into squares and serve whilst still slightly warm.

SHY CAKE

Serves 6-8

How this cake acquired its name is unclear, although it is certainly a very old Gloucestershire recipe, appearing in many traditional cookery books. The cake is made with a quantity of ground rice, giving it a short texture, and the subtle use of spices certainly makes it a plain honest cake.

115 g/4 oz butter	175 g/6 oz self raising flour
175 g/6 oz soft brown sugar	$^1/_2$ teaspoon ground ginger
Zest of one lemon	$^1/_2$ teaspoon mixed spice
2 large eggs, lightly beaten	175 g/6 oz ground rice

Preheat the oven to 160°C/325°F/Gas Mark 3.

Cream the sugar and butter until fluffy, stir in the lemon zest. Add the lightly beaten eggs, the flour, spices and ground rice a little at a time, stirring thoroughly with a wooden spoon.

Spoon the mixture into a greased and lined 900 g/2 lb loaf tin and bake in the oven for approximately 1 hour or until golden, well risen and firm to touch.

Turn onto a wire rack to cool.

RIPON SPICE CAKE

Makes 2 loaf cakes, each serves 6-8

Whilst appearing in various old recipe books, even the reference librarians in Ripon have been unable to help me locate a background history for this lightly fruited spiced cake. Baked in a loaf shape and traditionally served with Wensleydale cheese, it is a simple but delicious recipe well worth trying.

225 g/8 oz butter	175 g/6 oz currants
225 g/8 oz soft brown sugar	175 g/6 oz sultanas
450 g/1 lb self raising flour	175 g/6 oz raisins
1 teaspoon ground mixed spice	50 g/2 oz chopped glace peel
1 teaspoon ground mace	75 g/3 oz glace cherries, halved
50 g/2 oz ground almonds	Zest of one lemon
3 eggs, lightly beaten	150 ml/^{1}/4 pint milk

Preheat the oven to 160°C/325°F/Gas Mark 3.

Cream the butter and sugar until light and fluffy. Sift the flour and spices into a bowl, adding the ground almonds. Gently beat the flour and eggs alternately into the butter and sugar until well mixed. Then gently fold in the fruits and lemon zest, adding enough milk to give a dropping consistency.

Spoon the mixture into two greased and lined 900 g/2 lb loaf tins, smoothing the surface lightly. Bake in the oven for about 1 hour or until well risen, golden brown and a skewer inserted into the centre comes out clean.

Allow to cool in the tin before turning onto a wire rack.

This cake keeps well if stored in an airtight tin.

SALLY LUNN CAKE

AVON AND SOMERSET   *Serves 6-8*

Sally Lunn was a west country lass, who supposedly owned a house and shop in Lilliput Alley in Bath. She was famed for the teacakes named after her, which she was said to have sold on the streets of the city.

Although they became known as Sally Lunn Cakes, a more likely explanation is that what the lass was actually crying, in west country French, was *sol et lune* or *soleil lune* meaning sun and moon.

There are many versions of this very famous teacake, which can either be baked as one large round cake or smaller individual buns. Round and golden they closely resemble a good French brioche, and although there are arguments as to whether they should be made with cream, or milk and butter, personally I prefer the latter.

When baked they are split horizontally and can be spread with whipped or clotted cream or lightly toasted, buttered and reassembled. The cake is then sliced into triangular wedges, which gives an interesting visual effect traditional to this cake.

25 g/1 oz fresh yeast	600 ml/1 pint milk
1 tablespoon caster sugar	2 large eggs
675 g/1 1/2 lb plain flour	
1 teaspoon salt	**Topping**
175 g/6 oz butter	1 egg yolk, lightly beaten

Preheat the oven to 200°C/400°F/Gas Mark 6.

Cream the yeast together with the sugar in a small bowl. Sift the flour and salt into a large bowl and make a well in the centre.

In a medium size saucepan, melt the butter and milk over a very low heat and then set aside until it is tepid (it should be no hotter than blood heat). Pour the cooled milk and butter onto the creamed yeast, stirring thoroughly before adding the two eggs. Stir into the well in the flour, beating again thoroughly until a smooth dough is formed.

Turn onto a lightly floured surface and knead gently until light and springy. Replace in a bowl and leave in a warm place, covered with a clean cloth, until doubled in size. Knead again until smooth and then shape into a round loaf.

Place on a greased baking sheet and brush over with the beaten egg yolk. Bake in the oven for about 25-30 minutes, or until golden brown and well risen. The cake should feel firm when pressed. Return to the oven for a little longer if necessary.

When baked, place on a wire rack to cool.

Best eaten slightly warm, spread with either cream or butter.

SINGIN' HINNIE

NORTHUMBERLAND   *Serves 6-8*

A large round, aromatic cake, baked on a griddle, the Singin' Hinnie is widely made in the northern counties of England. It derives its name from the 'singing' sound it makes when cooking as the fat reaches a very high temperature. Delicious split and spread with unsalted butter.

350 g/12 oz strong plain flour	75 g/3 oz butter
1/2 teaspoon bicarbonate of soda	115 g/4 oz currants
1 teaspoon cream of tartar	150 ml/1/4 pint milk
1/2 teaspoon salt	

Sift the flour, bicarbonate of soda, cream of tartar and salt together into a large bowl. Rub in the butter and stir in the currants. Pour in the milk slowly, stirring with a pallet knife, until a soft dough is formed.

Turn onto a lightly floured work surface and knead gently before rolling into a large round approximately 1 cm/1/2 inch thick. Dust the top with a little flour and transfer it carefully onto a preheated, greased griddle, which should be fairly hot.

Cook for about 7 to 8 minutes and turn gently to cook on the other side for a similar time.

The Singin' Hinnie should be nicely browned and singing merrily.

Remove onto a wire rack to cool slightly. This cake is best eaten fresh from baking, split and served with butter.

MARMALADE CAKE

IRELAND   *Serves 6-8*

Whilst Marmalade Cake can be found in various places, it does particularly seem to have its roots in Ireland, where it can be readily found on the shelves of their many truly excellent baker's shops.

The best cakes are made with one of the stronger types of orange marmalade such as chunky orange or whiskey orange marmalade. Do not be tempted to add 'a little extra' as this will change the consistency of the cake and may make it very heavy.

A marmalade cake may be made without vine fruits but usually it contains a small amount, such as a handful of sultanas.

115 g/4 oz butter	225 g/8 oz self raising flour
115 g/4 oz soft brown sugar	2 large eggs
115 g/4 oz marmalade	115 g/4 oz sultanas

Preheat the oven to 150°C/300°F/Gas Mark 3.

Cream the butter and sugar together until light and fluffy and then add the remaining ingredients, stirring thoroughly with a wooden spoon, until well mixed.

Spoon into a greased and lined 900 g/2 lb loaf tin and bake in the centre of the oven for about 1½ hours or until well risen, golden brown and a skewer inserted into the centre comes out cleanly.

Allow to cool for 30 minutes before turning out onto a wire rack to cool.

When cold, this cake is excellent sliced and buttered.

BELVOIR CAKE

LEICESTERSHIRE   *Serves 6*

Very similar to the Bever Cake of Suffolk, this fruited teacake was either shaped into buns or baked in a large round. Traditionally these teacakes were often eaten at harvest time, to celebrate the gathering of the crops.

The Belvoir Cake is a simple recipe deriving its flavour from the fruit rather than any spices. Originally it would probably have been made from pork lard, but in recent years butter has replaced the less healthy lard. Note that the word Belvoir is always pronounced 'beaver' meaning 'beautiful view' and as I can see Belvoir Castle from my garden, I feel rather an authority on how to pronounce the word!

450 g/1 lb strong plain flour	75 g/3 oz pale brown sugar
75 g/3 oz butter	50 g/2 oz sultanas
15 g/^{1}/2 oz fresh yeast	50 g/2 oz chopped mixed peel
1 teaspoon caster sugar	50 g/2 oz currants
50 ml/2 fl oz tepid milk	

Preheat the oven to 200°C/400°F/Gas Mark 6.

Sift the flour into a bowl and rub in the butter.

In a separate smaller bowl, cream the yeast and the caster sugar together, adding the tepid milk and stirring thoroughly. Leave for 15 minutes and then pour onto the flour, mixing thoroughly.

Knead gently on a lightly floured board until the dough becomes smooth, working in the sugar and fruits. Cover and leave in a warm place to double in size. Knead again lightly, shaping it into a round and place on a lightly greased baking tray. Leave to rise again for 30 minutes and then brush the top with a little milk and bake in the centre of the oven until dark golden brown, which will take approximately 25 minutes. When cooked, the cake will sound hollow if tapped underneath.

BLACK CAKE

CORNWALL

Serves 10

Like many of the Cornish fruit cakes, Black Cake partly derives its name from the quantity of currants used, giving it a dark appearance. Still widely baked this old recipe is delicious and keeps well, the ground rice giving it an interesting texture.

450 g/1 lb currants	$^1/_2$ teaspoon cinnamon
115 g/4 oz raisins	1 level teaspoon baking powder
115 g/4 oz chopped mixed peel	115 g/4 oz ground rice
225 g/8 oz butter	50 g/2 oz ground almonds
225 g/8 oz dark brown sugar	4 eggs, lightly beaten
115 g/4 oz plain flour	115 g/4 oz flaked almonds
1 teaspoon mixed spice	2 tablespoons brandy

Preheat the oven to 160°C/325°F/Gas Mark 3.

Wash all the fruit and drain thoroughly.

Cream the butter and sugar until light and fluffy.

Sift the flour, spices and baking powder into a bowl and stir in the ground rice and ground almonds before adding to the butter mixture together with the lightly beaten eggs.

When well incorporated, stir in the fruit, nuts and brandy.

Spoon into a greased and lined 20 cm/8 inch round cake tin and place in the centre of the oven. Bake for about 1$^1/_2$ hours or until the cake is firm and a skewer inserted into the centre comes out cleanly.

Allow to cool in the tin, then place on a wire rack until totally cold. Store in an airtight tin until required.

NORFOLK CAKE

Serves 8-10

A lightly fruited cake, this simple recipe is enhanced by finely grated orange and lemon rind and a little cocoa, giving it an interesting character.

115 g/4 oz butter	3 eggs
115 g/4 oz caster sugar	115 g/4 oz sultanas
225 g/8 oz self raising flour	50 g/2 oz currants
1 tablespoon cocoa	50 g/2 oz raisins
1/2 teaspoon ground mixed spice	Finely grated rind of one large orange
1/2 teaspoon mace	Finely grated rind of one large lemon

Preheat the oven to 160°C/325°F/Gas Mark 3.

Cream the butter and sugar until light and fluffy. Sift the flour, cocoa and spices together. Add the eggs and flour mixture to the butter and sugar, beating to ensure they are well incorporated.

Stir in the vine fruits and the grated rind of the lemon and orange.

Spoon the mixture into a greased and lined 18 cm/7 inch cake tin and bake in the oven for 2 hours or until a skewer inserted into the centre comes out cleanly and the cake is well risen and golden. If the cake browns too quickly, cover the top with a layer of brown paper.

Allow to cool in the tin for 30 minutes, before turning onto a wire rack to become completely cold.

CHOCOLATE RUM CAKE

Chocolate Rum Cake was said to have originally been baked in Cornwall; the alcohol used having been brought by ships from the West Indies who put into port with their cargoes of rum and spices.

225 g/8 oz butter
225 g/8 oz soft dark brown sugar
225 g/8 oz plain flour
1 teaspoon baking powder
115 g/4 oz cocoa
4 eggs, lightly beaten
115 g/4 oz ground almonds

3 tablespoons dark rum
A little milk if necessary

Filling
225 g/8 oz icing sugar
115 g/4 oz softened butter
2 tablespoons rum

Preheat the oven to 150°C/300°F/Gas Mark 2.

Cream the butter and sugar together until light and fluffy. Sift the flour, baking powder and cocoa into a separate bowl and then slowly incorporate it into the butter mixture, together with the beaten eggs.

Finally stir in the ground almonds and rum. Add a little milk if necessary, until the mixture forms a soft dropping consistency.

Spoon the cake mix into a greased and lined 20 cm/8 inch cake tin and bake in the centre of the oven for about 1½ hours or until the top is firm and a skewer inserted into the centre, comes out cleanly.

Allow the cake to cool slightly before turning out onto a wire cooling rack and leave to become cold.

Meanwhile prepare the filling by creaming the icing sugar, butter and rum together until smooth and creamy, adding a little extra rum if necessary.

Slice the cake in half and sandwich together with the filling, spooning a little onto the top of the cake and smoothing it over, if liked.

SELKIRK BANNOCK

SCOTLAND   *Serves approximately 6*

Famed for their high teas, a Scottish table would hardly be complete without a Selkirk Bannock and although they originated in the town of Selkirk, they are now widely made throughout southern Scotland.

Yeast was originally the only raising agent and therefore many of the good teacakes are closely related to bread.

Baked in one large round, as are all 'Bannocks', this straight forward recipe is easy and worth trying. I did recently buy one in an English supermarket, it simply did not compare with the Selkirk Bannocks tucked away in my memory from the days we spent living in the Highlands of Scotland.

450 g/1 lb strong white flour	1 teaspoon sugar
1/2 teaspoon salt	150 ml/1/4 pint tepid milk
75 g/3 oz butter	175 g/6 oz sultanas
75 g/3 oz caster sugar	25 g/1 oz chopped glace peel
15 g/1/2 oz fresh yeast	1 egg, lightly beaten

Preheat the oven to 200°C/400°F/Gas Mark 6.

Sift the flour and salt into a bowl and rub in the butter. Stir in the sugar and set aside.

In a small bowl cream the yeast with the teaspoon of sugar until creamy and pour on the tepid milk, stirring thoroughly.

Form a well in the centre of the flour mix and pour in the milk and yeast stirring with a pallet knife until it forms a ball of soft dough. Turn onto a lightly floured board and knead gently until the dough becomes smooth and elastic. Place in a clean bowl, cover with a cloth and leave somewhere warm to double in size.

When well risen, return to the floured board and knead in the fruit until evenly distributed, then form the dough into a round and place on a greased baking sheet, glazing with a little of the beaten egg.

Leave in a warm place to rise for about 45 minutes and then bake in the centre of the oven for 30 minutes, turning the oven down slightly if the cake begins to brown too quickly. When golden, tap the base and if it sounds hollow the cake is cooked. If not return it to the oven for a few more minutes until cooked through. Remove to a wire rack to cool.

Best served sliced and buttered.

PLUM CAKE LOAF

LINCOLNSHIRE   *Serves 6-8*

Cake-like in texture, this simple recipe is quick to make and not to be confused with the yeasted plum bread variations. Like many cakes going back centuries, there are numerous recipes in existence, often carrying the tag 'original' and there is no doubt at all that each and every recipe as it has been passed down through families and bakeries has been loyally adhered to.

This recipe really is worth trying and baked in the traditional loaf tin is an excellent teacake sliced and buttered.

225 g/8 oz butter	1 teaspoon mixed spice
225 g/8 oz caster sugar	225 g/8 oz raisins
3 eggs, lightly beaten	50 g/2 oz currants
450 g/1 lb self raising flour	50 g/2 oz peel

Preheat the oven to 160°C/325°F/Gas Mark 3.

Cream the butter and sugar until light and fluffy, adding the eggs, flour and spice a little at a time, beating with a wooden spoon until smooth.

Add the fruit and peel, fold in gently and then spoon into a 900 g/2 lb loaf tin, which has been greased and lined. Bake in the oven for 1 hour reducing the temperature to 140°C/225°F/Gas Mark 1 for a further hour or until the cake is golden brown and firm to touch. A skewer inserted into the centre of the cake should come out clean.

Remove from the oven when baked and turn onto a wire rack to cool.

SEED CAKE

Serves 8

Many recipes for Seed Cake can been found over the centuries in English cookery books, ranging from the rather plain through to much more elaborate versions which benefited from the addition of lemon peel, orange peel, ground almonds or a little nutmeg and cinnamon. In Ireland where they were also widely made, they were often known as 'Seedy Cakes'. But caraway seeds, which were widely used in Elizabethan cooking and have been traced as far back as prehistoric times, have largely gone out of favour in cakes these days. One recipe book compiled in the 19th century, gave no less than six versions of the Seed Cake, showing how tastes have changed.

It is however, well worth trying this recipe, which is rich enough to give a good moist cake, and as long as you do not add too much caraway, it is absolutely delicious with tea or coffee.

115 g/4 oz butter	50 g/2 oz ground almonds
115 g/4 oz caster sugar	50 g/2 oz chopped mixed peel
3 eggs, lightly beaten	1 tablespoon milk
175 g/6 oz self raising flour	2 teaspoons caraway seeds

Preheat the oven to 160°C/325°F/Gas Mark 3.

Cream the butter and sugar together until light and fluffy. Add the eggs and flour a little at a time, until completely incorporated. Fold in the remaining ingredients and spoon into the greased and lined 15 cm/6 inch cake tin.

Bake in the centre of the oven for approximately 1 hour or until the top springs back when lightly pressed in the centre and a skewer, inserted into the middle of the cake, comes out cleanly.

Leave to cool in the tin for 30 minutes and then turn onto a wire rack and leave to become cold.

SEED CAKE

Serves 8

Like all seed cakes the Irish recipe is now seldom baked except perhaps in the older households. I sometimes wonder if this is because caraway seed is rather an adult flavour. My father-in-law John often comments on the seed cakes of his childhood memories, but I can't remember my mother ever baking one, so I suspect you must go back quite a long way to find a generation that enjoyed them.

A Welsh Seed Cake or *Bara Carawe* is identical to this recipe without the ground almonds and sultanas. It just has a little milk added to the mixture, to make a soft dropping consistency, which is then cooked in a 900 g/2 lb greased and lined loaf tin.

A seed cake is well worth trying and certainly used with care, they are unusual and interesting, reminding me rather more of the cooking to which we were so often treated by our Polish friends.

175 g/6 oz butter	50 g/2 oz ground almonds
175 g/6 oz soft pale brown sugar	2 teaspoons caraway seeds
3 large eggs, lightly beaten	50 g/2 oz sultanas
225 g/8 oz self raising flour	

Preheat the oven to 160°C/350°F/Gas Mark 4.

Cream the butter and sugar until light and fluffy, folding in the eggs and flour a little at a time until well mixed together.

Stir in the ground almonds, caraway seeds and the sultanas and spoon the mixture into a 18 cm/7 inch round cake tin.

Place the cake in the centre of the oven and bake for about 1 hour or until the cake is golden brown and feels firm when pressed lightly. A skewer inserted into the centre will come out cleanly when the cake is cooked.

Turn onto a wire rack to cool before serving.

VINEGAR CAKE

NORFOLK   *Serves 10*

The history of Vinegar Cake is unclear and difficult to trace, but this light fruitcake appears to have originated in Norfolk. Egg-less and sometimes made with dripping instead of butter, it is none the less an excellent inexpensive cake for weekday teatimes. This recipe was very probably the same one as the egg-less cake so necessary in wartime Britain or simply when the hens were off lay. The vinegar reacting with the bicarbonate of soda, acts as a raising agent.

225 g/8 oz butter or dripping
450 g/1 lb plain flour
275 g/10 oz caster sugar
225 g/8 oz raisins
115 g/4 oz sultanas

115 g/4 oz currants
1 teaspoon bicarbonate of soda
225 ml/8 fl oz milk
2 tablespoons vinegar

Preheat the oven to 180°C/350°F/Gas Mark 4.

In a large bowl, rub the fat lightly into the flour until it resembles breadcrumbs.

Add the sugar and fruit stirring thoroughly.

In a small bowl, mix the bicarbonate of soda with 1 tablespoon of the milk, pour the remaining milk into a large jug and add the vinegar.

Stir the bicarbonate of soda mixture into the jug of milk and vinegar, the liquid will froth up, so working quickly, add to the dry ingredients beating well.

Pour straight away into a greased and lined 18 cm/7 inch round cake tin and place in the centre of the oven and bake for 30 minutes then lower the oven to 150°C/300°F/Gas Mark 2 and bake for a further 1 hour. If the top begins to darken too much, cover with a sheet of brown paper.

The cake is cooked when the top feels firm when lightly pressed and a skewer inserted into the middle comes out cleanly.

Leave to cool for 20 minutes in the tin, before turning onto a wire rack to cool.

Not being credited with the title 'Regional' does not make these small country cakes any less interesting. In fact most of the recipes are undoubtedly still baked today, an example in our house being the enduring pleasure given by a plate of Butterfly Cakes, the sight of which is undeniably enhanced by memories of childhood.

The Cat's Tongue Cakes always make me smile, whilst the Wigs, Sugar Cakes and Macaroons all seem to me to have connections with funerals, when the family and friends of the deceased would make a considerable effort, bearing in mind the expense of some of the ingredients, to take a plate of seemingly 'suitable' cakes as a contribution to the funeral food.

Many of the cake recipes will probably remind you of family baking sessions rather than a particular area of the country, which in a lot of ways makes them nicer to bake.

Often used as an introduction to the fun of cake making, many of them are suitable for small children to bake with a little adult help and supervision. I can certainly still remember the pleasure my own children, Sian and Andrew, derived from preparing, baking and decorating Fairy Cakes. That's without mentioning the enjoyment they gained from eating them, often picking off the decorations, which they had so painstakingly chosen and arranged on top of the glace icing, before consuming the soft pale vanilla sponge cakes from inside their paper cases.

So do try some of the recipes, the Raspberry Buns, the Fondant Fancies, the Rock Cakes and perhaps even the irresistible Cat's Tongue Cakes.

**SMALL
COUNTRY CAKES**

HASTY CAKES

I found this recipe so intriguing that I could not believe it would work, until I made a batch myself. They are so quick to make and bake, that they live up to their name and are well worth trying as an alternative to breakfast toast.

450 g/1 lb self raising flour	25 g/1 oz of sultanas (optional)
A good pinch of salt	Milk, to mix

Preheat the oven to 160°C/325°F/Gas Mark 3.

Sieve flour and salt into a bowl, adding the sultanas if required. Stirring with a pallet knife add enough milk to form a stiff dough. Knead gently, cut into four to five pieces and shape into round cakes. Flatten slightly with a fork and place on a greased baking sheet.

Bake in the oven, for about 10 to 15 minutes until golden. Split and serve with fresh butter.

ELEVEN O'CLOCK BUNS

Makes 10-12

Long before the days of convenience snacks, these simple fruited buns were popped into packed lunch boxes to be enjoyed with coffee or tea at eleven o'clock.

225 g/8 oz self raising flour
50 g/2 oz butter
(Lard may be used if preferred)
50 g/2 oz caster sugar
50 g/2 oz sultanas

25 g/1 oz candied peel
Zest 1 lemon
1 large egg, lightly beaten
Milk

Preheat the oven to 190°C/375°F/Gas Mark 5.

Sift flour and rub in butter or lard, stir in sugar, sultanas, peel and lemon zest. Mix well and beat in the egg, if necessary adding enough milk to form a soft dough.

Spoon into greaseproof paper cases placed in a bun tin and bake in the centre of the oven for 20 minutes or until firm when lightly pressed.

Lift carefully from the bun tin and allow to cool on a wire rack.

CAT'S TONGUE CAKES

Makes about 20

Baking a batch of these light, airy little cakes, you will be in no doubt as to how they acquired their name. The long thin cakes, with slightly brown edges, closely resemble the delicate tongue of the family cat.

Although possibly French in origin, they have however, been made in Britain for so long as to have become traditional, often being served with ice cream or sorbet. Recently, when looking at several beautifully illustrated Irish cookery books, I found Cat's Tongues included among the recipes – so obviously the family 'moggy' travelled widely.

75 g/3 oz butter	75 g/3 oz plain flour
75 g/3 oz caster sugar	2 large egg whites, lightly beaten

Preheat the oven to 200°C/400°F/Gas Mark 6.

Cream the butter and sugar together until pale and fluffy. Sift the flour and add alternately with the egg whites, a little at a time, folding them in carefully to ensure they are well blended and free from any lumps.

Grease two baking trays and set aside. Fill a large piping bag with the mixture and pipe strips 5 cm/2 inches long and about 5 mm/1/4 inch wide. Bake in the centre of the oven for 5 to 7 minutes, until golden at the edges.

Allow to cool for a minute, then using a spatula lift them very carefully from the baking sheets onto a wire rack.

FUNERAL CAKES

Makes about 16

Sponge fingers, long and narrow with a little fruit and peel, were traditionally baked for funerals and served with sherry or wine.

Right up until the earlier part of the 20th century, Funeral Cakes were specially prepared for these sad gatherings and it would have been considered a very great insult for a mourner to refuse to eat these delicacies.

The funeral tea after the service would have included yet more cakes, in particular seed cakes, which were always served hot and buttered. Macaroons, Wig Cakes and Sugar Cakes were also documented as having been part of traditional funeral meal teas, which would often have been brought by the mourners as gifts for the family, in memory of the deceased.

Recipes for all these cakes can be found in this book.

75 g/3 oz plain flour
3 large eggs, separated
75 g/3 oz caster sugar
25 g/1 oz currants

Finely grated rind of 1 lemon

Topping
2 tablespoons icing sugar

Preheat the oven to 180°C/350°F/Gas Mark 4.

Line a baking tray with greaseproof paper, brush lightly with corn oil and set aside.

Sift the flour into a medium bowl. In a separate bowl whisk the egg yolks and sugar until pale and creamy. In a third bowl whisk the egg whites until stiff and able to stand in peaks.

Fold the flour a little at a time into the egg yolk mixture, using a metal tablespoon and then add the egg whites, folding in very gently to keep all the air you have just worked so hard to whisk in! Lastly, very carefully, fold in the currants and grated lemon rind.

Spoon the mixture into a large piping bag and using a 1 cm/$1/2$ inch plain nozzle, pipe 7.5 cm/3 inch fingers onto the prepared baking sheet, allowing space to expand as they bake.

Place the cakes in the centre of the oven and bake for about 10 minutes, or until they are pale golden brown. Do not over cook.

Leave the cakes to cool a little before lifting with a spatula onto a wire rack and dusting lightly with icing sugar. Place the icing sugar in a fine sieve and tap the edge lightly to give an even finish.

Store in an airtight container.

JUMBLES

Despite a fairly modern sounding name, the recipe for Jumbles appears in many old cookery books, long out of print. Lady Clark of Tillypronie, in her book of recipes collected until she died in 1897, mentions an almond variety. Other books and documents liken them to Brandy Snaps, or even mention a lemon flavoured Jumble, but the one unifying thing is that they all detail the traditional presentation as being 'knots, twists or twirls'.

The lemon variety is particularly delicious and very summery.

115 g/4 oz butter	Zest of 1 large lemon
115 g/4 oz caster sugar	250 g/9 oz self raising flour
2 eggs, lightly beaten	

Preheat the oven to 180°C/350°F/Gas Mark 4.

Cream the butter and sugar until light and fluffy. Beat in the eggs one at a time together with the lemon zest. Stir in the flour, using a metal spoon. The mixture will form a stiff dough.

Turn onto a lightly floured board and divide the mixture into 12 pieces. Roll them into 'sausages' and twist, knot or twirl using your artistic skills. Lift them gently onto a lightly greased baking sheet and bake for 15 to 20 minutes in the oven.

When pale golden brown, allow to cool for 5 minutes and then using a spatula, lift the Jumbles onto a wire cooling rack.

BUTTERFLY CAKES

Makes 18

As a child I used to like pulling off the wings and licking the butter cream filling from these pretty little cakes. My granny, Dora Blinman, was an expert at these, making vanilla ones with vanilla butter cream and a delicious chocolate variation by the addition of a tablespoon of cocoa to the mixture and the filling.

However, without doubt my absolute favourites were the orange butterfly cakes. Just adding orange zest to the cake mixture and freshly squeezed orange juice to butter cream, makes for an aromatic, mouth watering confection which is in my opinion, incomparably delectable.

115 g/4 oz butter
115 g/4 oz caster sugar
115 g/4 oz self raising flour
1 teaspoon baking powder
2 large eggs, lightly beaten
Flavours of your choice:
orange zest *or* cocoa *or* vanilla extract

Butter Cream Filling
(ingredients vary according to variety baked)
300 g/10 oz icing sugar
150 g/5 oz butter
Fresh orange juice *or* cocoa *or* vanilla extract

Preheat the oven to 190°C/375°F/Gas Mark 5.

Cream the butter and sugar together in a large bowl until light and fluffy. Sift the flour and baking powder and add alternately with the eggs, folding into the butter mixture. At this point add the flavour of your choice (either 2 teaspoons of orange zest, 1 tablespoon of cocoa or 1 teaspoon of vanilla). When blended and smooth, pile the mixture into bun tins, lined with greaseproof paper cases, filling each case to about two thirds full.

Bake in the centre of the oven until the cakes are well risen, firm to touch and pale golden brown which will take about 20 minutes. Remove from the oven and lifting them out of the bun tin, place on a wire rack to cool.

To make the butter cream filling, place the icing sugar and butter in a medium sized bowl and beat until smooth and lump free, by this time is will also become light and fluffy.

If you wish, add 1 tablespoon of orange juice or 1 tablespoon of cocoa or 1 teaspoon of vanilla extract, not allowing the butter cream to change too much in texture. It will in any case set firmly after if has been piped onto the cakes so do not worry.

When cold cut a slice horizontally from the peaked top of each fairy cake and divide it in half. Spoon or pipe a little butter cream filling onto the centre of the top of each cake replacing the two halves of the cake vertically, to form butterfly wings.

FONDANT FANCIES

Makes about 8-9

These dainty little cakes may be iced with glace icing if preferred but the fondant icing gives them a more consistent appearance and also makes them more easily handled and eaten. Good quality fondant icing is available from most supermarkets and specialist cake decorating shops.

I clearly remember making a large batch of these for my daughter Sian's sixth birthday party, unfortunately, I got so carried away that although they looked very beautiful when finished – it took me a whole afternoon and evening to decorate 24 cakes – it took 2 minutes for the children to eat them.

175 g/6 oz butter	3 large eggs lightly beaten
175 g/6 oz caster sugar	
175 g/6 oz self raising flour	**Topping**
1 teaspoon baking powder	Icing and decorations of your choice

Preheat the oven to 180°C/350°F/Gas Mark 4.

In a large bowl cream the butter and sugar together until light and fluffy and then add the remaining ingredients, beating well together until smooth and thoroughly blended.

Pile into a greased and lined 15 cm/6 inch square cake tin, allowing enough mixture for 4 cm/1 1/2 inch depth when baked. Place in the centre of the oven and cook for about 30 to 40 minutes or until the cake is firm to touch and pale golden brown. Carefully turn the cake out onto a wire rack to cool.

Leave the sponge, in its greaseproof paper to rest overnight in order to let it become a little firmer, then after removing its lining paper, turn the cake upside down to ensure as flat a top as possible. Finally cut into the required squares, rounds or diamonds, depending on your artistic whim. From here there is no limit to your ideas.

If liked, cut the cakes in half horizontally and sandwich together with a little jam or butter cream. Or using a piping bag, pipe a little 'blob' of butter cream onto the top of each cake. If using glace icing, ensure it is entirely smooth but thick enough to coat the cakes. A little colouring may be used if you would like pink or lemon cakes. Mauve and pink fondant fancies look really lovely and are my own personal favourites. Place the cakes on a wire rack and spoon the icing over, taking care that it completely covers the sides. Leave to dry.

Alternatively if using fondant icing, roll thinly and cut into shapes to fit easily over the cakes, tucking the fondant in carefully around the sides.

When completely dry, decorate the cakes with crystallised roses or violet petals, silver dragees or suitable sweets.

SLY CAKES

Sly Cakes appear to have acquired their rather odd name due to the very plain outward appearance of the pastry squares, except for a few odd currants peeping slyly through the surface.

In reality it hid a delectable filling of apples, currants, sultanas, sugar and spices and I recently came across a variation, which even included figs and walnuts and seemed well worth trying.

So despite the rather comical name, these little cakes are actually rather good.

225 g/8 oz Puff Pastry (page 20)	Zest of one lemon
75 g/3 oz sultanas	1 teaspoon mixed spice
75 g/3 oz currants	25 g/1 oz melted butter
1 large Bramley apple, grated	If liked a small quantity of chopped figs and
50 g/2 oz pale brown sugar	walnuts may be added
Zest of one orange	A little milk

Preheat the oven to 180°C/350°F/Gas Mark 4.

Roll the pastry thinly into an oblong and cut into two equal sized squares, laying one of the squares on a greased baking tray.

To prepare the filling, combine the fruits, sugar, zest, spice and the melted butter, stirring thoroughly. Then spread the filling onto the sheet of pastry, leaving a small band at the edges. Damp and seal the edges well to prevent the filling escaping.

Mark the top lightly into squares using a knife and then brush with a little milk and place in the oven for about 45 minutes or until brown and well puffed.

Leave to cool and cut into squares with a sharp knife.

BLOSSOM CAKES

Makes 18

When reading one of my grandmother's very ancient handwritten cookery books I came across this delightful recipe for these delicate little cakes, which when decorated look really exquisite, the name 'Blossom Cakes' being an excellent description. I can remember my grandmother Elsie baking them and my being allowed to place the 'blossom' on top of the iced cakes, I must have been about four or five years old at the time.

Basically a Fairy Cake mixture, these little buns are iced on top with the palest pink glace icing and decorated with a little angelica, cut into the shape of leaves and either crystallized violet or rose petals.

Traditionally, the cake mixture would also have been coloured with a little pink food dye – but this is optional. Personally I would recommend seeking out one of the safe food colours now available from specialist stores and departments.

115 g/4 oz butter	**Topping**
115 g/4 oz caster sugar	225 g/8 oz icing sugar
115 g/4 oz self raising flour	A little pink colouring
1 teaspoon baking powder	A little hot water
2 large eggs, lightly beaten	Crystallised rose petals
	Angelica 'leaves'

Preheat the oven to 190°C/375°F/Gas Mark 5.

Cream the butter and sugar in a large bowl and add the sifted flour and baking powder alternately with the eggs. When the mixture is well blended, add a couple of drops of food colouring to obtain the very palest pink tint. Spoon the cake mixture into bun trays lined with greaseproof paper cases, filling each cake case to about two thirds full.

Bake in the centre of the oven until well risen and firm to touch, this will take about 15 to 20 minutes.

Remove from the oven and taking the cakes from the bun trays, leave them to cool on a wire rack.

Meanwhile mix the icing sugar and a little pink colouring, with a drop of hot water to form a coating consistency and spread a little of the icing over the top of each of the cold cakes. Decorate them with the crystallised rose petals and angelica 'leaves'. Leave to set before placing on a serving plate.

TANSY CAKES

Serves 8-10

Tansy Cakes were considered a great treat in 18th century England but tansy, a wild herb, has fallen out of favour and is rarely used now. This is a herb with an extremely strong taste – a small quantity gives a pleasant flavour to cakes, but do not be tempted to add a little extra. The tansy plant I bought recently from our local herb nursery enabled me to try this recipe and I was enchanted to learn from them about the many medicinal uses for this historical herb.

Fried in butter, Tansy Cakes are delicious at teatime but would also make a very good pudding, served with some cream. It is important however to ensure that the mixture is thickened with enough macaroon crumbs. The cakes resemble drop scones in appearance but are sweet and slightly crunchy in texture.

6 Macaroons (see page 174)
2 large eggs, lightly beaten
75 ml/3 fl oz double cream
1 tablespoon sherry
50 g/2 oz caster sugar
1 teaspoon chopped fresh tansy

Zest of 1 large lemon
Zest of 1 large orange
50 g/2 oz melted butter

Topping
A little extra caster sugar for dredging

Crush the macaroons in a large bowl. Add all the other ingredients, whisking together until completely blended. Leave for 30 minutes.

In a large frying pan melt some butter and olive oil to a depth of 1 cm/^{1}/2 inch, then drop tablespoons of the mixture into the oil and fry a few at a time, cooking each side for 3 or 4 minutes, until golden brown.

Lift the cakes out onto kitchen roll to drain. Dredge with caster sugar and serve whilst still warm.

HIRING FAIR CAKES

Makes 8

Right up until the early part of the 20th century, Hiring Fairs, nowadays often called Mop Fairs, were held in many country areas during May and November. These sombre gatherings where farm workers, servants and very often children were hired for labour, were enlivened by festivities, entertainment and traditional eating and drinking.

Hiring Fair Cakes were very often gingerbreads such as the Norfolk Fair Buttons (see page 264) but there were also regional specialities such as the Keswick Fair Cakes and Wiltshire Fairings. Old historical manuscripts provide us with a great insight into the ingredients used and the large variation of cakes coming under the general name of Hiring Fair Cakes or Fairings.

I have chosen one recipe from the many available, which is really rather good.

450 g/1 lb plain flour
175 g/6 oz butter (lard may be used if preferred)
12 g/$^1/_2$ oz fresh yeast
50 g/2 oz soft brown sugar
150 ml/$^1/_4$ pint tepid water

Filling
225 g/8 oz currants

225 g/8 oz sultanas
225 g/8 oz soft brown sugar
50 g/2 oz chopped glace peel
50 g/2 oz chopped glace cherries
$^1/_2$ teaspoon mace
$^1/_2$ teaspoon mixed spice
2 tablespoons rum

Preheat the oven to 200°C/400°F/Gas Mark 6.

Sift the flour into a bowl and rub in the butter (or lard) making a well in the middle. Cream the yeast with the sugar, pour on the tepid water and stir, leaving for a little while until froth forms (about 15 minutes). Pour the yeast mix into the centre of the flour and mix with your hands until a ball is formed.

Knead for 5 minutes on a lightly floured surface until smooth, place in a bowl, cover and leave to rise until doubled in size. Turn again onto a lightly floured board, knead again for a few minutes and roll out into a thin oblong, cutting the dough into approximately 7.5 cm/3 inch squares, set aside. You should have at least 16 to make the 8 cakes.

Place the ingredients for the filling into a bowl and combine thoroughly. Then put a spoonful of the mixture onto each of 8 squares, leaving a little space at the edges for sealing, dampening them with a little water.

Finally place the remaining squares of dough over the top of the bases and press the edges firmly together, lifting the cakes onto a greased baking tray.

Bake in the centre of the oven for about 30 minutes or until risen and golden brown.

Using a spatula transfer carefully onto a wire rack and leave to become cool, bearing in mind that the filling will be extremely hot if you are tempted to try one too hastily.

MARCHPANE CAKES

Makes about 15-20

Marchpane Cakes with their gold leaf decorations were frequently served at the end of lavish Tudor banquets, although there is some evidence that these cakes go back even further in history.

At Christmas the cakes formed an eye-catching centrepiece, often decorated with or nestled in amongst glace fruits and silvered sugared almonds. The forerunner to our marzipan, marchpane (from the French *marce pain*), made from ground almonds and finely crushed sugar, had the added ingredient of rosewater which prevents the almonds from becoming too 'oily' during handling – a tip that I have found very useful when incorporated into today's baking.

Elaborate shapes were cut from the marchpane mixture, the most common being hearts, diamonds, animals, triangles and circular shapes. Once baked and the cakes cold, they were decorated with crystallised flowers, sugared almonds, dragees and almost always the gold leaf.

There is some evidence that marchpane was sometimes baked as a large iced cake before being endowed with its traditional elaborate decorations and whilst it is speculation, there is every reason to believe that these iced versions were eventually added onto the Victorians' rich fruit cake bases, becoming the Christmas cakes that we know today.

The following recipe is easy, but do not overwork the mixture or it will become very sticky.

450 g/1 lb ground almonds	Rosewater
300 g/10 oz caster sugar	A little extra ground almond for rolling out
1 egg yolk	

Preheat the oven to 150°C/300°F/Gas Mark 2.

Place the ground almonds, sugar and egg yolk in a bowl, adding enough rosewater to form a soft but not sticky paste. Pat the mixture into a ball and transfer to a board, which has been lightly 'floured' with ground almonds.

Shape into a sheet approximately 2.5 cm/$^1/_2$ inch thick and cut into shapes of your choice, using metal cutters if liked.

Prepare a baking sheet by covering with rice paper and carefully lift the marchpane shapes onto the sheet. Bake in the oven for 20 minutes or until set but not browned. The cakes will be ready when they are firm to touch.

Lifting carefully with a spatula, place them on a wire rack and leave to become completely cold.

Trim the rice paper from the edges and decorate with silver or gold leaf, gold or silver dragees or even crystallised roses.

Place on a plate and use as a centrepiece for a dinner party – they are sure to attract considerable attention, both with their appearance and their interesting history.

BERKELEY BUNS

Serves 12

Despite considerable detective work, I have been unable to find any real history behind Berkeley Buns, which for obvious reasons I thought may be connected with the village of Berkeley in Gloucestershire, but all searching proved unsuccessful. The recipe constantly crops up in old cookery books and therefore I felt these intriguing little buns were a worthy addition to our list of recipes.

225 g/8 oz self raising flour
1/2 teaspoon mixed ground spice
115 g/4 oz butter
115 g/4 oz soft pale brown sugar

50 g/2 oz glace cherries
50 g/2 oz crystallised ginger
Zest of one lemon
1 large egg, lightly beaten

Preheat the oven to 200°C/400°F/Gas Mark 6.

Sift the flour and ground spice into a bowl and rub in the butter to form a breadcrumb texture, stir in the sugar.

Chop the cherries and ginger into small pieces and together with the lemon zest add to the mixture, stirring to ensure they are evenly distributed.

Add the beaten egg and stir with a pallet knife to form very soft dough.

Grease a flat baking sheet and using a tablespoon, drop little heaps of the mixture onto the tray, spacing them evenly.

Bake in the centre of the oven for approximately 15-20 minutes and when golden brown, remove from the oven and gently lift them onto a cooling rack.

PRINCE OF WALES CAKES

Makes 8-9

Not the modern recipe you would imagine – these cakes were named after the previous Prince of Wales, who became King Edward VIII briefly in 1936.

Shaped into knots, these little cakes are extremely delicious and their appearance is rather different. I certainly enjoyed trying this recipe and the resulting cakes disappeared very rapidly.

50 g/2 oz butter	225 g/8 oz self raising flour
50 g/2 oz sugar	25 g/1 oz ground rice
1 egg	1 lemon

Preheat the oven to 180°C/350°F/Gas Mark 4.

Cream the butter and sugar together until fluffy. Beat in the egg, add the sifted flour, the ground rice and the grated rind of the lemon (reserving the lemon juice for use later).

Mix thoroughly, adding a little lemon juice if necessary, to form a soft dough. Cut the dough into even sized pieces and roll them into 15 cm/6 inch long 'sausages'. Tie the 'sausages' into knots and lift onto a greased baking tray. Brush with a little water and sprinkle with caster sugar.

Bake in the oven for about 15 minutes until golden brown.

Leave to cool for 5 minutes before lifting carefully, with a spatula, onto a wire rack.

RASPBERRY BUNS

Makes 12

An old recipe which deserves a revival. Raspberry Buns with their jam centres are absolutely delicious and popular with children and adults alike. I was delighted to come across a very good version in a handwritten cookery book dating back to 1923, by Ivy Peatman, lent to me by her son Neville Peatman who assures me it was one of his mother's favourite recipes.

225 g/8 oz self raising flour
35 g/1 ^{1}/2 oz Raisley *
(substitute 1 teaspoon baking powder)
75 g/3 oz butter
75 g/3 oz caster sugar

1 large egg, lightly beaten
A little milk
Raspberry Jam
A little extra milk
A little extra caster sugar

Preheat the oven to 180°C/350°F/Gas Mark 4.

Sift the flour and baking powder into a bowl and rub in the butter until it resembles fine breadcrumbs. Stir in the sugar. Add the beaten egg and enough milk to form a soft dough. Divide the dough into 12 even sized pieces and roll them into balls.

On a lightly floured board, flatten each one slightly and place half a teaspoon of raspberry jam in the centre. Dampen the edges with a little milk and close the dough over the jam. Turn the buns over and place them on a greased baking sheet. Brush with a little milk and sprinkle with sugar. Bake in the oven for 15 to 20 minutes.

Cool on a wire rack and serve when cold, but do be careful if tempted to eat straight from the oven, the jam will be very, very hot.

* **Raisley** – I had great trouble tracing this product, which is very old and no longer in production. However, having traced it as far as Brown and Polson who were famous for their cornflour, I managed to contact their Customer Service Department (they are now owned by Unilever Best Foods) who were very enthusiastic and dug out an old advertisement for Raisley from their archives.

The nearest thing today would probably be baking powder, Raisley being described in the advertisement as 'for home baking, specially for improving cakes and scones, used 1 part to 6-8 parts of flour'. Whilst of course, we would not need to use as much baking powder, it would appear to be a similar baking ingredient.

ROUT CAKES

Serves 15-20

Like so many of the old recipes, I have found several mentions of Rout Cakes, none of the recipes bearing any similarity to each other.

One excellent book from which I have made many cakes over the years, although now long out of print, was by Helen Jerome entitled *Cake Making* and first published in 1932, in which she refers to Rout Cakes as being the probable forerunners of Marchpane Cakes (see page 160) and detailing a recipe given in 1736. And indeed her recipe does use almonds rather than flour and orange flower water to bind.

A recipe in a much more recent book enchantingly entitled *The Jane Austen Cookbook* by Maggie Black and Deirdre Le Faye whilst using rosewater, which was a major ingredient in the original Marchpane Cakes, omits any ground almonds and bases their Rout Drop Cakes on a flour base. Therefore like so many very old recipes the ingredients and variations do in fact vary considerably, although doubtless all made with the same enthusiasm.

The following recipe, using almonds, is one which seems to form a happy compromise of the various recipes I have found over the years and as I admit to a weakness for almonds in any shape or form, I can heartily recommend them.

350 g/12 oz grounds almonds	1 small egg, lightly beaten
175 g/6 oz caster sugar	
175 g/6 oz icing sugar	**Topping**
1 teaspoon rosewater	50 g/2 oz currants if liked
1/2 teaspoon almond extract	

Preheat the oven to 140°C/275°F/Gas Mark 1.

Place all the ingredients into a bowl, including the lightly beaten egg and knead the mixture until it forms a soft pliable dough. This may take some time but do not be put off. The ground almonds naturally exude oil, which the rosewater will help to balance.

When the ball of mixture is formed, lightly dust a cool surface with icing sugar and roll the dough to about 1 cm/1/2 inch thickness. Cut into rounds, or any preferred shape, using metal cutters, kneading any remaining dough and gently rolling out again until all the mixture has been used.

Place the shapes onto a lightly greased baking sheet dotting the top with a few currants if liked.

Bake in the centre of the oven for about 15 minutes or until very slightly golden brown and firm when pressed lightly in the centre.

Remove the cakes with a spatula and place on a cooling rack.

If liked the Rout Cakes may be decorated in the manner of Marchpane Cakes (page 160), using silver balls or crystallised flowers.

SUGAR CAKES

Makes 18

It was something of a surprise to find that these dainty little cakes were once fashionable at funerals, although Sugar Cakes were also baked for 'special' teatime occasions, having been very popular for several centuries. They seemed to find their way into the very best of cookery books, probably due to the high cost of their ingredients, so it is doubtful that they would have been baked by the 'lower classes' except perhaps as a gift for the funeral meal.

Rather sweet by today's standards, they would none the less be excellent served with something like a fruit mousse.

275 g/10 oz butter
450 g/1 lb plain white flour
350 g/12 oz of the best ground sugar
(icing sugar would be used nowadays)

4 eggs, lightly beaten
Zest of 1 orange
$^1/_2$ teaspoon mace

Preheat the oven to 140°C/275°F/Gas Mark 1.

Cream the butter into the flour until it forms a ball. Add the icing sugar continuing to knead gently until it forms a dough. Add enough of the lightly beaten eggs to allow the mixture to become soft and pliable and then add the zest and mace, kneading gently.

The mixture should be a stiff dropping consistency, but not runny.

Drop dessertspoonfuls of the cake mix onto greased baking trays, leaving room for expansion and bake in the centre of the oven for approximately 10 to 15 minutes or until very, very pale brown and well risen. They will feel quite firm when pressed lightly in the centre.

Remove gently from the baking tray using a spatula and allow to cool on a rack. When cold store in an airtight tin until required.

SILVER CAKES

Makes approximately 12

Wonderfully delicate almond cakes, perfect for lazy summer picnics or with an after dinner coffee. The pale appearance of these little cakes is achieved by using only the whites of egg, the yolks being the 'Gold' ingredient in Gold Cakes (see page 170). Some recipes even use lard, presumably to keep the colour of the cakes 'silver', but I admit to using butter even if that does make the cakes slightly less pale.

Gold and Silver Cakes were said to have been much loved by Queen Victoria, although their history is actually rather hazy but they were certainly very popular and are mentioned in many old cookery books. The richness of their ingredients however, suggests that they were probably only eaten in middle and upper class homes.

115 g/4 oz butter (or lard if preferred)	1 level teaspoon baking powder
115 g/4 oz caster sugar	50 g/2 oz ground almonds
5 egg whites	1/2 teaspoon almond extract
115 g/4 oz plain flour	

Preheat the oven to 160°C/325°F/Gas Mark 3.

Cream the fat and sugar until light and fluffy. Whisk the egg whites until they are stiff and gently fold them into the sugar mixture, using a large metal spoon. When fully incorporated sift the flour and baking powder together and add a little at a time, finally stirring in the ground almonds and almond extract.

Spoon the mixture into a bun tin lined with paper cases, filling each to about two thirds. Bake in the centre of the oven for about 15 to 20 minutes. The cakes should remain very pale but feel firm when gently pressed.

Cool on a wire rack.

Opposite: Silver and Gold Cakes

GOLD CAKES

The companion cakes to Silver Cakes, use egg yolks (the whites having been used in the Silver Cakes) and oranges ensuring delectable, aromatic dainty golden cakes. Gold Cakes were particularly popular in the Victorian era when 'tea time' was a most fashionable time of the day.

115 g/4 oz butter	5 egg yolks, lightly beaten
115 g/4 oz caster sugar	3 tablespoons of fresh orange juice
115 g/4 oz plain flour	Zest of one orange
I teaspoon baking powder	

Preheat the oven to 180°C/350°F/Gas Mark 4.

Cream butter and sugar together until light and fluffy. Sift the flour and baking powder and together with the egg yolks and using a metal spoon, fold gently in to the butter mixture, a little at a time.

Finally lightly stir in the orange juice and zest ensuring it is well mixed.

Line a bun tin with greaseproof paper cases and spoon the mixture to about two thirds full.

Bake in the centre of the oven for about 20 minutes until well risen and firm to touch.

Remove from the tin but leave in their greaseproof cases and cool on a wire rack.

LADY'S FINGERS

Makes approximately 10

Light, finger cakes which are perfectly suited to eating with ice-cream or a summer fruit mousse. This very old recipe, for some reason, always reminds me of the elegance of the teas of Jane Austen's era. It is however, important to point out that you should not over cook them, as they must remain pale and delicate in appearance.

115 g/4 oz butter	Whites of 2 large eggs, lightly beaten
50 g/2 oz icing sugar, sifted	115 g/4 oz self raising flour
50 g/2 oz caster sugar	1/2 teaspoon vanilla extract

Preheat the oven to 160°C/325°F/Gas Mark 3.

Cream the butter, icing sugar and caster sugar until light and fluffy. Add the beaten egg whites stirring well. Lightly fold in the flour and vanilla extract making sure that the ingredients are thoroughly mixed.

Fill a large piping bag and pipe the mixture into 7.5 cm/3 inch lengths onto a greased baking tray.

Bake in the oven for approximately 10 minutes, watching carefully, allowing them to become only the very palest of brown.

Cool for a moment on the baking tray and then using a spatula, lift them carefully onto a wire rack to cool. As the Lady's Fingers become cold, they will be less delicate to handle.

FAIRY CAKES

Serves 12-15

Whilst it is unclear how these delectable little cakes acquired their name, I like to think it is due to their light texture and colourful decorations. Not unlike the fairies of our imagination.

Using a Victoria Sandwich mixture the little cup cakes are not dissimilar to the very much older recipe for Queen Cakes, except that no vine fruits are added.

They are popular with children; my own Sian and Andrew used to thoroughly enjoy mixing, baking and decorating Fairy Cakes, using glace icing and an assortment of sweets such as dolly mixtures for decoration. Alternatively you can use frosted rose or violet petals – for a sophisticated artisan finish, great for adult children.

Perhaps it was down to this early emphasis on design that my son Andrew later obtained a degree in landscape design, now there's a thought.

225 g/8 oz butter	**Topping**
225 g/8 oz caster sugar	225 g/8 oz icing sugar
4 eggs, lightly beaten	Lemon zest *or* orange zest
225 g/8 oz self raising flour	Juice of the lemon *or* orange
1/2 teaspoon vanilla extract	*or* flavouring of your choice
	Dolly mixtures *or* similar dainty sweets
	Crystallised petals

Preheat the oven to 190°C/375°F/Gas Mark 5.

Cream the butter and sugar together until light and fluffy, add the eggs and flour alternately, beating gently until fully incorporated. Add the vanilla extract, stirring thoroughly.

Line a bun tin with greaseproof paper cases, spooning enough mixture into each case to fill them two thirds full. Bake in the centre of the oven for 15-20 minutes or until well risen and golden brown. They should feel firm to touch if pressed lightly.

Leave them in their paper cases, remove from the bun tin and cool them on a wire rack.

When cold, ice each cake with the glace icing of your choice, using the icing sugar, zest and juice, which should be mixed to give a smooth coating consistency. Finish by decorating with your chosen toppings.

MACAROONS

Makes approximately 24

Almond macaroons have been adding elegance to the English tea table for several centuries. Crisp and melting, these delectable cakes are nectar for the almond lovers amongst us. The recipe appears to have changed very little over the centuries, simply ground almonds, sugar and egg white, but it is essential to obtain wafer or rice paper before attempting this recipe as the macaroons would stick like glue to a baking tray. Although it is important not to over bake, they will look very professional with little skill, just care. I can still remember the great feeling of success when I baked my first batch of macaroons.

4 large egg whites
225 g/8 oz ground almonds
450 g/1 lb caster sugar
1 teaspoon almond extract

Topping
1 egg white, lightly beaten
24 whole blanched almonds, for decoration

Preheat the oven to 160°C/325°F/Gas Mark 3.

Beat egg whites until frothy. Add the ground almonds and sugar, beating them well together. Add the almond extract and beat again.

Place the sheets of rice paper onto baking trays and drop a teaspoonful of the mixture onto the paper flattening slightly, allowing sufficient space for them to spread a little. Brush each cake with some of the beaten egg white and place an almond into the centre of each macaroon.

Bake in the oven for approximately 15 minutes or until very lightly browned. Lift the macaroons together with the rice paper onto a wire rack. The rice paper will crumble between the cakes but when cold you will easily be able to neaten the rice paper around the edges of the macaroons.

WIGS, WIGGS, WIGGES OR WHIGS   *Serves 8*

Originally a Lenten speciality, Wigs are recorded as far back as the 15th century; mention being found in many books including Samuel Pepys Diary for 8th April 1664 where he refers to them as being part of a 'Lenten Supper of Wiggs and Ale'.

Few recipes can be found until more recently, although Mrs Raffald (*The Experienced English Housekeeper, 1769*) does give a recipe for 'Light Wigs' and talks of toasting them to serve with melted cheese.

Different parts of the country had their own traditions and recipes for these particular cakes, which to our 21st century eye, often appear to be more like sweet bread than a cake. But it must be remembered that yeast was used to 'raise' cakes for hundreds of years before our more familiar raising agents.

In Bedfordshire they were eaten on St Catherine's Day, 25th November and in Dorset as a breakfast snack but always the unifying ingredient appears to have been caraway seeds.

The shape of Wigs varied as much as the recipes have over time, records showing that they were often large round buns, marked with a cross. Sometimes they were baked on enamel plates or saucers, the edges browning more than the centre, and curling slightly, giving the impression of a Wig. I have read that this version were also called Christmas Eve Wigs. Dorset Wigs were certainly individual round buns but without doubt the most commonly recorded shape, which seemed to be seen as the 'correct' shape, was a small wedge or triangle.

There is some evidence that Wigs were commonly eaten at funerals, but I have been unable to confirm the accuracy of this, despite speaking to several funeral directors.

Rarely if ever being baked today, they certainly had their place in our cake history.

450 g/1 lb strong plain flour	1 teaspoon caraway seeds
115 g/4 oz butter	300 ml/^{1}/2 pint tepid milk
115 g/4 oz sugar	15 g/^{1}/2 oz fresh yeast
^{1}/2 teaspoon mixed spice	1 large egg

Preheat the oven to 200°C/400°F/Gas Mark 6.

Place the flour in a bowl and rub in the butter to breadcrumb consistency. Add the sugar, spice and caraway seeds and stir.

Pour the tepid milk onto the yeast and stir thoroughly, adding to the flour mixture, continue stirring with a pallet knife and then mix in the beaten egg. Knead gently to a soft, smooth dough.

Form into a large circle and cut a little way into the top, to form wedges, which will become the triangles when baked and split into portions. Leave to rise uncovered, in a warm place for 15 minutes and bake in the oven until well risen and golden brown.

Cool on a wire rack and break into triangles as needed. May be eaten plain or served buttered with jam or cheese.

ROCK CAKES

Makes 12

I remember my mother Thelma making these for tea, and very good they were too. The traditionally 'rocky' appearance being achieved by ensuring that very little liquid, if any, is added other than eggs. On the other hand I have tasted some very bad rock cakes – those closely resembling their name.

The recipe for rock cakes dates back a long way; Lady Clark of Tillypronie mentions them in her recipes collected during the 1800's, flavoured with lemon peel. It is easy to imagine how these little cakes must have been simplicity itself to bake, bearing in mind the far from easy conditions for baking in cottages.

An old fashioned rock cake should be light and crumbly, with enough fruit and peel to give it its characteristic 'fruity' fragrance. In fact I defy you to resist eating them still warm from the oven – clearly reminiscent of childhood.

225 g/8 oz self raising flour	115 g/4 oz sultanas
1 teaspoon baking powder	50 g/2 oz chopped glace peel
115 g/4 oz butter	Zest of an orange (optional)
75 g/3 oz caster sugar	2 large eggs

Preheat the oven to 200°C/400°F/Gas Mark 6.

Sift the flour and baking powder into a large bowl and rub in the butter until it resembles breadcrumbs.

Stir in the sugar, fruit, peel and zest.

Whisk the eggs and add to the dry ingredients. Stir with a pallet knife to bind together to form a stiff dough.

Grease a large baking sheet and allow 2 teaspoonfuls of the mixture for each cake, leaving a little space between each one.

Bake in the oven for 15 to 20 minutes until golden brown and firm to touch.

Do not overcook. Remove from the baking sheet and allow to cool on a wire rack.

SHROVE TUESDAY BUNS

Makes 14 buns

Traditionally a time of jollity leading up to Lent, Shrove Tuesday Buns were made, like pancakes, to use up the food in the store cupboard. Once the surplus food had been consumed this removed temptation and ensured frugal eating during Lent.

Simple yeast buns with an almond filling, they are easy to make and the result is delicious. They are a little time consuming but worth the effort.

15 g/1/2 oz fresh yeast
1 teaspoon sugar
5 tablespoons tepid water
350 g/12 oz plain flour
1 teaspoon mixed spice
50 g/2 oz caster sugar
50 g/2 oz ground almonds
2 eggs, lightly beaten
150 ml/1/4 pint milk

Topping
A little extra milk

Filling
75 ml/3 fl oz single cream
115 g/4 oz ground almonds
50 g/2 oz caster sugar

Preheat the oven to 180°C/350°F/Gas Mark 4.

Place the yeast in a small bowl and cream together with the teaspoon of sugar, add the water and stir. Set aside for 10 to 15 minutes in a warm place until a froth is formed.

Sift the flour and spice into a bowl and stir in the sugar and ground almonds. Make a well in the centre and pour in the yeast, lightly beaten eggs and the milk. Using your hands mix all the ingredients together until a soft dough is formed.

Turn onto a lightly floured surface and knead until smooth, this will take about 5 to 10 minutes. Place into a clean bowl, cover and place in a warm place, leaving to double in size.

When well risen turn out onto a floured surface and knead lightly for 5 minutes, when the dough will be reduced in size.

Pull into 14 pieces, rolling them gently between your hands to form smooth balls. Place them onto a greased baking sheet, leaving enough space between them for them to expand a little during cooking, and lightly coat the tops with the milk. Bake in the oven for about 20 minutes or until the buns are well risen and golden brown. The buns are done when they sound hollow if tapped underneath. If necessary return to the oven for a further 5 minutes.

When cooked, transfer to a wire rack and leave to become completely cold.

Meanwhile in a small bowl mix together the filling ingredients. Cut the buns in half, remove a spoonful of the centre of each bun, breaking it into cake crumbs. Add this to the almond filling and stir well. Finally spoon the mixture into the buns and serve.

JUBILEE BUNS

Makes 12

Queen Victoria's Golden Jubilee in 1897 kindled many ideas for celebration recipes and these little buns were just perfect for children's parties or adult teas.

Simple and inexpensive to make, this recipe for 12 buns would have cost around 5p.

450 g/1 lb self raising flour
115 g/4 oz butter
115 g/4 oz caster sugar
350 g/12 oz currants
2 large eggs, lightly beaten
1 teaspoon almond extract

A little milk

Topping
1 egg white, lightly beaten
115 g/4 oz ground almonds

Preheat the oven to 180°C/350°F/Gas Mark 4.

Sift the flour into a bowl and rub in the butter until the mixture resembles breadcrumbs. Stir in the sugar. Add currants, beaten egg and almond extract, mixing thoroughly. Add a little milk if necessary to form a soft dough.

Divide into 12, shape into rounds and place on a greased baking tray.

Brush with egg white and sprinkle liberally with the ground almonds.

Bake in the oven for 20 minutes or until lightly brown and firm to touch.

Remove from the baking tray and cool on a wire rack.

MERINGUES

It was difficult to decide whether to include Meringues, but who can argue that they belong to the cake family? A good meringue should be crisp on the outside but delectably chewy on the inside and when sandwiched together with fresh whipped cream, they are in a class of their own.

Easy to make, yet with pitfalls if the method is not followed carefully, however if you approach the task slowly and with care you will find few problems.

4 large egg whites	**Filling**
225 g/8 oz caster sugar	Whipped double cream

Preheat the oven to 100°C/200°F/Gas Mark ¼.

In a very clean cold bowl, whisk the egg whites until they are stiff.

Fold in half the sugar, using a metal spoon and whisk again until the meringue mixture becomes very stiff and dry.

Finally fold in the remaining sugar, very gently, so as not to lose all the air you have so carefully incorporated.

On a lightly greased baking sheet drop spoonfuls of the meringue, leaving a little gap between each spoonful and place in the centre of the oven for about 3 hours or until completely dry. Don't worry if it takes a little longer.

Cool on a wire rack. The meringues will store well in an airtight container until required.

Sandwich together, with whipped cream, just before serving.

MADELEINES

Traditionally made in dariole moulds (small, cylindrical moulds), these light Genoese sponge cakes are coated with a little apricot or raspberry jam, rolled in desiccated coconut, placed upright and topped with half a glace cherry.

A great favourite at the Victorian tea table, these pretty little cakes are well worth making.

225 g/8 oz butter	**Topping**
225 g/8 oz caster sugar	Raspberry or apricot jam
225 g/8 oz self raising flour	Desiccated coconut
4 large eggs, lightly beaten	Red glace cherries, halved
I teaspoon vanilla extract	

Preheat the oven to 160°C/325°F/Gas Mark 3.

Cream the butter and sugar together until light and fluffy. Add the flour and lightly beaten eggs a little at a time, until fully mixed. Add the vanilla and stir well.

Grease moulds and flour lightly. Fill to about two thirds full and stand upright on a baking tray.

Bake in the centre of the oven for about 10-15 minutes or until firm to touch and golden brown.

When baked, remove from the oven, tap the tins firmly on the work surface and gently turn out onto a wire rack and allow to cool.

When cold, brush with a little warmed jam and roll gently in desiccated coconut. Stand upright and top with half a red glace cherry.

Perhaps one of the most interesting sections of the book; for many of the recipes are linked to the passage of the year such as the farming cakes with a Threshing, a Shearing, or a Harvest Cake. Many of course are celebrations of the church year and are therefore religiously and historically symbolic like Christmas Cake and Simnel Cake, which are part of our lives today.

Particularly fascinating was the wide variety of recipes for the same cake; some of them such, as the Plum Cake, have seven or eight different variations, often with widely differing ingredients. The Luncheon Cake for example, boasts at least a dozen recipes of which I have tried several, including a yeast based variation. Collecting the recipes and the research necessary to trace the background stories of the cakes, has been enchanting and always incredibly absorbing. I have baked the recipes and enjoyed every moment of it – although I have to say, some of the cakes have been a good deal more tasty than others, but it is very humbling to remember the times and social conditions under which the cakes would have been made and so every cake has its own importance within the scheme of history. The Oven Bottom Cake is the perfect example, it would have been made from left over odds and ends and baked as the heat was fading from the oven, doubtless being seen as a real treat to enliven days when food was often not easily varied.

I recall reading a little book, issued by the Royal English Agricultural Society in 1843, which gave advice to estate owners and wealthy employers on the recommended feeding for 'labourers'. Potatoes featured heavily, with a little meat 'passed through' giving flavour, although the luckier labourers would have had the space to keep a pig, thus improving their diet enormously. Cakes most certainly did not feature. One particular paragraph summed up the tone perfectly 'Close economy is the very life and existence of a poor man's comforts. Without it he will run in arrear with every one with whom he deals, starvation will stare him in the face; the wretchedness of his wife and children will drive him in despair to the beer-shop; and that finally, as a drunkard, pilferer and a poacher, to the workhouse.' The sad thing is that this was in England and not that long ago. But what such a booklet does is help to understand that a cake baked on a griddle over a cottage fire would have provided real interest to the dreary diet and doubtless been a very real treat for such a down-trodden family.

On a jollier note there is undeniably something wholesome and good about an invitingly aromatic cake being cooled on a wire rack and then placed on a plate ready to cut into wedges and we can only begin to think about the importance such cakes would have assumed in families where cooking facilities were inadequate, sometimes just a pot by the fire, ingredients often hard to come by and indeed the money to buy the ingredients even harder to find. It is therefore easy to see how a cake would so easily illustrate the status of the family baking and eating it.

It is not that different today, there is always pride accompanying the making of a splendid cake put in its place in the centre of the table. A pride you will not feel with a shop bought cake.

**LARGE
COUNTRY CAKES**

QUEEN CAKE

Serves 6-8

Dating from the Victorian era, this delightful recipe is rather different from the small Queen Cakes detailed in the Small Regional Cakes section in that it contains chopped glace fruits of any variety, such as cherries, ginger, pineapple, peaches, apricots etc, added to a basic Victoria Sponge recipe. It is delicious, really different and very imaginative.

175 g/6 oz butter
175 g/6 oz caster sugar
4 eggs, lightly beaten
175 g/6 oz self raising flour

225 g/8 oz chopped glace fruits
(Comprising any of the fruits mentioned)

Filling
Raspberry jam

Preheat the oven to 190°C/375°F/Gas Mark 5.

Cream the butter and sugar together until light and fluffy and stir in the eggs and sifted flour a little at a time, until fully mixed.

Fold in the finely chopped glace fruits (washed and dried if necessary) using a large metal spoon.

Transfer the mixture to two 18 cm/7 inch greased sandwich tins and smooth the surface lightly. Place in the oven for 25 to 30 minutes or until firm to touch and pale golden brown.

Turn carefully onto a wire rack and leave to cool before sandwiching together with fresh raspberry jam.

SPONGE CAKE FROM 1895

Serves 6

To me this recipe illustrates perfectly an age gone by, not only is it impossible to buy sugar by the block, but the time taken to make this sponge by hand, would have been phenomenal. I suppose using sugar cubes may produce a similar effect.

This cake does not rise as much as we would expect today from one made with more modern ingredients but it is none the less a very good cake, which I think I am justified in leaving in the original pounds and ounces measurements.

$^3/_4$ lb of block sugar
$^1/_2$ teacup water
5 eggs
$^1/_2$ lb flour

Filling
Jam

Preheat the oven to 150°C/350°F/Gas Mark 4.

Break up the block sugar and together with the water bring to the boil in a medium saucepan. Allow the syrup to cool slightly.

Beat the eggs in a bowl until pale and creamy, and then slowly add the sugar water in a constant stream, whisking all the time. Continue whisking until the mixture is completely cold; this may take some considerable time.

Finally sift the flour and fold it gently into the mixture using a large metal spoon.

Divide the mixture evenly between two 15 cm/7 inch sandwich tins and bake in the centre of the oven for about 25 to 30 minutes until risen and firm to touch.

Turn onto a wire cooling rack and leave to become cold, before sandwiching together with a jam of your choice.

SIMNEL CAKE

MOTHERING SUNDAY AND EASTER   *Serves approximately 10-12 portions*

The earliest version of this traditional cake appears to have been a bun made of dough which was illustrated in a 15th century dictionary and known as the Shrewsbury Simnel, although I recently read that Simnels have been traced back as far as 1280, having a scalloped edge which is particularly identified with Shropshire. Lancashire was also famed for having a similar yeast bun, known as a Barn Simnel, and Bury in Lancashire had a cake rather like the Simnel of today, known as the Bury Simnel. Perhaps the strongest claim and probably the most documented is that the cake is a Mothering Sunday Cake (mid-Lent) which was baked and taken home by servant girls when visiting their mothers on what has become known as Mothering Sunday. Often saved for Easter in households where a cake would be a real treat, it later also became our traditional Easter cake. The 11 Apostle balls represent the disciples, with the 12th disciple, Judas, being omitted from the cake.

Several theories abound as to how the cake got its name, but the most likely explanation is that it was derived from the word *simila,* the Latin for 'fine white flour'. Another popular, but rather unlikely explanation which is none the less amusing, is that a baker called Simon and his wife Nell devised the cake and to keep marital harmony when a dispute about the name to be given to the cake threatened their marriage, they named it a 'Sim-nel' cake. What is undeniable however, is that carefully made, it is a most delectable treat for almond lovers and, decorated with spring flowers in the centre of the Apostle Balls, brings joy to an Easter table.

175 g/6 oz softened butter	175 g/6 oz raisins
175 g/6 oz pale muscovado sugar	75 g/3 oz chopped glace peel
3 large eggs	2 tablespoons Amaretto
225 g/8 oz plain flour	
50 g/2 oz ground almonds	**Topping**
1 teaspoon mixed spice	550 g/1^{1}/2 lb almond paste
75 g/3 oz flaked almonds	(may be purchased ready made)
175 g/6 oz sultanas	2 tablespoons apricot jam
115 g/4 oz currants	

Preheat the oven to 160°C/325°F/Gas Mark 3.

Cream the butter and sugar together until light and fluffy, lightly beat the eggs and together with the flour, ground almonds and spice add a little at a time, stirring thoroughly. Fold in the flaked almonds, the fruits and the peel, beating gently with a wooden spoon until thoroughly mixed and adding the 2 tablespoons of Amaretto.

Divide the almond paste into half, and divide one of the halves in half again. Roll one of the smaller portions into a circle approximately 18 cm/7 inches round and place the remaining 2 balls of paste in a polythene bag.

Grease and line a 18 cm/7 inch round cake tin and pile half of the cake mixture into the bottom, smoothing it carefully. Place one of the circles of almond paste on top and then spoon the remaining cake mixture into the tin.

Bake in the oven for 1½ hours and then covering the cake with a sheet of brown paper, reduce the temperature to 140°C/275°F/Gas Mark 1. Continue baking for a further 1 to 1½ hours or until the cake is well risen and feels firm to touch.

Because of the layer of marzipan in the centre of the cake, it is difficult to insert a skewer to check in the normal manner, that the cake is cooked, as it is liable to come out 'sticky'. However, it should be possible to make a sensible judgement when the cake looks golden brown and baked. Leave in the tin until completely cold.

The following day, remove from the tin, and carefully peel away the greaseproof paper. Lightly brush the surface of the cake with warmed apricot jam and apply the second circle of almond paste to the cake top.

Roll the remaining almond paste into 11 equally sized balls and position them on top around the edge of the cake. You may then place the cake briefly under a warm grill until browned, or, as I prefer, use one of the now readily-available chef's blowtorches to brown the top of the cake and Apostle Balls. When the cake is finished, place a small posy of spring flowers in the centre.

RATION BOOK CAKES   *Serves 6*

During wartime food rationing, unless you were able to keep a few chickens, fresh eggs were almost impossible to find; dried egg being the alternative. Cakes therefore, were often the first things noticeably absent from the tea table. My mother-in-law Beryl Duff tells me that 2 oz of butter per person, per week, was the norm which is why dripping from the roast was so valuable. But ingenuity and wartime spirit saw the rise of egg-less cakes and here are two of the most popular recipes.

MADEIRA-TYPE CAKE

150 g/5 oz caster sugar	1 level teaspoon cream of tartar
225 g/8 oz dripping	1/2 teaspoon salt
450 g/1 lb plain flour	Zest of one orange
1 level teaspoon bicarbonate of soda	300 ml/1/2 pint milk

Preheat the oven to 190°C/375°F/Gas Mark 4.

Cream the sugar and dripping together until light and fluffy.

Sift the flour, bicarbonate of soda, cream of tartar and salt and then add to the sugar and dripping mixture together with the remaining ingredients, beating thoroughly.

Spoon the mix into a greased and lined 15 cm/6 inch cake tin and bake in the oven for approximately 1 1/2 hours or until golden brown and firm to touch.

GENOA-TYPE CAKE   *Serves 8*

This recipe uses dried egg powder, still found in some supermarkets.

350 g/12 oz plain flour	50 g/2 oz chopped glace peel
1/2 teaspoon mixed spice	115 g/4 oz sugar
1 level tablespoon egg powder	50 g/2 oz ground almonds
225 g/8 oz margarine or lard	50 g/2 oz flaked almonds
225 g/8 oz sultanas	300 ml/1/2 pint milk
175g/6 oz currants	

Preheat the oven to 180°C/350°F/Gas Mark 3.

Sift the flour and spice into a large bowl and sprinkle in the dried egg powder. Add the margarine or lard and rub in lightly. Stir in the remaining dry ingredients and then add the milk mixing thoroughly.

Spoon into a greased and lined 18 cm/7 inch cake tin, smooth the top and place in the centre of the oven. Bake for approximately 2 1/2 hours or until a skewer inserted into the centre comes out cleanly. If it begins to brown too rapidly, cover with a piece of brown paper.

Allow to cool in the tin for 30 minutes before carefully turning out onto a wire rack.

CONDENSED MILK CAKE   *Serves 10*

A recipe from World Wars I and II, this cake came into its own at a time when sugar and butter were very limited. It was almost invariably made without any fat and certainly no sugar, thus avoiding using precious rations.

A surprisingly good cake, it is however, important to cover it with a damp tea towel when it is removed from the oven, and leave it over the tin until the cake is cold. This ensures that the cake does not form a crusty surface, by returning the steam back onto the cooling cake.

I have added a little butter to the recipe as it really does improve the texture and flavour, but of course, you can leave it out if you want to be authentic.

400 g/14 oz can of condensed milk	225 g/8 oz self raising flour
50 g/2 oz butter	1 teaspoon mixed spice
800 g/1 lb 12 oz mixed fruits	2 eggs, lightly beaten
(choose from whatever is available,	
e.g., currants, raisins, sultanas, peel, cherries)	

Preheat the oven to 150°C/300°F/Gas Mark 2.

In a large saucepan, gently melt the condensed milk and butter together. When dissolved add the fruits and stir thoroughly. Set aside to cool slightly.

Meanwhile sift the flour and spice, and together with the lightly beaten eggs, stir into the fruit mixture, ensuring that it is well blended.

Spoon the mixture into a greased and lined 18 cm/7 inch cake tin and bake in the centre of the oven for about 1½ hours or until firm to the touch and a skewer inserted into the centre comes out cleanly. If the top begins to darken too quickly, cover the cake with brown paper whilst cooking.

When baked, remove from the oven and cover with a damp tea towel. Allow to become completely cold before turning onto a serving plate.

TWELFTH NIGHT CAKE

Serves approximately 10

The feast of Epiphany on 6th January is also known as Twelfth Night, celebrating the time when the Three Wise Men, Gaspar, Melchior and Balthazar came bearing gifts to the baby Jesus who was lying in a manger in a stable in Bethlehem.

The Twelfth Night Cake is still served today. The recipe is a rich fruitcake, to which the baker adds silver charms. When the cake is sliced, the recipients of the charms are bestowed good luck for the coming year. Originally a 'lucky bean' was baked into the cake, the finder being crowned King Bean.

Almost 200 years ago an actor named Robert Badderley, left a legacy to the Drury Lane Theatre in London, so that performers appearing on Twelfth Night would share a traditional cake and toast the actor. I spoke to the manager of the Drury Lane Theatre, who confirmed that this enchanting tradition still continues today.

225 g/8 oz butter	225 g/8 oz raisins
225 g/8 oz dark muscovado sugar	225 g/8 oz currants
1 tablespoon black treacle	225 g/8 oz sultanas
225 g/8 oz plain flour	50 g/2 oz chopped mixed peel
1 teaspoon mixed spice	50 g/2 oz cherries, halved
1/4 teaspoon salt	50 g/2 oz ground almonds
4 large eggs	1 tablespoon brandy

Preheat the oven to 160°C/325°F/Gas Mark 3.

Cream the butter and sugar together until light and fluffy and then beat in the treacle.

Sift the flour, spice and salt into a bowl. Lightly whisk the eggs with a fork and then beat them gently into the butter and sugar mixture, together with the flour. When thoroughly mixed, stir in the fruits*, nuts and brandy and then pile the cake mixture into a greased and lined 18 cm/7 inch round cake tin.

Place in the centre of the oven. Bake for approximately 1 1/2 hours, then reduce the temperature to 120°C/250°F/Gas Mark 1/2 and bake for a further 1 hour, or until the cake is well risen, golden brown and firm to touch. A skewer inserted into the centre should come out cleanly.

Leave the cake to cool in the tin, covered with a clean cloth. Turn out when completely cold.

* If you would like to continue with the tradition of the centuries, you may of course bake a 'bean' into the cake, which would be added at the same time as you add the fruit.

MATRIMONY CAKE

Serves 8

In the era of Jane Austen, a wedding procession would usually have walked to the church for the marriage ceremony and back home afterwards, led by one of the guests carrying a Matrimony Cake or Marriage Cake signifying good luck and lives of plenty. The cake would have been carried at the head of the procession, on a pole with a platform on the top supporting the cake, giving it a place of significance in the proceedings.

Very few recipes for these cakes exist now but one from the south western part of the country includes apples and dried fruit and we thoroughly enjoyed it. Whilst not perhaps a cake as we recognise it, it was certainly seen and baked as such during the 18th century, so do try it.

450 g/1 lb Shortcrust Pastry (page 21)	50 g/2 oz breadcrumbs
450 g/1 lb cooking apples	1 teaspoon mixed spice
50 g/2 oz sultanas	Juice and zest of one lemon
50 g/2 oz currants	50 g/2 oz soft brown sugar
50 g/2 oz chopped mixed peel	

Preheat the oven to 180°C/350°F/Gas Mark 4.

Roll out half of the pastry and place into a lightly greased 23 cm/9 inch flan dish.

Peel, core and slice the apples and arrange evenly on the flan base, spreading the remainder of the ingredients evenly over the top.

Finally roll the remaining half of the pastry into a large circle and lift carefully over the top of the cake, firmly sealing the edges.

Brush the top with a little milk and decorate with cut out shapes such as hearts, or initials of the couple.

Finally bake in the centre of the oven for 30 to 40 minutes or until golden brown.

Best served warm, but if you do decide to carry the cake in front of a marriage procession this may not be possible!

WEDDING CAKE 1920

Serves many

Who could possibly read this recipe without being overcome with wonder at the sheer enormity of coping with baking a cake of this size, $43\frac{1}{2}$ lbs of mixture? In addition to the magic of the size of the recipe, we are then assured that it will keep for 20 years. I don't doubt that for a minute.

Mr Roger Latter kindly lent me a handwritten book of recipes, which his mother, Mrs Gertrude Latter who is now 91, had faithfully recorded throughout her younger days. The book is well used and falling to pieces, exactly as you would expect an old, much loved notebook to be after so many years. I found it so absorbing as the introduction to another era.

I am not suggesting that you try to bake this cake, but certainly if you can find a large enough bowl, well why not?

50 eggs	10 lbs currants
5 lbs of sugar	1 pint brandy
5 lbs butter	$\frac{1}{4}$ oz cloves
5 lbs flour	1 oz cinnamon
15 lbs raisins	4 oz mace
3 lbs citron peel	4 oz nutmeg

The procedure for making the cake has not been given, but if you wish to attempt it, I suggest making it in the same way as a Christmas Cake, but be sure you will be able to cope with the quantities first.

COCONUT POUND CAKE

Serves 8

Traditionally coloured a very pale pink and finished with a white butter cream icing, sprinkled with desiccated coconut, this is a delicious cake, simple and quick to make. I'm quite sure I remember from childhood, it would have been finished by topping with a red glace cherry placed in the centre.

225 g/8 oz self raising flour
225 g/8 oz caster sugar
225 g/8 oz butter
2 large eggs, lightly beaten
115 g/4 oz desiccated coconut
A few drops of pink colouring

Topping
225 g/8 oz icing sugar
115 g/4 oz butter
2-3 tablespoons desiccated coconut
I red glace cherry

Preheat the oven to 180°C/350°F/Gas Mark 4.

Place all the cake ingredients in a large mixing bowl and using a wooden spoon, beat until thoroughly mixed together.

Pile into a greased and lined 18 cm/7 inch cake tin and bake in the centre of the oven until well risen and firm to touch. A skewer inserted into the centre will come out cleanly when the cake is cooked, which will take about I hour.

Turn out carefully onto a wire rack and leave to become cold.

For the topping, cream together the icing sugar and butter until smooth and creamy and spread onto the top of the cold cake. Immediately sprinkle the topping with 2 or 3 tablespoonfuls of desiccated coconut and finish by placing a cherry in the centre.

SCRIPTURE CAKE

Serves 10-12

This 'divine' cake is great fun to fathom out and perfect for Sunday tea. There are several versions, some called Bible Cakes, but the following recipe is one that I have spent time looking through the Bible and deciphering the ingredients, so I know it works.

115 g/4 oz	Jeremiah	Chapter I	v11
350 g/12 oz	Jeremiah	Chapter XXIV	v2
350 g/12 oz	I Chronicles	Chapter XII	v40
500 g/1lb 2 oz	Leviticus	Chapter II	v2
2 teaspoons	Galatians	Chapter V	V9
I teaspoon	Solomon	Chapter IV	v14
Pinch	St Matthew	Chapter V	v13
6	Job	Chapter XXXIX	v14
350 g/12 oz	Isaiah	Chapter VII	v15
450 g/1 lb	Jeremiah	Chapter VI	v20
2 tablespoons	I Samuel	Chapter XIV	v29
1/2 breakfast cup	Solomon	Chapter IV	v11

Preheat the oven to 140°C/275°F/Gas Mark 1.

Chop the first three ingredients.

Sift the Leviticus and the Galatians into a bowl together with the Solomon Chapter IV v14 and Matthew.

Lightly beat Job. Cream Isaiah and Jeremiah together until light and fluffy, gradually mixing in the beaten Job and sifted ingredients, using a wooden spoon, until smooth.

Fold in the I Samuel, Solomon Chapter IV v11 and remaining ingredients. Spoon the mixture into a greased and lined 20 cm/8 inch cake tin and bake in the oven for approximately 2 to 2 1/2 hours. If the cake begins to brown too quickly, cover the top with a sheet of brown paper. When the cake is well risen and firm to touch, insert a skewer into the centre, if the cake is cooked it will come out cleanly.

Leave to cool in the tin for 30 minutes before turning out onto a wire rack.

Note: A translation of the recipe can be found at the end of the book on page 284 but it is much more fun looking through the bible for the ingredients.

PASSION CAKE

Serves 9

Written on a piece of now very tatty notebook paper, this recipe has been tucked away in my baking scrapbook for many years. Every so often it is brought out and baked, always with the same enthusiasm that I felt when I first read the recipe although sadly I can no longer trace the original source.

When the children were small, I felt rightly or wrongly that it was good for them, containing as it does bananas, carrots, sultanas, nuts and corn oil instead of butter. Certainly the resulting cake used to disappear with great speed in our household, sometimes before it had been decorated, although I admit to liking it with the cream cheese icing!

Perhaps it is the very speed with which this version of a carrot cake disappears that led to its name Passion Cake, but I really urge you to try it as you can hardly be anything but impassioned by the result!

275 g/10 oz plain wholemeal flour
I level teaspoon bicarbonate of soda
I heaped teaspoon baking powder
$^1/_2$ teaspoon cinnamon (optional)
25 g/I oz chopped pecan nuts
25 g/I oz flaked almonds
175 g/6 oz finely grated carrot
175 g/6 oz pale muscovado sugar
3 large eggs

3 mashed bananas
175 ml/6 fl oz corn oil
I tablespoon fresh orange juice

Topping
75 g/3 oz cream cheese
175 g/6 oz icing sugar
I teaspoon fresh orange juice

Preheat the oven to 180°C/350°F/Gas Mark 4.

Sift the flour, bicarbonate of soda, baking powder and cinnamon if liked, into a medium sized bowl. Stir in the pecan nuts, almonds, grated carrot and sugar.

Add the eggs to the banana, corn oil and orange juice and beat thoroughly before stirring into the flour mixture. Continue stirring until all the ingredients are thoroughly combined. The mixture will be fairly runny.

Pour into a greased and lined 20 cm/8 inch cake tin and place in the centre of the oven and bake for about 1$^1/_4$ hours or until the cake is golden brown and feels firm if pressed lightly in the centre.

Leave to cool in the tin for about $^1/_2$ hour before turning carefully onto a wire rack to become cold.

Place the cream cheese in a small bowl and add the sifted icing sugar, beating until it becomes smooth.

Finally, remove greaseproof paper, spoon the icing onto the top of the cake and spread with a pallet knife, leaving a rough effect. Allow the icing to set.

The cake should be stored in an airtight tin, in the refrigerator.

WARTIME CARROT CAKE

Serves 8–10

I was surprised at first to discover that a cake which I had always considered very up to date, perhaps due to its considerable popularity at the present time, was actually an old recipe. It certainly was promoted in wartime recipe leaflets during World War II. Not surprising really as there was the easy accessibility of carrots, which could be grown at home, compared to sugar which was severely rationed during the war years and the carrots add both sweetness and a moist texture, particularly if grated finely.

This particular recipe includes eggs, but if they were unavailable during wartime, then vinegar would have been used as a raising agent.

225 g/8 oz self raising flour
2 teaspoons baking powder
150 g/5 oz butter
150 g/5 oz soft brown sugar
50 g/2 oz sultanas

50 g/2 oz walnut pieces
150 g/5 oz finely grated carrot
^{1}/2 teaspoon vanilla essence
2 large eggs, lightly beaten

Preheat the oven to 180°C/350°F/Gas Mark 4.

Sift the flour and baking powder into a bowl and rub in the butter to form the texture of fine breadcrumbs.

Stir in the sugar, sultanas, walnut pieces, carrot, vanilla extract and lightly beaten eggs, stirring until thoroughly mixed together.

Spoon into a greased and lined 18 cm/7 inch square cake tin and bake in the centre of the oven for about 1 hour or until well risen and firm to touch.

Remove from the oven and allow to cool in the tin for 30 minutes before carefully turning out onto a wire rack to cool.

FIGGY CAKE

Approximately 9 portions

Palm Sunday was also known as Figgy Sunday and during Elizabethan times was celebrated with Figgy Pudding and Figgy Cake.

If is doubtful that either of these traditional items of Palm Sunday celebrations are still baked today, Figgy Pudding having transferred its allegiance to Christmas festivities as one of the forerunners of today's 'Christmas Pudding'.

Palm Sunday Cake is however, a simple recipe, which would be well worth reviving, although I confess to enjoying it warm with cream, rather than sliced cold at teatime.

75 g/3 oz butter	150 g/5 oz finely grated carrot
75 g/3 oz caster sugar	$1/2$ teaspoon mixed spice
175 g/6 oz self raising flour	Pinch of salt
150 g/5 oz soft brown sugar	2 eggs, lightly beaten
50 g/2 oz sultanas	Finely grated rind and juice of 1 small lemon
50 g/2 oz walnut pieces	175 g/6 oz figs (ready to eat variety)

Preheat the oven to 180°C/350°F/Gas Mark 4.

Cream the butter and sugar together in a medium bowl, until light and pale. Sift the flour, spice and salt into a bowl. Add the eggs and flour mixture, a little at a time, to the butter and sugar, beating with a wooden spoon until smooth and thoroughly mixed.

Add the lemon rind and juice together with the chopped figs, mixing well.

Spoon into a 15 cm/6 inch square cake tin, which has been greased and lined, and smooth the top carefully.

Place in the oven and bake for approximately 45 minutes or until it is well risen, golden brown and feels firm to touch.

Leave to cool in the tin for 20 minutes, before turning carefully out onto a cooling rack.

CHEWY SPICED FRUIT CAKE

Serves 8

A 1941 copy of *The Farmer and Stock Breeder* revealed this Chewy Spiced Fruit Cake recipe. I am not entirely sure how it got its name, but it is certainly very fruity and the use of wholemeal flour gives it an interesting density of texture. I thoroughly enjoyed making and eating it.

175 g/6 oz butter or margarine
150 g/5 oz soft pale brown sugar
115 g/4 oz plain flour
1 teaspoon baking powder
1/2 teaspoon mixed spice
3 eggs, lightly beaten

175 ml/6 fl oz milk
225 g/8 oz wholemeal flour
225 g/8 oz sultanas
50 g/2 oz chopped mixed peel
50 g/2 oz glace cherries, halved

Preheat the oven to 150°C/300°F/Gas Mark 2.

Cream the butter and sugar together until light and fluffy.

Sift the flour, baking powder and spice into a bowl and together with the eggs and milk, beat gently into the butter mixture.

Finally stir in the wholemeal flour, sultanas, peel and cherries, ensuring that the cake is well mixed.

Spoon into a greased and lined 18 cm/7 inch cake tin and bake in the centre of the oven for about 1 1/2 hours, or until well risen and firm to touch. A skewer inserted into the middle will come out cleanly when the cake is cooked.

Leave to cool in the tin for 30 minutes before turning onto a wire rack.

ORANGE SANDWICH CAKE

Serves 8

I freely admit to having a soft spot for orange cakes and this recipe from 1935 is no exception, it is simple to make and truly delectable. Trying out the recipe, frequently made by my grandmother Dora, took me straight back to childhood (albeit I was not even thought of in 1935) and the cakes standing on the marble slab in her pantry. It has once more become a firm favourite in our house.

115 g/4 oz butter	**Filling**
175 g/6 oz caster sugar	175 g/6 oz icing sugar
175 g/6 oz plain flour	75 g/3 oz butter
1/2 teaspoon baking powder	Zest of 1 orange
2 eggs, lightly beaten	Juice of orange
Zest and juice of 1 large orange	

Preheat the oven to 180°C/350°F/Gas Mark 4.

Cream the butter and sugar together until light and fluffy.

Sift the flour and baking powder together. Add with the eggs, orange zest and juice to the butter mixture a little at a time, beating thoroughly.

Grease two 15 cm/6 inch sandwich tins and divide the mixture evenly between them. Place in the centre of the oven and bake for 20 to 25 minutes or until well risen and firm to touch. Do not over bake.

Remove from the oven and turn carefully onto a wire rack, leaving to become cold.

In a separate bowl cream together the icing sugar, butter and orange zest, adding enough orange juice to soften, to a light fluffy mixture. If you overdo the juice, you can always add a little icing to stiffen the mixture.

Finally sandwich the cakes together and smooth the remaining icing on to the top of the cake. Leave to set before serving.

SAVOY CAKE

Serves 8-9

How this cake acquired its name is unclear but it is without doubt delicious. It is useful to remember that all the whisking involved with making this cake would have been done with a hand whisk, so I can only be grateful that when making it, I had access to an electric mixer.

I large lemon	Water
2 or 3 lumps of sugar	8 eggs
225 g/8 oz sugar	225 g/8 oz self raising flour

Preheat the oven to 150°C/300°F/Gas Mark 2.

Rub the lumps of sugar over the lemon skin, these will absorb the lemon oil. Place them in a medium saucepan together with the remaining sugar and the juice of the lemon, making the liquid up to 300 ml/$^1/_2$ pint with the water.

Bring the liquid to the boil and heat continuously until a syrup is formed. Remove from the heat and set aside.

In a large bowl whisk the eggs until pale and creamy, they will have increased considerably in volume.

Then continuously whisking, pour the syrup in a steady thin stream into the eggs, continuing to whisk until the mixture is cool.

Carefully fold in the sifted flour, a little at a time, using a large metal spoon and working in a figure of eight.

Pour into a greased and lined 18 cm/7 inch cake tin and place immediately in the centre of the oven and bake for about 30 minutes or until well risen, golden brown and firm to the touch if pressed gently in the centre.

Remove from the oven and leave in the tin to cool for about 10 minutes before turning carefully out onto a wire rack.

LUNCHEON CAKE

Serves 8

Recipes for Luncheon Cake appear to be as diverse as the many cooks who created them, indeed the oldest I found was yeast based, which was rather like tea bread.

The Victorians who were great cake eaters, provided us with Luncheon Cakes which were rather different and lighter in texture, although often made with dripping rather than butter, they contained a little dried fruit, spices and almost always citron peel. Mrs Beeton's original Luncheon Cake recipe in her *Book of Modern Household Cookery*, 1861 has the addition of caraway seeds.

The following recipe is a very representative example of this good plain cake.

450 g/1 lb plain flour	350 g/12 oz sultanas
1 teaspoon mixed spice	Zest of one lemon
1 teaspoon mace	1^1/2 teaspoons bicarbonate of soda
115 g/4 oz butter	300 ml/^{1}/2 pint buttermilk
225 g/8 oz pale brown sugar	

Preheat the oven to 180°C/350°F/Gas Mark 4.

Sift the flour and spices into a bowl and add the butter. Rub in lightly with the finger tips until the mixture forms the consistency of fine breadcrumbs.

Stir in the sugar, sultanas and lemon zest.

Add the bicarbonate of soda to the buttermilk and stir, quickly adding to the cake mixture continuing to stir until all the ingredients are thoroughly mixed together.

Turn immediately into a greased and lined 18 cm/7 inch cake tin and bake in the centre of the oven. After 1 hour check the cake by pressing lightly on top with your fingers to see if it is firm to touch. If not return to the oven for a further 30 minutes or until a skewer inserted into the centre comes out cleanly.

Allow the cake to cool in the tin for 30 minutes before turning out carefully onto a wire rack to become cold.

This cake is best left for a couple of days before eating.

CHRISTMAS CAKE

Serves 12 approximately

Oddly enough nobody seems to know how the most loved cake of the year came about in its present form but communities all over the world have their own very special cakes to celebrate the birth of Christ: the German *Christstollen*, the Danish *Julekage* or the *Buche de Noel* of France. The most likely explanation for ours seems to be that the rich yeasted cake breads, which were eaten during the 15th-17th centuries, gave way to the dark, aromatic fruit cake, invariably steeped in alcohol, which is now the traditional Christmas Cake in Britain. (See Marchpane Cakes page 160).

Prince Albert, the husband of Queen Victoria, who changed our festivities with the advent of the Christmas tree from his native Germany and the introduction of the round plum pudding, was most probably also behind the introduction of Christmas cakes as we know them today. The following recipe is based on a rich dark brandy fruitcake.

225 g/8 oz currants	1 dessertspoon black treacle
225 g/8 oz raisins	225g/8 oz plain flour
225 g/8 oz sultanas	1 heaped teaspoon ground mixed spice
50 g/2 oz chopped glace peel	50g/2 oz ground almonds
50 g/2 oz glace cherries, halved	4 large eggs
4 tablespoons brandy	Zest of one large lemon
225 g/8 oz butter	1 tablespoon lemon juice
225 g/8 oz dark muscovado sugar	50 g/2 oz flaked almonds

The night before you bake the cake, wash the dried fruit, peel and cherries, draining thoroughly. There is no need to dry the fruit, simply place it in a bowl, add the brandy, stir well, cover and set aside overnight.

Preheat the oven to 140°/275°F/Gas Mark 1. Place the butter and sugar in a large bowl creaming together until light and fluffy and then beat in the black treacle. In a separate bowl, sift the flour and spice, stirring in the ground almonds. Lightly beat the eggs and add them to the butter and sugar, a little at a time, adding a tablespoon of the flour if the mixture begins to curdle. Fold in the remaining flour, together with the lemon zest and juice. Finally, add the fruit and flaked almonds stirring gently but thoroughly.

When the ingredients are thoroughly mixed together, spoon into a greased and lined 20 cm/8 inch round cake tin and place on a low shelf in the oven. After 2 hours lower the temperature to 120°C/250°F/ Gas Mark ½ covering the top of the cake with brown paper and bake for a further 1 hour or until the top feels firm and a skewer inserted into the centre comes out cleanly.

When the cake is cooked, leave in its tin and cover with a clean cloth. Allow it to become completely cold – at least 24 hours. Remove from the tin and leaving it in its greaseproof wrapping, over wrap with a clean sheet of greaseproof, finally wrapping it tightly in foil. The cake will remain in excellent condition for 3 or 4 months if stored in a cool, dry place, until required. Decorate as you like with bought marzipan or Almond Paste (page 214) and royal icing.

CHRISTMAS CAKE

Serves 10-12

FROM THE MINISTRY OF FOOD LONDON SW1, FOOD FACTS NO 333

During World War II, the Ministry of Food published Food Fact Sheets, and Number 333 detailed Christmas Cake, Mincemeat and a Christmas Pudding. It was based on their premise that 'Christmas must be traditional, it must be the best we can provide, but above all it must be colourful'. The recipe makes a rather good fruitcake.

75 g/3 oz sugar	1 teaspoon cinnamon
115 g/4 oz margarine	1 teaspoon mixed spice
1 tablespoon golden syrup	2 to 4 eggs (fresh or dried)
225 g/8 oz plain flour	450 g/1 lb mixed dried fruit
2 teaspoons baking powder	1/4 teaspoon lemon substitute
Pinch of salt	Milk to mix (fresh or household)

Preheat the oven to 140°C/275°F/Gas Mark 1.

Cream the sugar and margarine. Add the syrup.

Sift the flour, baking powder, salt and spices together in a separate bowl and then add alternately with the lightly beaten eggs into the creamed sugar mixture and beat well. Add the fruit and lemon substitute and enough milk to give a dropping consistency.

Line an 18 cm/7 inch round cake tin with greased paper, put in the mixture and bake in a moderate oven. I suggest baking for 2 to 2 1/2 hours or until well risen, golden brown and a skewer inserted into the centre comes out cleanly.

MOCK MARZIPAN

50 g/2 oz margarine	225 g/8 oz plain cake crumbs
50 g/2 oz caster or icing sugar, sifted	(Madeira would be perfect)
1 to 2 teaspoons almond extract	

Preparation time 10 minutes
No Cooking
Quantity – enough to cover the top of a 18 cm/7 inch Christmas cake

Cream the margarine and the sugar with the extract until light and fluffy.

Add the cake crumbs and knead the mixture to a pliable dough.

Roll out into a 18 cm/7 inch round and lift carefully onto the top of the fruitcake, which you should coat with a little jam or lemon curd first.

This recipe made a very good wartime substitute for almond paste.

WARTIME WHITE ICING

I came across this lovely old recipe cut from a wartime newspaper column, whilst I was looking through a handwritten cookery book of 1923, so this was clearly a recipe from the First World War. It is however, very engaging and although I have not tried it, I am assured that it is an excellent substitute for icing sugar. Incidentally, since writing this recipe out, I have seen it in two or three other handwritten recipe books from the same era, so its popularity is in no doubt.

2 dessertspoonfuls of sugar	Powdered milk
3 dessertspoonfuls of hot water	

Dissolve the sugar in the hot water, adding enough powdered milk to form an 'icing' consistency, stir constantly to ensure that it is lump free and then spread onto the cake as required.

SPINSTER CAKE   *Serves 6-8*

It is not clear how this cake acquired its name, but it is a really good fruitcake, which was perhaps made by eligible ladies for gentleman callers.

Not unlike a Grasmere Eggless Fruitcake, it is just a little more heavily fruited.

350 g/12 oz self raising flour	115 g/4 oz raisins
1 teaspoon mixed spice	115 g/4 oz currants
1/2 teaspoon ground cinnamon	115 g/4 oz sultanas
1/2 teaspoon ground ginger	50 g/2 oz flaked almonds
1 heaped teaspoon bicarbonate of soda	25 g/1 oz caraway seeds
115 g/4 oz butter	50 g/2 oz chopped glace peel
225 g/8 oz soft brown sugar	300 ml/1/2 pint soured milk or buttermilk

Preheat the oven to 190°C/375°F/Gas Mark 5.

Sift flour, spices and bicarbonate of soda into a bowl and rub in the butter. Add all the other dry ingredients and stir well with a pallet knife.

Lastly add in enough of the soured milk or buttermilk to make a soft consistency.

Spoon into a 18 cm/7 inch square lined cake tin and bake in the centre of the oven for the first 30 minutes, reducing the heat to 160°C/325°F/Gas Mark 3 for a further 1 1/2 hours or until the cake is firm to touch and a skewer inserted into the centre comes out cleanly.

Leave to cool in the tin for 30 minutes before turning onto a wire rack and leaving to become cold.

COFFEE CAKE

Serves 10

Long having been a favourite amongst cakes, Coffee Cake is traditionally sandwiched together, topped with coffee butter cream and decorated with walnut halves.

My husband Malcolm adores iced coffee on warm summer days, made with the bottled Camp coffee essence and I find it perfect for making coffee cakes. If you are however, unable to lay your hands on any in your local shops or supermarket, then coffee granules dissolved in a little hot water will be fine.

225 g/8 oz butter
225 g/8 oz caster sugar
225 g/8 oz self raising flour
4 large eggs, lightly beaten
50 ml/2 fl oz Camp coffee essence or dissolved
   granules

Filling
225 g/8 oz icing sugar
115 g/4 oz butter
2 teaspoons Camp coffee essence or
   dissolved granules

Decoration
7-8 walnut halves

Preheat the oven to 180°C/350°F/Gas Mark 4.

Cream the butter and sugar together until light and fluffy and then beat in the flour and eggs a little at a time. Finally beat in the coffee.

Spoon the mixture into two greased and lined 18 cm/7 inch sandwich tins and bake in the centre of the oven for about 25-30 minutes or until well risen and golden. The top should feel firm when pressed gently.

Carefully turn onto a wire cooling rack and leave to become cold.

Meanwhile cream the icing sugar and butter together with the coffee until light and creamy. When the coffee cakes are cold, sandwich them together with the butter cream and ice the top with the remaining icing, if liked you may ice the sides of the cake. Finally decorate the top with the halved walnuts and leave the cake to set before serving.

ALMOND CAKE

Serves 10-12

A delightful, very talented lady, Gladys Pickard, who in her eighties still thoroughly enjoys baking and making shortbread to put me to shame, gave me this recipe for Almond Cake, which has been passed down through several generations of her family. I had great pleasure in baking it; as a serious almond lover, I can assure you it was an exceptional treat.

175 g/6 oz butter	115 g/4 oz plain flour
225 g/8 oz caster sugar	$^1/_2$ teaspoon baking powder
4 medium eggs	$^1/_2$ teaspoon almond extract
115 g/4 oz ground almonds	

Preheat the oven to 160°C/325°F/Gas Mark 3.

Cream the butter and sugar together until light and fluffy. Beat the eggs and add slowly, together with half of the ground almonds.

Sift the flour and baking powder together and together with the remaining ground almonds fold gently into the mixture. Stir in the almond extract.

Spoon the mixture into a greased and lined 18 cm/7 inch round cake tin and bake in the oven for about $1^3/_4$ hours, covering the top of the cake with a sheet of brown paper if the cake begins to darken too quickly.

When the cake is firm to touch and a skewer inserted into the centre comes out cleanly, remove the cake from the oven, leaving it to cool in the tin.

When cold you may add the following homemade marzipan, decorating it with flaked almonds, which you could lightly toast.

ALMOND PASTE

This recipe does not contain eggs

225 g/8 oz ground almonds	1 tablespoon lemon juice
115 g/4 oz icing sugar	1 teaspoon vanilla extract
115 g/4 oz caster sugar	1 tablespoon brandy

Place all the ingredients into a large bowl and using a wooden spoon, slowly incorporate all the ingredients together. Then using your hands, form into a ball, kneading very gently, so that the almond oil in the nuts does not become 'greasy' making the dough unmanageable.

Wrap the ball in film and place in the refrigerator until you are ready to roll it out to fit the cake, on a surface lightly dusted with icing sugar. Then after spreading a little warmed apricot jam onto the top of the cake, gently lift the almond paste onto the cake, trim if necessary and decorate as liked. This can be used too for the top of the Christmas Cake on page 208. Spread cake first with warm apricot jam.

ROSEYLANGEN CAKE

Serves 6

This lovely old-fashioned fruit cake is made with brown ale, giving it a robust character.

225 g/8 oz butter
225 g/8 oz pale brown sugar
5 large eggs, lightly beaten
450 g/1 lb plain flour
1/2 teaspoon mixed spice
1/2 teaspoon mace

450 g/1 lb raisins
115 g/4 oz chopped mixed peel
Zest of one large orange
Small bottle of brown ale
1 level teaspoon bicarbonate of soda

Preheat the oven to 160°C/325°F/Gas Mark 3.

Cream the butter and sugar together until light and fluffy. Add the lightly beaten eggs a little at a time together with the flour and spices, beating thoroughly with a wooden spoon until smooth. Stir in the raisins, peel and orange zest.

Warm the ale slightly and add the bicarbonate of soda, stirring vigorously. Pour immediately onto the cake mixture and beat until well mixed.

Working quickly, spoon the mixture into a greased and lined 900 g/2 lb loaf tin and place in the centre of the oven and bake for 1 1/2 to 2 hours or until a skewer inserted into the centre comes out cleanly. If the top starts to brown too much, cover the cake with brown paper.

Cool the cake in the tin for 20 minutes before turning out onto a wire rack and when completely cold wrap in greaseproof and store in a tin for a day or two to allow the flavour to mature before eating.

SWISS ROLL

Serves 6 – 8

From the very name of this delicious sponge cake, I realise that it probably did not have its origins in this country. But from the length of time it has been served on our tea tables it was hard and a little sad to leave it out of this section of the book. A good homemade Swiss Roll bears no resemblance to one bought from a supermarket. They are certainly a little time consuming but are well worth the effort and again like the sponge cake, the finished result corresponds exactly to the care taken in preparation.

75 g/3 oz plain flour
3 large eggs
75 g/3 oz caster sugar
1 tablespoon hot water

Filling
Raspberry jam or lemon curd
A little extra caster sugar

Preheat the oven to 200°C/400°F/Gas Mark 6.

Half fill a saucepan with boiling water and place a large mixing bowl on the top. Break the eggs into the bowl and add the sugar, whisking constantly until the mixture is thick enough to leave a trail when the whisk is held above the bowl. By this time the egg mixture will be very pale and have increased in volume.

Removing the bowl from the heat, sift the flour a little at a time over the mixture and using a large metal spoon, carefully fold in the flour using a figure of 8 motion. Once the flour has been added, working quickly, add the hot water to slacken the mixture and immediately pour the mixture into a greased and lined Swiss Roll tin. Allow the mixture to run into the corners of the tin, by tilting but do not smooth the top. Once it uniformly covers the tin, bake immediately in the oven for 10 to 15 minutes, until well risen and firm to touch.

Do not overcook.

Meanwhile dredge a sheet of greaseproof paper with caster sugar and immediately invert the cake onto the paper, removing the tin and allow to cool for 10 minutes. Gently peel the greaseproof paper from the base of the cake and trim the edges slightly, to make it easier to roll.

Spread the Swiss Roll with the jam or lemon curd, smoothing it to the edges.

Lift the greaseproof paper, from the short edge and roll. Don't worry if the surface cracks, it really doesn't matter, it all adds to the 'homemade' charm. Dredge lightly with caster sugar and place on a plate to serve.

SHEARING CAKE

Serves approximately 12

Seasons of the year bring with them rituals in the farming calendar, often celebrated with food. One such event is sheep shearing which takes place in May to June, although it is doubtful that Shearing Cakes are made in farmhouse kitchens today (the farmer's wife is more likely to be helping with the shearing or working at a second income job). They certainly had their place in times past however, and how lovely it would be to see these cakes re-introduced, certainly when we shear our small flock this year, I will bake a Shearing Cake.

225 g/8 oz butter
350 g/12 oz pale muscovado sugar
450 g/1 lb self raising flour
1 teaspoon mixed spice
Finely grated rind of one lemon
2 large eggs

300 ml/^{1}/2 pint milk

Topping
225 g/8 oz icing sugar
Lemon juice

Preheat the oven to 180°C/350°F/Gas Mark 4.

Cream the butter and sugar together until light and fluffy. In a separate bowl mix the spices into the flour and stir in the lemon rind. Lightly beat the eggs into the milk.

Add the spiced flour, milk and eggs to the creamed butter and sugar, beating gently until thoroughly mixed.

Spoon the mixture into a greased and lined 23 x 23 cm/9 x 9 inch square cake tin, smoothing gently.

Bake in the oven until golden brown and the top feels firm.

Leave the cake to cool in the tin and turn out when completely cold.

Meanwhile mix the icing sugar in a small bowl, with the juice of the lemon, until a smooth coating consistency is reached. Pour the icing over the sponge, spreading it to the outer edges. Leave to set, cutting into squares 7.5 x 7.5 cm/3 x 3 inch before serving.

SHEARING CAKE/*Cacen Gneifio*

WALES   *Serves 6-8*

Another traditional recipe for a Shearing Cake, varying from the one previously given, in that it is rather more highly spiced and has its roots in Wales, where it is known as *Cacen Gneifio*.

Due to the decreasing popularity of caraway seeds this cake is seldom baked today but is none the less well worth trying as it is wonderfully aromatic and has a really old-fashioned flavour.

225 g/8 oz plain flour	175 g/6 oz soft brown sugar
1 teaspoon baking powder	2 teaspoons caraway seeds
1/2 teaspoon mace	Zest 1/2 large lemon
1/2 teaspoon nutmeg	1 beaten egg
125 g/4 oz butter	125 ml/1/2 pint milk

Preheat the oven to 180°C/350°F/Gas Mark 4.

Sift the plain flour and baking powder into a bowl, stir in the freshly grated nutmeg. Rub in the butter, add the sugar, caraway seeds and lemon zest, stirring thoroughly. Making a well in the centre, pour in the egg and milk, beating with a wooden spoon until well incorporated.

Transfer into a 15 cm/6 inch greased and lined cake tin and bake in the oven for approximately 1 hour or until a skewer inserted into the centre comes out cleanly.

Leave to cool for 30 minutes before turning out of the tin onto a wire rack.

HARVEST CAKE

Serves 10

Just as there are different harvests in the farming calendar, there are lots of harvest cakes and at a time when there are so many extra hands on the farm, cakes are always welcome.

The Suffolk Harvest Cake, made with vine fruits, candied peel, pork lard and yeast, is rather like a Lardy Cake, very fruity and sugary and probably not too good for the figure. Another rather different cake is the Harvest Betsy Cake, made with barley flour, the result being an excellent golden fruitcake packed with sultanas.

275 g/10 oz plain white flour	115 g/4 oz pork lard
1 teaspoon baking powder	125 ml/4 fl oz milk
1/4 teaspoon bicarbonate of soda	1 beaten egg
1/2 teaspoon ground nutmeg	225 g/8 oz sultanas
1/2 teaspoon mixed spice	50 g/2 oz raisins
12 g/1/2 oz fresh yeast	50 g/2 oz chopped glace peel
225 g/8 oz soft brown sugar	

Preheat the oven to 180°C/350°F/Gas Mark 4.

Sift the flour, baking powder, bicarbonate of soda and spices into a large bowl. Crumble the yeast and rub in, stir in the sugar.

Rub the lard into the flour mixture, until it resembles breadcrumbs.

Finally, add the remaining ingredients, including the milk, stirring thoroughly with a pallet knife.

Grease and lightly flour a 18 cm/7 inch square cake tin. Pile in the cake mixture, smoothing the top lightly. Cover and leave in a warm place for one hour to rise. Bake in the oven for 1 1/2-2 hours or until golden brown.

Leave for 10 minutes to cool slightly in the tin and then turn out onto a wire rack.

HARVEST CAKE/*Teisen y Cynhaeaf*

WALES   ***Serves 8***

The Welsh variation of a Harvest Cake is made with apples, sultanas and cinnamon and closely resembles the Irish Apple Cake which is baked with a layer of fruit through the centre. This is another superb Welsh cake which is highly recommended, bearing in mind that you do not have to either be a farmer or wait until harvest time to try it.

175 g/6 oz butter	1/2 teaspoon cinnamon
175 g/6 oz soft brown sugar	450 g/1 lb cooking apples
2 large eggs, lightly beaten	50 g/2 oz sultanas
225 g/8 oz self raising flour	50 g/2 oz currants
1/2 teaspoon mixed spice	50 g/2 oz flaked almonds

Preheat the oven to 180°C/350°F/Gas Mark 4.

In a small saucepan melt the butter and soft brown sugar. Allow to cool slightly before beating in the eggs.

Sift the flour and spices into a bowl. Finally adding the melted ingredients, beat gently together.

Peel, core and chop the apples into small pieces and mix together with the fruit and almonds.

Spoon half the cake mixture into a greased and lined 18 cm/7 inch cake tin and top with the fruits and nut mix, finally spooning the remaining cake mix over the top.

Smooth the cake gently and place in the centre of the oven for about an hour or until firm to touch and a skewer inserted into the centre comes out cleanly.

Remove from the oven and leave to cool in the tin for 30 minutes before turning onto a wire rack to become completely cold.

THRESHING CAKE/*Cacen Ddyrnu*

WALES   ***Serves 7-8***

Of all the Threshing Cakes, this one appears to be the most interesting, probably because the ingredients clearly reflect what was readily available and inexpensive. An old recipe using dripping and buttermilk, it gives a clear insight into cakes of the past.

Unlike shearing and harvest time, sadly there really is no longer a threshing time; today combine harvesters remove the grain as they gather the crops.

450 g/1 lb plain flour	225 g/8 oz pork or bacon dripping
225 g/8 oz sultanas	3 eggs, lightly beaten
225 g/8 oz currants	1 teaspoon bicarbonate of soda
225 g/8 oz soft brown sugar	Buttermilk, to mix

Preheat the oven to 190°C/375°F/Gas Mark 5.

Sift the flour into a bowl and stir in the sultanas, currants and sugar. Gently melt the dripping and stir into the mixture, adding the lightly beaten eggs. Mix thoroughly.

Add the bicarbonate of soda to a little buttermilk and quickly add to the cake mixture stirring until a soft dough is formed.

Spoon the mixture into a greased and lined 900 g/2 lb loaf tin and place in the centre of the oven. Bake for about 1½ hours or until the cake is well risen and a skewer inserted into the centre comes out cleanly, if it takes a little longer do not worry, just turn the oven down a little and try again after 15 minutes.

Turn onto a wire rack to cool. Excellent served sliced and buttered.

ALE CAKE

Over the centuries ale was often brewed for the farm workers and I have a really potent recipe for home brewed ale, given to me by a farmer's wife, which had passed through many generations of the family.

Certainly in the farmhouse where I live the ale was brewed in the 'wash house' and piped into the dairy cellar where it was left to mature, before serving to the farm workers at harvest time. I have since made the recipe often, although not in the washhouse and the resulting ale is excellent both for drinking and cake making.

This Ale Cake recipe is one I have baked on many occasions. It is excellent served with coffee or tea, but also very good eaten warm accompanied by cream or custard, as a pudding. What more could you ask of a cake? Oh and incidentally, it keeps and keeps, stored in an airtight tin.

A couple of years ago I was commissioned by a major broadsheet to bake several very large Ale Cakes which were sent out to the BBC Radio 4 cricket commentators and players in the West Indies – I gathered they were very well received, although I am unclear as to whether they affected the cricket.

225 g/8 oz raisins	225 g/8 oz dark brown muscovado sugar
225 g/8 oz sultanas	1 tablespoon black treacle
350 g/12 oz currants	4 large eggs, lightly beaten
75 g/3 oz citrus peel	225 g/8 oz plain flour
250ml/9 fl oz strong English ale	1 teaspoon mixed spice
225 g/8 oz butter	

Preheat the oven to 180°C/350°F/Gas Mark 4.

In a large bowl, steep the fruits and the citrus peel in the ale, leaving it for at least 24 hours, stirring occasionally.

In a separate bowl, cream the butter and sugar together until light and fluffy, beat in the treacle and then slowly add the eggs, flour and spice, a little at a time until thoroughly mixed together. Stir in the steeped fruits and pile the mixture into a greased and lined 20 cm/8 inch round cake tin. Bake in the centre of the oven for one hour, reducing the temperature to 120°C/250°F/Gas Mark ¹/2 for a further 2 hours or until a skewer inserted into the centre comes out cleanly. Because of the quantity of liquid used in making this cake, it may take a little longer to cook, but don't worry, this is perfectly normal.

Cover with a cloth and leave the cake in the tin to become cold, then turn it out and peel the greaseproof paper away.

This cake improves if it is left for 24 hours before eating.

BOILED FRUIT CAKE

Serves 8-10

Boiled fruit cake is a really old-fashioned cake which is still very popular today and it is virtually impossible to pick up a cookery book from any time during the last two centuries, detailing fruit cakes, without finding an excellent recipe.

I always thought they sounded rather dull and uninteresting until my mother, who often wrote recipes for the staff magazine of a very large bakery, put one into print and I thought I had better try it. Excellent – no wonder this recipe has remained popular through the generations.

225 g/8 oz sultanas	175 g/6 oz soft brown sugar
225 g/8 oz currants	Generous teaspoon mixed spice
225 g/8 oz raisins	350 g/12 oz self raising flour
50 g/2 oz chopped citrus peel	Pinch salt
175 g/6 oz butter	3 large eggs, lightly beaten

Preheat the oven to 150°C/300°F/Gas Mark 2.

Place the fruit, peel, butter, sugar and spice in a large saucepan and slowly bring to the boil, stirring constantly. Boil gently for 4 minutes.

Remove from the heat and set aside to cool.

Sift the flour and salt into another bowl and making a well in the centre, pour the lightly beaten eggs into the flour. Pour the fruit mixture onto the flour and eggs, beating with a wooden spoon until the mixture is thoroughly combined.

Spoon into a greased and lined 18 cm/7 inch round cake tin. Bake in the centre of the oven for 2 – 2½ hours, or until the cake is firm to touch and a skewer inserted into the centre comes out cleanly.

Cover with a clean cloth and allow to cool in the tin.

CHURCH WINDOW CAKE
OR BATTENBURG

Serves 6

Rather like the chicken and the egg, which came first is unclear, Church Window Cake or Battenburg, but what is certain is that the cake has appeared frequently in British recipe books over the last two centuries. The finished cake resembles a church stained glass window and although the Prussian village of Battenburg may have played a part in the origins of the cake, it is nonetheless a firm favourite on the traditional English tea table and deserves inclusion in this book.

Very decorative and for almond lovers, a real treat, the Church Window Cake just requires a little artistic patience, but is well worth the effort. It is a pretty two coloured sponge cake with the strips of cake sandwiched together in a chequerboard effect. There is a pink layer above a white, using four equally sized strips of sponge and the finished cake is wrapped in an outer layer of almond paste.

175 g/6 oz butter	**Topping**
175 g/6 oz caster sugar	275 g/10 oz almond paste (purchased or
3 large eggs, lightly beaten	page 214)
175 g/6 oz self raising flour	A little warmed raspberry jam
A little red food colouring	

Preheat the oven to 160°C/325°F/Gas Mark 3.

There are several methods of preparing this mixture but I suggest the easiest is to use one tin, baking the two colour sponges alongside each other.

Cream the butter and sugar together until light and fluffy, then add the lightly beaten eggs and flour, a little at a time, beating until completely smooth.

Grease and line a 18 cm/7 inch square cake tin and spoon half of the mixture into the left hand side, then add a little red food colouring to the remaining sponge mix and stir thoroughly. Spoon the pink mixture into the other half of the tin and smooth gently.

Bake in the oven for approximately 30 to 35 minutes or until firm when lightly pressed in the centre.

Carefully turn out of the tin onto a wire rack and leave to cool.

When cold, trim the edges of the cake and divide it equally into 4 long sections, which will give you two strips of each colour.

Using a little of the warmed raspberry jam, place one of each colour on the bottom and the remaining two on top, alternating the colours to give a chequerboard effect.

Roll the marzipan out thinly into oblong, using the cake as a measurement for length. Spread a thin layer of jam over the marzipan then roll it around the block of sponge, sealing it with a little jam. Trim the edges neatly at each end.

Place it onto a plate with the 'seam' underneath and lightly mark the top in the traditional crisscross pattern.

HUNT CAKE

Serves 10-12

Probably the most famous Hunt Cake is the Melton Hunt Cake, which can still be bought in the market town of Melton Mowbray, Leicestershire and was served before a meet as long ago as 1854.

Although the Melton Hunt no longer exists they were certainly not the only hunt to have a cake. They are served at the end of a hard day's hunting as part of a high tea table, creaking with goodies, to tired and hungry hunt followers. The Blackmore Vale had its own cake, which has been served for over a century and I can remember cake being served to the Chiddingfold Farmers' Hunt members at their meets in Surrey 50 years ago.

What the cakes do have in common though is that a hunt cake is always a good old-fashioned fruitcake, packed with nuts and cherries and made with a liberal helping of sherry, rum or brandy.

225 g/8 oz raisins	1 tablespoon black treacle
225 g/8 oz sultanas	225 g/8 oz plain flour
275 g/10 oz currants	1 teaspoon mixed spice
50 g/2 oz chopped glace peel	1/2 teaspoon salt
50 g/2 oz red cherries, halved	4 large eggs, lightly beaten
3 tablespoons sherry, rum or brandy	50 g/2 oz ground almonds
225 g/8 oz butter	50 g/2 oz flaked almonds
225 g/8 oz dark muscovado sugar	1 tablespoon lemon juice

Preheat the oven to 140°C/275°F/Gas Mark 1.

Wash all the fruit, drain and put it into a large bowl. Add the preferred alcohol and mix thoroughly. Cover and leave overnight to steep.

In a separate bowl, cream the butter and sugar together until light and fluffy and beat in the black treacle. Sift the flour, spices and salt and together with the eggs add a little at a time, stirring well. Fold in the ground and flaked almonds together with the lemon juice, stirring until mixed. Finally add the steeped fruits, folding in thoroughly.

Spoon the mixture into a greased and lined 20 cm/8 inch cake tin and place in the centre of the oven for 1 hour. Reduce the oven temperature to 120°C/250°F/Gas Mark 1/2 for a further 2 1/2 hours. If the cake appears to be browning too quickly, cover with a layer of brown paper.

The cake is ready when it is firm to touch and a skewer inserted into the middle comes out cleanly.

Cover with a clean tea cloth and allow the cake to cool overnight in the tin before turning out onto a wire rack. This cake is best wrapped in greaseproof and foil and allowed to mature for several days before eating.

MINCEMEAT CAKE

Serves 8-10

The first Mincemeat Cake I made 30 years ago seemed an up-to-the-minute idea but I have since been surprised how often this recipe crops up in cookery books during the early part of the last century. Although it would not have been a good idea to use mincemeat made with meat as the original mincemeats were. An excellent way of using up any left over mincemeat after Christmas, the resulting fruitcake is delicious, and topped with vanilla butter cream icing, makes a lovely family cake.

Because the cake is very moist, it will only keep 2 or 3 days so I always keep mine in the refrigerator, in an airtight container, although it seldom remains uneaten long enough to warrant such attention.

175 g/6 oz butter	Zest of one large orange
225 g/8 oz pale brown sugar	225 g/8 oz fruit mincemeat
275 g/10 oz self raising flour	
1 teaspoon baking powder	**Topping**
175 ml/6 fl oz buttermilk	115 g/4 oz soft butter
2 eggs, lightly beaten	225 g/8 oz icing sugar
Zest of one large lemon	1/2 teaspoon vanilla extract

Preheat the oven to 160°C/325°F/Gas Mark 3.

Cream the butter and sugar together until light and fluffy. Sift the flour and baking powder together and with the buttermilk and eggs add to the butter mixture, a little at a time, beating with a wooden spoon until completely smooth.

Stir in the lemon and orange zest, together with the mincemeat and spoon into a 20 cm/8 inch greased and lined cake tin.

Bake in the oven for 1 1/2 to 2 hours or until the top feels firm when lightly pressed and a skewer inserted into the centre comes out cleanly.

Cool for 30 minutes in the tin before turning out onto a wire rack and leaving to become completely cold.

Meanwhile beat the butter, sifted icing sugar and the vanilla extract together in a bowl until soft and creamy and spread onto the top of the cold Mincemeat Cake, leaving to set for a couple of hours, before serving.

FRESH ORANGE FRUIT CAKE   *Serves 10-12*

Made with fresh orange juice and Cointreau liqueur, this truly delectable fruitcake is based on our award-winning cake. It has featured in Fortnum & Mason's leading hampers on many occasions and is sold in the store each year during the festive period.

I think the charm of this cake is that whilst packed with the finest vine fruits, it is paler than the traditional rich fruitcake. Using pale muscovado sugar and omitting the treacle, enables the aromatic spices and delicate flavour of oranges to shine through. Undecorated it is suitable for both summer teatimes and picnics but the addition of baked orange slices and spice bags gives it a wonderful visual, wintery warmth for special occasions.

I developed the cake for Church Farmhouse by simply adapting the fruitcake recipe used throughout her life by my grandmother Elsie.

250 g/8 oz sultanas	^{1}/2 teaspoon mixed spice
250 g/8 oz golden sultanas	1 teaspoon ground mace
115 g/4 oz currants	1 teaspoon ground coriander
115 g/4 oz raisins	50 g/2 oz ground almonds
115 g/4 oz chopped mixed peel	4 large eggs
250 g/8 oz butter	2 tablespoons fresh orange juice
250 g/8 oz pale muscovado sugar	1 tablespoon Cointreau
250 g/8 oz plain flour	Finely grated rind of one orange

The day before you make the cake rinse all the fruits thoroughly. Drain and put into a bowl, cover and set aside until required. There is no need to dry the fruit, if thoroughly drained; it will absorb the moisture and give a better texture to the cake.

Cream the butter and sugar in a large bowl until light and fluffy.

Sift the flour and spices and stir in the ground almonds.

Whisk the eggs and add alternately with the flour mixture to the butter and sugar, using a wooden spoon to stir thoroughly between each addition. Continue stirring whilst adding the orange juice and cointreau. Finally add the prepared fruits, together with the freshly grated orange rind, stirring until the cake mixture is thoroughly combined.

Spoon the mix into a greased and lined 20 cm/8 inch cake tin. Tie two layers of brown paper around the outside of the tin. Finally covering the top of the cake tin with a piece of brown paper, place the cake in the centre of a preheated oven 160°C/325°F/Gas Mark 3 for one hour before turning the oven to 140°C/275°C/Gas Mark 1 for a further 2 to 2^1/2 hours. Remove the brown paper from the top of the cake for the last hour of baking. The cake will be cooked when it feels firm and a skewer inserted into the centre, comes out cleanly.

Remove the cake from the oven and place it, still in the tin, on a wire cooling rack. Cover with a clean cloth and leave until cold before carefully turning out.

The cake may be decorated with glace orange slices if liked.

NAVY CAKE

Whilst the origins of this cake are unclear, the connection to the Navy is in little doubt. Until 31st July 1970, when the practice was discontinued, sailors had received a daily 'tot' of rum in a ritual which began in 1655. Hence this moist aromatic dark fruitcake is made with honey, vine fruits and a very large tot of rum. It makes an excellent special occasion cake but is best made the day before it is required.

450 g/1 lb sultanas	225 g/8 oz butter
450 g/1 lb raisins	225 g/8 oz dark muscovado sugar
675 g/1½ lb currants	225 g/8 oz plain flour
115 g/4 oz chopped glace peel	1 teaspoon mixed spice
115 g/4 oz glace cherries, halved	4 large eggs, lightly beaten
225 ml/8 fl oz dark rum	175 ml/6 fl oz clear honey

Preheat the oven to 160°C/325°F/Gas Mark 3.

Place all the fruits in a large bowl and add the rum. Stir thoroughly and leave overnight to steep.

In a separate bowl cream the butter and sugar together until light and fluffy. Add the sifted flour and spice together with the lightly beaten eggs, a little at a time, until thoroughly combined.

Stir in the steeped rum fruits and honey, mixing well. Pile into a greased and lined 23 cm/9 inch cake tin, smoothing the top carefully.

Bake in the oven for about 2½ hours or until the top feels firm and a skewer inserted into the middle of the cake comes out cleanly. If the top begins to brown too much, cover the cake with brown paper for the last 30 minutes.

Leave the cake in the tin to become completely cold.

PLUM CAKE

A very old recipe, which was often used as the base for traditional wedding cakes, this is one of our most loved cakes, even the title conjures up thoughts of a bygone era.

Elizabeth Raffald in her excellent book *The Experienced English Housekeeper*, 1769, lists no less than three versions: The Good Plum Cake, The White Plum Cake, and The Little Plum Cakes.

Thought to have originated in Gloucestershire, I suspect from the many versions available that the title 'Plum Cake' became widely used to describe any rich, almond fruit cake, which was steeped in brandy. However, Mrs Raffald adds ¹/₂ pint of sack (dry white wine or sherry) to her White Plum Cake and to the Irish Plum Cake found so often in old cookery books, adds stout.

225 g/8 oz butter	225 g/8 oz raisins
225 g/8 oz caster sugar	Zest of one large lemon
225 g/8 oz plain flour	50 g/2 oz chopped glace peel
¹/₂ teaspoon mixed spice	75 g/3 oz ground almonds
4 large eggs, lightly beaten	50 g/2 oz glace cherries, quartered
225 g/8 oz currants	2 tablespoons brandy
225 g/8 oz sultanas	

Preheat the oven to 140°C/275°F/Gas Mark 1.

Cream the butter and sugar together until light and fluffy. Sift the flour and spice and add to the mixture a little at a time, together with the lightly beaten eggs.

Fold in the fruits, lemon zest, peel, ground almonds, cherries and brandy using a metal spoon, stirring until thoroughly mixed.

Pile into a 18 cm/7 inch greased and lined cake tin and smooth the top gently.

Bake in the centre of the oven for 2 hours, reducing the temperature to 120°C/250°F/Gas Mark ¹/₂ for a further 1 hour or until the cake is firm when pressed lightly on top, and a skewer inserted into the centre comes out cleanly.

Leave to cool in the tin overnight. When completely cold remove from the tin and wrap in a layer of greaseproof, followed by a layer of foil and store in a cool dry place until required.

SAND CAKE

Serves 6-8

Very similar to a Rice Cake, having ground rice as a fundamental part of the recipe, but a Sand Cake has an even crumblier texture, as a result of using cornflour rather than flour.

Butter and the addition of orange or lemon zest add flavour to the cake, which is a good plain teatime cake and an interesting talking point.

115 g/4 oz cornflour
25 g/1 oz ground rice
1/2 level teaspoon baking powder
115 g/4 oz butter

115 g/4 oz caster sugar
Zest of one orange
2 large eggs

Preheat the oven to 180°C/350°F/Gas Mark 4.

Put the cornflour, ground rice and baking powder into a bowl.

In a separate bowl cream the butter and sugar together until light and fluffy, adding the orange zest towards the end. Beat the eggs lightly and add a little at a time until fully incorporated, then fold in the dry ingredients gently using a large metal spoon.

Place the mixture in a greased and lined 15 cm/6 inch cake tin and bake in the oven for about 1 hour or until golden and firm to touch. A skewer inserted into the centre should come out cleanly.

Cool for 15 minutes in the tin and turn onto a wire rack to become cold.

The Sand Cake is also very good served sliced and buttered.

HONEY CAKE

Honey has been used since before medieval times to sweeten our traditional British cakes, especially gingerbreads, which were made from a spiced honey mixture, thickened with breadcrumbs.

Cerebus the three-headed, dragon-tailed dog of Roman mythology was subdued by the Trojan Prince, Aeneas and the beautiful maiden Psyche by them offering honey cake. Perhaps worth trying similarly on one's enemies?

Until the 18th century honey was the main source of sweetening but the introduction of loaf sugar, enabled the wealthy to replace it in their cooking, sadly resulting in the many variations of honey cakes becoming less popular, although they are enjoying a limited revival today, as honey is seen as a healthier product than sugar.

From the endless recipes available, I have chosen my own personal favourite.

450 g/1 lb wholemeal self raising flour	50 g/2 oz currants
1 teaspoon bicarbonate soda	50 g/2 oz sultanas
1 teaspoon mixed spice	50 g/2 oz raisins
175 g/6 oz pale muscovado sugar	50 g/2 oz chopped glace peel
225 g/8 oz clear honey	
75 ml/3 fl oz vegetable oil	**Topping**
3 large eggs	4 tablespoons extra honey
2 tablespoons milk	A little sliced crystallized ginger
50 g/2 oz glace cherries	

Preheat the oven to 160°C/325°F/Gas Mark 3.

Sift the flour, bicarbonate of soda and spice into a mixing bowl and stir in the sugar. Melt the honey and oil together in a saucepan until the two are combined and then set aside to cool. Beat the eggs and milk together and whisking constantly, add to the honey and oil mixture.

Make a well in the centre of the flour and slowly add the liquid ingredients, stirring constantly with a wooden spoon. Stir in the remaining ingredients.

Spoon the mixture into a greased and lined 18 cm/7 inch cake tin, smoothing the top. Bake on the lowest shelf of the oven for approximately 1 1/2 hours or until the top is firm when pressed gently, and a skewer inserted into the centre comes out cleanly. If the cake begins to brown too quickly, before it is completely cooked, cover with a sheet of brown paper.

Meanwhile gently melt the 4 tablespoons of honey, and when the cake is cooked, remove from the oven and gently pour it over the cake. Decorate with sliced crystallized ginger if liked.

Allow the cake to cool for 30 minutes before carefully removing from the tin and placing on a wire rack to cool. When cold remove the greaseproof paper.

VICTORIAN FRUIT CAKE

Serves 6-7

Passed down from my great-grandmother Helen Caroline to my grandmother Elsie, this very old and economical fruit cake recipe was widely made in Victorian days, being simple to mix using the all-in-one method. Having made the recipe many times, always with success and attracting compliments, it would have been hard to leave such a very easy recipe, which goes back several generations, out of the book.

115 g/4 oz butter
115 g/4 oz caster sugar
2 eggs, lightly beaten
150 ml/¼ pint milk
350 g/12 oz mixed dried fruit
50 g/2 oz chopped mixed peel

50 g/2 oz chopped glace cherries
225 g/8 oz self raising flour (or plain flour adding ½ teaspoon baking powder)
Pinch salt
1 level teaspoon mixed spice

Preheat the oven to 160°C/325°F/Gas Mark 3.

Place all the ingredients into a large bowl and beat with a wooden spoon until well mixed.

Spoon into a greased and lined 15 cm/6 inch cake tin and bake on the middle shelf of the oven for 1½ to 1¾ hours or until golden brown and a skewer inserted into the centre comes out cleanly.

Leave for 30 minutes before turning on to a wire rack to become cold.

POUND CAKE

Serves 8

A very old recipe which can be found in cookery books dating as far back as the 1700's, it continued to be baked right through the Victorian period, until recently when the quantities required to bake a true Pound Cake, were simply seen as colossal within the smaller family unit. The Pound Cake derived its name from the weight of the ingredients used to bake the cake; 1lb butter, 1 lb sugar, 1 lb flour, 1lb vine fruits with the addition of a little peel, spice and eggs.

The following recipe, to which I have added a little mace, comes from *The Ideal Cookery Book* by M. A. Fairclough. Whilst certainly based on the old pound cakes, it is more manageable and makes a very good teatime cake. Interestingly this recipe we are told, will cost 1s 8d (about 9p) and 4 hours to make. I have never been able to trace or date this lovely old book, but at 1s 8d for a really generous cake, we can assume it is quite old. Incidentally, such a cake would cost about £3.50 to bake today. I unashamedly leave the weights for this recipe in pounds and ounces. Although the recipe calls for 6 eggs I did find that it was rather too many, so I suggest you add the eggs one at a time until a soft but not runny consistency is reached. You may find you do not need them all.

1/2 lb butter	1/2 teaspoon mace
1/2 lb caster sugar	1/2 lb currants
6 eggs, lightly beaten	1/2 lb raisins
1/2 lb plain flour	2 oz peel
1/2 teaspoon baking powder	

Preheat the oven to 150°C/300°F/Gas Mark 2.

Cream the butter and sugar together in a large bowl until light and fluffy. Add the eggs, lightly beaten, one at a time, together with the sifted flour, baking powder and mace. When mixed, add the remaining ingredients and stir thoroughly.

Spoon into a 18 cm/7 inch greased and lined cake tin, smoothing the top lightly. Bake in the centre of the oven for 1 1/4 to 1 1/2 hours, or until the cake is well risen and golden brown. A skewer inserted into the centre should come out cleanly, if not allow a little longer. If the cake begins to brown too quickly, cover it with a sheet of brown paper to reduce the top heat.

When baked, leave in the tin for 15 minutes and then turn out onto a wire rack and leave to cool.

RICE CAKE

Serves 6–8

Whilst I was not successful in unearthing an intriguing history to these cakes, they appear in several very old cookery books and lots of more modern ones, the rice in question being ground rice.

Mrs Raffald, in 1769, gives a splendid version using 15 eggs, however, a more manageable quantity using 3 eggs will bake an excellent cake, with a light, slightly crumbly texture, ideal for afternoon tea.

175 g/6 oz butter	115 g/4 oz plain flour
175 g/6 oz caster sugar	175 g/6 oz ground rice
Zest one lemon	1 level teaspoon baking powder
3 eggs	1 tablespoon hot water

Preheat the oven to 180°C/350°F/Gas Mark 4.

Cream the butter and sugar together until light and fluffy. Stir in the lemon zest. Add the eggs, flour, ground rice and baking powder a little at a time, folding until thoroughly mixed, pour in the water and stir until the mixture is smooth. Add a little extra water if necessary, until a dropping consistency is achieved.

Spoon the mixture into a lightly greased and floured 900 g/2 lb loaf tin and bake until golden brown and firm to touch. Approximately 1 hour. Leave to cool in the tin for 10 minutes before carefully turning onto a wire rack to cool completely.

PRINCESS CAKE

Serves 8

I was disappointed to find a lack of consistency in the cakes bearing this title, certainly there did not appear to be a basic recipe, albeit most of them sounded very good. One in particular, well worth trying, reminded me of the Irish Apple Cake, where the fruit is layered in the centre.

When making this cake do not worry if some of the fruits sink to the bottom, it makes no difference to the interesting textures and flavours within the cake.

225 g/8 oz butter	175 g/6 oz currants
225 g/8 oz caster sugar	50 g/2 oz chopped glace cherries
6 large eggs, lightly beaten	50 g/2 oz chopped glace peel
565 g/1 lb 4 oz self raising flour	25 g/1 oz flaked almonds
225 g/8 oz sultanas	

Preheat the oven to 160°C/325°F/Gas Mark 3.

Cream the butter and sugar together until light and fluffy. Add the lightly beaten eggs a little at a time, beating in thoroughly. If they begin to curdle add a spoonful of flour. Sieve the flour and fold it gently into the mixture.

Prepare a 18 cm/7 inch cake tin, line it carefully and put half of the cake mixture into the tin, spreading it evenly. Sprinkle, in turn, the various fruits and almonds over the surface of the cake spreading them equally around the cake, and then spoon the remaining mixture on top, smoothing the top gently.

Bake for 1½ hours or until golden brown and well risen. The cake should feel firm when pressed lightly in the centre.

Leave in the tin for 30 minutes and then turn out carefully onto a wire rack, leaving to cool completely.

SPONGE CAKE

Serves 8

A perfectly made, fresh sponge cake, sandwiched with homemade raspberry jam or lemon curd, seems to typify the most delectable of teatime cakes. Recipes can be found through the centuries although the advent of 'the mechanical whisk' has greatly lessened the hours spent preparing by hand.

There are no shortcuts to the very best of sponge cakes, the process being straightforward and simple, as long as time is taken at each stage. The final texture is entirely relative to the amount of air whisked into the eggs.

75 g/3 oz plain flour	**Filling**
3 large eggs	Raspberry jam or lemon curd
75 g/3 oz caster sugar	Caster sugar or icing sugar

Preheat the oven to 190°C/375°F/Gas Mark 5.

Grease two 15 cm/6 inch sandwich tins, placing a circle of greaseproof into the bottom of each tin. It is important to prepare them in advance to prevent loss of air in the mixture once it is ready to bake.

Half fill a saucepan with water and bring to the boil, turn off the heat (or you will end up with scrambled eggs) and place a large mixing bowl over the top. Break the eggs into the bowl, add the sugar and start whisking until the mixture is thick enough to leave a trail when the whisk is held above the bowl. At this stage the mixture will have become very pale and increased in volume.

Remove the bowl from the saucepan and sift the flour, a little at a time over the mixture. With a large metal spoon carefully fold in the flour using a figure of 8 motion, to lessen the risk of lumps forming.

Divide the mixture evenly between the sandwich tins, smooth the top gently and immediately place in the centre of the oven baking for 20 minutes or until the cakes are pale golden brown and feel firm when lightly pressed in the centre.

Turn onto a wire rack and carefully peel the paper from the cakes, leaving them to become quite cold.

Sandwich them together with the filling of your choice, sprinkling the top with a little caster sugar or dredged icing sugar.

Best eaten on the same day it is baked.

GENOA CAKE

Serves 8

A traditional light fruit cake, popular in Victorian times, when afternoon tea was an important part of the day in genteel households.

225 g/8 oz caster sugar	50 g/2 oz glace cherries, halved
225 g/8 oz butter	Grated rind of one lemon
4 large eggs, lightly beaten	50 g/2 oz flaked almonds
275 g/10 oz self raising flour	1 tablespoon sherry or rum (optional)
175 g/6 oz sultanas	

Preheat the oven to 160°C/325°F/Gas Mark 3.

Cream the butter and sugar together until light and fluffy, add the eggs a little at a time, beating thoroughly. If they begin to curdle, add a little flour and beat again.

Sift the flour and then fold in together with the sultanas, cherries, lemon rind and almonds. Add the sherry or rum, if liked. Continue stirring until well mixed.

Grease and line an 18 cm/7 inch cake tin and spoon in the mixture, smoothing the top. Bake in the centre of the oven for about 1¹/₂ to 1³/₄ hours, or until a skewer inserted into the centre, comes out cleanly and the top feels firm if lightly pressed.

If the cake begins to brown too quickly, cover with a layer of brown paper.

Allow to cool in the tin for 30 minutes before gently turning out onto a wire rack and leaving to become cold.

COLLEGE CAKE

Serves 8-10

I have come across several versions of this old recipe, all very similar, one with the inclusion of caraway seeds and a little ginger, another with the addition of dates. But basically they are all very much lard or dripping based cakes with grated orange rind and a variety of vine fruits.

I have chosen a version without caraway seeds but of course you may add a teaspoonful if you like.

250 g/9 oz plain flour	Grated rind of one large orange
1 1/2 teaspoons baking powder	3 large eggs
75 g/3 oz butter	1/4 teaspoon vanilla extract
75 g/3 oz lard or dripping	A little milk
115 g/4 oz caster sugar	
75 g/3 oz currants	**Topping**
75 g/3 oz chopped dates	175 g/6 oz icing sugar
75 g/3 oz raisins	Juice of the orange

Preheat the oven to 180°C/350°F/Gas Mark 4.

Sift the flour and baking powder together into a large bowl and rub in the butter and lard or dripping, to a fine breadcrumb consistency. Stir in the sugar, currants, dates, raisins and orange rind.

Lightly beat the eggs and add together with the vanilla extract, mixing thoroughly. Add enough milk to form a dropping consistency and spoon into a 18 cm/7 inch greased and lined cake tin. Place in the oven and bake for about 1 3/4 hours or until the top is firm to touch and a skewer inserted into the centre comes out cleanly.

Turn onto a wire rack and leave to cool.

If liked a little orange icing can be drizzled over the top of the cake before serving. Simply squeeze out the juice of the orange and stirring well to eliminate any lumps, add enough icing sugar to form a pouring consistency. Spoon over the top of the cake and allow the icing to run down the sides a little.

PRINCE ALBERT CAKE

Serves 16

Prince Albert had a wide variety of dishes named after him, probably the most famous being the Prince Albert Pudding, so I can only think that he must have been a real foodie.

The Prince Albert Cake has several variations but is always baked in a square tin and cut into smaller square portions. The following recipe is the one that appears most commonly.

8 eggs	175 g/6 oz sultanas
275 g/10 oz caster sugar	Grated rind of one lemon
350 g/12 oz self raising flour	

Preheat the oven to 160°C/325°F/Gas Mark 3.

As with a sponge cake, start by beating the eggs and sugar over a bowl of hot water until a trail forms if the whisk is held above the mixture. Then using a large metal spoon, gently fold in the flour ensuring there are no lumps. Add the sultanas and lemon rind, stirring carefully in a figure of eight, so as not to lose all the air you have added to the mixture.

Working quickly, pour the cake mixture into a greased and lined 25.5 cm/10 inch square cake tin and bake for 20 to 25 minutes or until well risen and firm when lightly pressed. Allow to cool in the tin for 30 minutes and then turn out carefully onto a wire rack and leave until completely cold. Then using a sharp knife, cut into sixteen, 6 cm/2¹/₂ inch squares before serving.

VICTORIA SANDWICH

Serves 8

Queen Victoria lent her name to this traditional cake, which she was said to have greatly enjoyed with afternoon tea.

Often confused with a sponge cake (which does not contain fat), it is baked in two shallow tins, sandwiched together with jam and the top is finished with a light dusting of caster sugar. A Victoria Sandwich is also excellent with a little butter cream sandwiched in along with the jam filling.

Incidentally, you can make this cake by the all-in-one method, but if you have time it is worth making it in the traditional way, as you will have a closer, better texture as the all-in-one method often results in large air holes.

115 g/4 oz butter	115 g/4 oz self raising flour
115 g/4 oz caster sugar	Jam
2 large eggs	A little extra caster sugar

Preheat the oven to 180°C/350°F/Gas Mark 4.

Cream the butter and sugar together until pale, light and fluffy. Fold in the lightly beaten eggs and the flour, a little at a time, until completely incorporated.

Spoon the mixture equally into two greased 15 cm/6 inch sandwich tins, smoothing the tops gently. Place in the centre of the oven until well risen and golden. The top when lightly pressed should spring back. This will take approximately 25 to 30 minutes.

Remove from the tins and turn onto a cooling rack immediately. When completely cold sandwich together with the jam and sprinkle the top lightly with the caster sugar.

SNOW CAKE

Serves 8

This very elegant cake is also known as a White Cake or Silver Cake and was very popular in Victorian times when teatime cakes were varied and imaginative, visual impact being as important as taste.

The absence of egg yolks makes the sponge virtually white, the flavour being enhanced by the addition of lemon zest, orange zest or vanilla extract, which maintain the delicate nature of the cake, not overpowering the basic ingredients.

Incidentally, lard was often used instead of butter, to keep the appearance of the cake 'whiter' (although I admit to not enjoying the cake very much when I used lard), and Mrs Gertrude Latter gives an interesting recipe, in her handwritten recipe book, using arrowroot instead of flour, arrowroot being very similar to tapioca. I have detailed this cake in the next recipe.

115 g/4 oz butter (or lard if preferred)	**Filling**
225 g/8 oz caster sugar	150 ml/^{1}/4 pint whipped cream
275 g/10 oz self raising flour	
150 ml/^{1}/4 pint milk	**Topping**
Zest of 2 large lemons	225 g/8 oz icing sugar
Pinch of salt	Lemon juice
4 egg whites	Silver balls or silver Smarties

Preheat the oven to 160°C/325°F/Gas Mark 3.

Cream the butter and sugar together until light and fluffy. Add the flour, milk, lemon zest and salt a little at a time, stirring until thoroughly incorporated.

In a separate bowl, whisk the egg whites until they are very stiff and using a metal spoon fold them gently into the mixture.

Spoon the cake mix into a greased and lined 18 cm/7 inch cake tin, working gently but quickly. Place in the oven and bake until risen and firm to touch approximately 1^1/4 hours, but this may vary between ovens. If it begins to brown, cover with a sheet of brown paper to lessen surface heat, the cake is cooked when a skewer inserted into the centre, comes out cleanly.

Leave to cool in the tin for 30 minutes and then turn out gently onto a wire rack. Leave until cold before peeling off the greaseproof paper.

When cold, slice in half horizontally and sandwich back together with the whipped cream.

In a separate bowl mix the icing sugar to a smooth coating consistency using a little water or the juice of one of the lemons. Spread evenly onto the top of the cake and leave to set before serving.

Decorations such as silver balls or silver Smarties may be used to decorate the icing when set.

SNOW CAKE

Not unlike the previous cake but this recipe uses arrowroot instead of flour, although it is doubtful if you would buy it to use today, as I have found arrowroot is generally only available in packs of fairly small quantity. It is however, interesting to read these very old recipes, this one dating from about 1920.

225 g/8 oz butter	1 teaspoon baking powder
225 g/8 oz caster sugar	3 eggs, lightly beaten
450 g/1 lb common arrowroot	Rind of 1 lemon

Preheat the oven to 150°C/300°F/Gas Mark 2.

Cream the butter and sugar together.

Sift together the arrowroot and baking powder, adding them together with the eggs and lemon rind to the creamed butter mixture. Beat until thoroughly incorporated.

Spoon the mixture into a greased and lined 18 cm/7 inch square cake tin and then having smoothed the top gently, place in the centre of the oven and bake for about 40 minutes or until well risen and firm to touch. If the cake begins to brown too quickly, cover with a sheet of brown paper.

When cooked, allow to cool slightly before turning onto a wire rack. When cold, cut into squares before serving.

RIBBON CAKE

Serves 6-8

You can imagine my delight when I first read an enchanting handwritten recipe book lent to me by a friend whose family had been Lincolnshire bakers. Compiled in 1923 by Ivy Peatman, it must have been really rather modern in its time and the recipe for Ribbon Cake was doubtless considered a real treat. The three-coloured cake contains an ingredient which was new to me called 'Raisley flour'; I have since learnt it was rather like baking powder.

115 g/4 oz butter	1 1/2 teaspoons Raisley flour
175 g/6 oz caster sugar	(substitute 1/2 teaspoon baking powder)
2 eggs, well beaten	A little milk
225 g/8 oz plain flour	Cochineal
	Cocoa powder

Preheat the oven to 180°C/350°F/Gas Mark 4.

Cream the butter and sugar together until light and fluffy. Add the well-beaten eggs. Stir in the flour gently and the Raisley flour (substitute the baking powder) and if necessary add a little milk to form a soft dropping consistency.

Divide the cake mix into three portions, to one add a few drops of cochineal to colour it pale pink, to the second portion add 1 dessertspoonful of cocoa. Leave the third part plain.

Grease and line two 15 cm/6 inch sandwich cake tins. Place spoonfuls of each colour randomly into each cake tin but dividing the mixture equally between the two tins, slightly swirling them together at the edges to form ribbons of colour. Bake in the oven until the cakes are firm to touch, approximately 20 to 25 minutes.

Turn out onto a cooling rack and when cold, sandwich the cakes together with a filling of your choice, either jam or butter cream would be suitable.

Note: For information on Raisley Flour see the recipe for Raspberry Buns (page 164).

LAWN TENNIS CAKE

Serves approximately 8

Whilst the exact origins of the Lawn Tennis Cake remain unclear, it is a recipe found in many cookery books of the 19th and 20th century including *Mrs Beeton's Cookery and Household Management*, 1861.

Based on a light sultana fruitcake and baked in an oblong loaf tin, they may be enriched with a generous measure of sherry.

When the cake is baked and is quite cold, the surface is levelled with a knife and then topped with a layer of almond paste before spreading with a smooth layer of royal icing and sprinkling liberally with finely chopped pistachios nuts, to give the effect of green grass.

Then a royal icing 'net' is piped onto greaseproof paper and when the 'net' and the cake are completely dry, gently position the 'netting' upright onto the centre of the cake, using a little icing to glue it into position.

Alternatively you may prefer to pipe white tennis court markings onto the 'pistachio' grass, giving an excellent visual effect.

How easy it is to imagine this cake forming a delightful centrepiece for a 1920's summer tennis party.

225 g/8 oz butter	**Decoration**
225 g/8 oz caster sugar	115 g/4 oz almond paste
4 large eggs, lightly beaten	225 g/8 oz royal icing
275 g/10 oz plain flour	(packet royal icing is excellent)
175 g/6 oz sultanas	115 g/4 oz pistachios
50 g/2 oz currants	
50 g/2 oz chopped cherries	
50 g/2 oz chopped glace peel	
2 tablespoons sherry	

Preheat the oven to 180°C/350°F/Gas Mark 4.

Cream the butter and sugar together until light and fluffy.

Add the beaten eggs and flour alternately to the mixture, beating thoroughly between each addition.

Gently fold in the fruit, peel and sherry and pile the mixture into a greased and lined 900 g/2 lb loaf tin. Bake in the centre of the oven, reducing the temperature to 150°C/300°F/Gas Mark 2 after 30 minutes. Bake for a further 45 minutes or until the top feels firm and a skewer inserted into the centre comes out cleanly.

Leave to cool in the tin for 20 minutes and then turn onto a wire rack and leave to become completely cold, before decorating as detailed above. Making up the royal icing according to the instructions on the packet, as if the cake is to be given to children or the elderly, it is a safer method than using raw egg white, which should be used with caution, following recent salmonella worries.

OVEN BOTTOM CAKE

Serves 6

Brick ovens heated with wood were used to bake bread, pies and cakes, before the advent of more modern ovens. Oven Bottom Cakes were exactly that, flat shallow cakes baked on the very bottom of the oven, often whilst other bakery goodies were cooking on the shelves above or at the end of the day, when the oven is empty and the heat ebbing away.

In Yorkshire and Lancashire these were often made into a form of tea bun, traditionally using any left over bread base which was then enriched with butter, sugar and vine fruits.

450 g/1 lb Yeast Dough (see page 21)	75 g/3 oz caster sugar
(Traditionally this would have been left over	50 g/2 oz chopped glace cherries
from the day's baking)	50 g/2 oz sultanas
75 g/3 oz butter	

Preheat the oven to 180°C/350°F/Gas Mark 4.

Roll out the bread dough thinly into an oblong. Dot with the butter, sprinkle over the caster sugar, cherries and sultanas, rolling carefully into a 'Swiss roll' shape. Cut into 6 pieces and arrange them flat onto a greased baking sheet. Place them in a circle with 5 pieces around a central piece of cake, leaving approximately 2.5 cm/1 inch between the cakes so that when baked the individual pieces will expand and join together, forming one large sectioned cake.

Leave to rise, uncovered, in a warm place, for 30 minutes and then place into the bottom of the oven. Check after 30 minutes. The Oven Bottom Cake will be ready when risen and golden brown.

Cool on a wire rack, best eaten whilst very fresh.

LEMON DRIZZLE CAKE

Serves 6-7

The recipe for this aromatic, delicious cake has been around for many, many years, and it is not dated, still being perfect to serve at teatime. Easy to make and although a little care is needed with the lemon icing, which should be quite runny, once finished the cake requires no more attention other than eating. Without doubt one of my favourite cakes, the sharpness of the lemon perfectly offsetting the sweet sponge of the cake.

115 g/4 oz butter	**Topping**
115 g/4 oz caster sugar	115 g/4 oz icing sugar
1 large egg, lightly beaten	Juice of the lemon
115 g/4 oz self raising flour	
Zest of 1 large lemon	

Preheat the oven to 180°C/350°F/Gas Mark 4.

Cream the butter and sugar together in a medium sized bowl until light and fluffy.

Fold in the egg and flour, a little at a time, together with the lemon zest, until thoroughly mixed.

Spoon the mixture into a greased 18 cm/7 inch shallow cake tin (a sandwich tin would be perfect) and place the cake in the centre of the oven and bake for about 25 minutes or until well risen and golden brown. The cake will be firm if lightly pressed in the centre.

Meanwhile in a small bowl place the juice of the lemon together with half of the icing sugar, beating thoroughly to eliminate any lumps. Add enough of the remaining icing sugar as needed to form a soft runny consistency to the icing.

Whilst still warm remove the cake from the tin and leave for 10 minutes to cool before drizzling the lemon icing over it and leaving to become cold before serving.

Note: It does not matter if the cake absorbs some of the icing, this is exactly how it should be.

CHOCOLATE CAKE

Serves 8

It may appear that in this book chocolate cakes have simply been forgotten, particularly in view of their popularity today, but they haven't. Chocolate or cocoa as we know it was not brought to Britain until the 16th century, where it remained for a long time very, very expensive and well beyond the reach of the average household or baker.

The first Chocolate House opened in London in 1657, Coffee Houses already being popular and not unlike Gentlemen's Clubs, where the business men of the day met to talk and relax. Chocolate Houses were considered very decadent and exclusive and the drinking of hot chocolate sweetened with vanilla rather took over from coffee and tea as the 'fashionable' drink.

It was not until 1853, when Gladstone lowered the tax on cocoa beans, which had up until that time been extortionate, that cocoa became more easily accessible for cooking, and in particular flavouring, cakes. This, combined with the happy fact that a Dutch scientist had in 1828, whilst experimenting with the cocoa bean, found a way of extracting the cocoa butter, leaving behind a solid block, which in its powdered form became cocoa powder, made its use in baking far simpler. We were of course, still some way from the production of chocolate as we know it today, but that's another story.

The following recipe was probably one of the first recorded recipes for a chocolate cake, which I am sure you will now understand, had not been particularly prolific up until the removal of the cocoa tax. I have adjusted it only very little, to ensure success with today's ingredients.

225 g/8 oz butter
225 g/8 oz soft brown sugar
8 eggs
225 g/8 oz plain chocolate (at least 70% cocoa solids)

115 g/4 oz self raising flour
115 g/4 oz ground almonds
1/2 teaspoon almond extract

Preheat the oven to 160°C/325°F/Gas Mark 3.

Cream the butter and sugar together until pale and fluffy.

Separate the egg yolks and whites. Add the yolks to the butter and sugar a little at a time, beating thoroughly. In a separate bowl whisk the egg whites until they are stiff and set aside.

Melt the chocolate in a bowl over a pan of very hot water and stir, together with the flour and ground almonds, into the cake mixture. Finally, using a metal spoon, fold in the whisked egg whites very gently.

Spoon into a greased and lined 18 cm/7 inch cake tin and place in the centre of the oven and bake for 2¼ hours or until the cake is firm and a skewer inserted into the centre, comes out cleanly.

Remove from the oven and after ten minutes, gently turn onto a wire cooling rack and allow to become completely cold.

HONEY SPONGE CAKE

Serves 8-10

This is an excellent honey sponge cake which is quick and easy to make and always a great favourite with adults and children alike.

Baked frequently in our house, I admit to being unable to resist a slice whilst still warm and in fact would have no hesitation in saying that although still excellent, I like it less once it has become cold. At least that is the excuse I am sticking to for being unable to delay eating this cake whilst still sticky from the warm honey. I always bake it in a ring tin and to me it does not look right baked in any other shape, so it has become something of a tradition in our household, but of course you may use a round cake tin instead.

175 g/6 oz butter	3 large eggs, lightly beaten
175 g/6 oz pale brown sugar	225 g/8 oz clear honey
175 g/6 oz wholemeal self raising flour	(Approx 1/2 jar)

Preheat the oven to 180°C/350°F/Gas Mark 4.

Cream the butter and sugar together until light and fluffy, add the flour and eggs, a little at a time, beating until thoroughly mixed.

Grease and lightly flour a 18 cm/7 inch ring tin and spooning the mixture evenly around the ring, smooth the top lightly.

Place in the centre of the oven for about 30 to 40 minutes or until well risen and firm to touch when pressed lightly.

Meanwhile in a small saucepan, melt the honey over a low heat and as soon as the cake is removed from the oven, make a few holes with a skewer around the cake and spoon half the honey over the sponge.

Shake the cake gently in the tin to loosen it from the sides and invert it onto a plate. Spoon the remaining honey over the top of the cake and leave to cool.

LADY CAKE

The use of only the whites of eggs, gives this pale elegant cake, a texture which lends itself very well to the fragrance given by the careful use of almond extract.

The Lady's Fingers recipe, which can be found in the Small Country Cakes section (page 171), whilst bearing a very similar name, differs in as much as it is never made with almond extract, only vanilla.

175 g/6 oz butter	150 ml/¹/4 pint milk
175 g/6 oz caster sugar	7 egg whites
1 teaspoon almond extract	450 g/1 lb self raising flour

Preheat the oven to 180°C/350°F/Gas Mark 4.

Cream the butter and sugar together until light and fluffy. Beat in the almond extract and milk.

In a separate bowl, whisk the egg whites until they are stiff and dry and using a large metal spoon fold them gently into the mixture.

Sift the flour and adding a little at a time stir it into the cake mix using a figure of 8 motion and immediately turn into a greased and lined 18 cm/7 inch cake tin. Bake in the centre of the oven for 1¹/4 hours or until firm to touch and a skewer inserted into the centre comes out cleanly.

Carefully remove the cake from the tin and turn onto a wire rack to cool. Remove lining paper when the cake is cold.

Ginger, a native of Asia, was one of the very first spices to be used, not only medicinally but also in cookery, the root being either dried and ground, preserved in syrup or crystallised. Brought to Europe more than 2000 years ago by traders, the spices could take years to reach Europe, often being passed from trader to trader and were a considerable source of income.

One of the oldest recorded cakes; the recipe used in the mid-15th century was quite unlike anything we know today, its main ingredients being honey and breadcrumbs. Interestingly, gingerbread did not always contain ginger and this cake was no exception, the flavour and aromatic quality being derived from cinnamon and black pepper.

The ingredients were warmed together, the breadcrumbs absorbing the honey and resulting in a dough-like mixture, which was then allowed to cool before cutting into shapes. Traditionally this gingerbread was decorated with box leaves and cloves.

Although I am not setting out an ingredient list, by melting honey until very hot and then stirring in enough breadcrumbs, together with the spices, to make a thick paste, it would be possible to make a modern day medieval gingerbread.

A 17th century Elizabethan gingerbread recipe gave a similar base of breadcrumbs (or manchets as they were called) but instead of honey they were formed into a dough by boiling them in claret wine before adding the spices and allowing the mixture to cool, finally cutting into shapes.

But through the centuries, each region developed its own variation adding wholemeal flour, treacle, vine fruits, eggs or oats. Some became thin and crisp, some deep, moist and sticky but all delicious. Regional varieties include Yorkshire Gingerbread, Nottingham Gingerbread, Grantham White Gingerbread, Grasmere Gingerbread and of course, wonderfully aromatic ginger cakes and Parkin which are traditionally cut into either squares or triangles.

Throughout the ages, gingerbread became associated with feast days and fairs, such as the Nottingham Goose Fair and St Bartholomew's Fair in London. Vendors hawking gingerbreads, which were often shaped into men or animals and carried in large baskets with accompanying cries, attracted fairgoers and their children, becoming a familiar part of such festivities. In Norwich part of the fun of the Easter Fair was the Ginger Fair Buttons and in the North of England, Parkin was and still is, traditionally served around the bonfire during the festivities on Guy Fawkes Night.

In the following section I have gathered together a small sample of some of the wonderful regional recipes and a little of their history. I hope that you will be tempted to try them and forgive me for not including more gingerbread recipes, which I am sure you will agree are actually a subject which could warrant a whole book.

GINGERBREADS AND GINGER CAKES

HONEY AND GINGER CAKE
/Teisen Fel a Sinsir

Serves 8

Although there are recipes for English Honey and Ginger Cake it does seem to have been particularly linked to Wales. Honey was often used before sugar became readily available, being relatively inexpensive and lending itself particularly well to a ginger cake, giving a moist texture and good flavour.

This Honey and Ginger Cake is also paler than usual as it does not contain treacle, but the addition of fruit makes it a very good teatime cake.

225 g/8 oz honey	$1/2$ teaspoon ground cinnamon
115 g/4 oz butter	50 g/2 oz sultanas
3 eggs, lightly beaten	50 g/2 oz chopped glace cherries
350 g/12 oz self raising flour	50 g/2 oz flaked almonds
1 teaspoon ground ginger	

Preheat the oven to 160°C/325°F/Gas Mark 3.

Melt the honey and butter in a saucepan over a very low heat, stirring gently. Allow to cool. Add the eggs, beating thoroughly.

Sift the flour and spices into a bowl and pour the honey mixture slowly into the centre, and using a wooden spoon, continue to beat thoroughly to avoid lumps. Stir in the fruits and almonds.

Pour into a greased, lined 18 cm/7 inch square cake tin and bake in the centre of the oven for $1^1/4$ hours or until firm to touch.

Cool in the tin for 30 minutes before turning onto a wire cooling rack.

When cold, peel off the greaseproof paper and cut into squares.

Keeps well if stored in an airtight tin and like all gingerbreads, improves with keeping.

NOTTINGHAM GOOSE FAIR GINGERBREAD

Makes 24

Sadly I have been unable to find any baker still making these traditional Nottinghamshire gingerbreads, or even an existing recipe and the Nottingham reference library was unable to come up with any original details.

But what we do know is, that gingerbread was hawked through Nottingham during the annual Goose Fair, which was first held in 1284, and is still in existence today. Now rather than farmers walking their geese to the fair to be sold, the geese often having had their feet dipped in tar to prevent them becoming sore during what was usually a considerable distance for them to walk, the fair consists almost entirely of funfair rides and stalls; and the Goose Fair Gingerbread seems to have faded into history.

Two different varieties of Nottingham Gingerbread emerged as favourites, one a round cake with a hole in the centre, the other a thinner version that was rolled into cones, rather like a brandy snap. Sadly neither recipe could be traced, but the one given below, will produce a very similar gingerbread to Nottingham Gingerbread, being based on a not dissimilar recipe.

350 g/12 oz plain flour	350 g/12 oz butter
2 teaspoons ground ginger	350 g/12 oz sugar
2 teaspoons cinnamon	225 g/8 oz treacle

Preheat the oven to 180°C/350°F/Gas Mark 4.

Sift the flour and spices into a large bowl and make a well in the centre.

In a medium saucepan melt the butter, sugar and treacle over a low heat, stirring occasionally and then set aside and allow to cool slightly.

Pour the melted ingredients into the flour and spices, beating with a wooden spoon, ensuring that it is smooth. The mixture will form into a ball of very soft dough.

Using a teaspoon, drop spoonfuls onto a greased baking sheet, leaving space between each for expansion. Bake in the centre of the oven for approximately 10 minutes or until golden brown and lacy in appearance.

Allow to cool very slightly until you are able to remove them from the tray without breaking, and one at time, 'curl' the biscuits around a dampened handle of a wooden spoon, before placing on a wire rack to cool.

NORFOLK FAIR BUTTONS   *Makes approximately 20*

Like many gingerbreads and cakes, Norfolk Fair Buttons trace their history to the many fairs held within a county, the Easter Fair in Norwich and the pre-Lent fair in Great Yarmouth being two of the largest in Norfolk.

These small round gingerbreads would have been sold during the 18th and 19th centuries by one of the many gingerbread merchants plying their trade. 'Come buy my Hot Spiced Gingerbread' being a typical accompanying street cry.

450 g/1 lb plain flour
1 teaspoon ground ginger
1/2 teaspoon bicarbonate of soda
225 g/8 oz pale muscovado sugar

150 g/4 oz lard or butter
150 g/4 oz black treacle
150 g/4 oz golden syrup

Preheat the oven to 180°C/350°F/Gas Mark 4.

Sift the flour, ginger and bicarbonate of soda into a bowl and stir in the sugar. Rub in the lard or butter to form fine breadcrumbs.

In a medium saucepan warm the syrup and treacle gently over a low heat until it is of pouring consistency and add it to the flour mixture, stirring thoroughly with a pallet knife to form a soft ball.

Turn onto a lightly floured slab and knead gently. Roll to 5 mm/1/4 inch thick and cut into 5 cm/2 inch rounds.

Carefully lift the Ginger Buttons onto a greased baking sheet and bake in the centre of the oven for approximately 10 minutes until well risen and golden.

Remove gently from the tray using a spatula and leave to cool on a wire rack.

Opposite: front, Norfolk Fair Buttons
          back, Nottingham Goose Fair Gingerbread

LANCASHIRE GINGERBREAD *Serves 12-14*

An excellent dark gingerbread, characterised by sultanas, mixed peel and the addition of orange marmalade which does add an interesting flavour to the traditional recipe. However, like all regional cakes, the recipe varies slightly from baker to baker, depending on which area of Lancashire you are buying your gingerbread from.

450 g/1 lb plain flour	225 g/8 oz butter
1 level teaspoon bicarbonate of soda	350 g/12 oz black treacle
2 heaped teaspoons ground ginger	225 g/8 oz dark muscovado sugar
1 teaspoon ground cinnamon	115 g/4 oz golden syrup
1 teaspoon mixed spice	150 ml/^{1}/4 pint milk
115 g/4 oz sultanas	1 tablespoon orange marmalade
50 g/2 oz chopped mixed peel	3 large eggs, lightly beaten

Preheat the oven to 180°C/350°F/Gas Mark 4.

Sift the flour, bicarbonate of soda and spices into a bowl. Add the sultanas and chopped mixed peel and stir, making a well in the centre.

In a medium sized saucepan melt the butter, treacle, sugar, golden syrup, milk and marmalade over a low heat, stirring until dissolved. Set aside to cool and then beat in the eggs.

Pour the melted ingredients into the flour mixture, beating with a wooden spoon to ensure it is thoroughly combined.

Spoon the gingerbread mixture into a greased and lined 23 cm/9 inch square cake tin, smoothing the top and bake on the lower shelf of the oven for about 1¼ hours, or until a skewer inserted into the centre comes out cleanly. As ovens vary considerably, this cake may take a little longer, but this is perfectly normal.

Remove from the oven and leave to cool in the tin.

When cold remove from the tin, carefully peeling off the greaseproof paper and cut into squares before serving. Like all gingerbreads, this cake improves with keeping.

CHRISTMAS GINGERBREAD

YORKSHIRE   *Serves 16*

Originating from the time when children called from door to door asking for pennies and pieces of gingerbread on Christmas Eve, this dark spicy gingerbread is often served with cheese.

Prepared with liberal amounts of vine fruits and peel, together with coriander, cloves, caraway seeds and ginger, the combination of ingredients creates an exceptionally delicious winter cake, which is also very good served buttered.

225 g/8 oz butter	2 tablespoons ground ginger
400 ml/14 fl oz treacle	1 tablespoon bicarbonate of soda
225 g/8 oz Demerara sugar	1 teaspoon caraway seeds
450 g/1 lb plain flour	175 g/6 oz sultanas
2 teaspoons ground coriander	175 g/6 oz raisins
2 teaspoons ground cloves	115 g/4 oz chopped glace peel

Preheat the oven to 150°C/300°F/Gas Mark 2.

In a medium sized saucepan melt the butter, treacle and sugar over a low heat and leave to cool.

Sift the flour, spices and bicarbonate of soda into a large bowl, finally stirring in the teaspoon of caraway seeds, make a well in the centre.

Using a wooden spoon, beat in the dissolved butter and treacle mixture, continue beating until smooth.

Add the fruits and beat again to ensure they are spread evenly within the mixture.

Grease and line a 23 cm/9 inch round cake tin. Pour the gingerbread into the prepared tin and place in the centre of the oven for 2$^{1/2}$ hours or until a skewer inserted into the middle of the cake comes out cleanly.

If the cake appears to begin to brown too much, cover with a sheet of brown paper for the last 30 minutes of cooking.

Allow to cool in the tin for 30 minutes before turning onto a wire rack to become cold. Like all gingerbreads, this cake improves if kept in an airtight tin for 2 or 3 days before eating.

STICKY GINGERBREAD LOAF

Serves 6-8

It seems appropriate that as I write, there should be a slice of this impressive, dark, sticky cake, on a plate beside me. Particularly tempting spread with fresh unsalted butter, it is difficult to imagine anything more suited to a winter's afternoon.

Ginger cakes have a propensity to sink in the middle when cooked, but that is exactly what should happen, giving the cake its characteristic appearance. No particular area of the country lays claim to this gingerbread, but it is one of the most frequently made variations and appears in many cookery books and baker's shops. Its origins are however, most likely to have been Yorkshire, where the dark sticky gingerbreads have always been eaten.

225 g/8 oz self raising flour	115 g/4 oz treacle
2 teaspoons mixed spice	115 g/4 oz butter
2 teaspoons ground ginger	115 g/4 oz dark muscovado sugar
1 teaspoon bicarbonate of soda	225 ml/8 fl oz milk
115 g/4 oz golden syrup	2 medium eggs, lightly beaten

Preheat the oven to 180°C/350°F/Gas 4.

Sift flour, spices and bicarbonate of soda together, making a well in the centre.

Place syrup, treacle, butter and sugar into a saucepan and melt over a gentle heat before setting aside and allowing to cool. Pour the mixture into the flour and beat until smooth.

Add the milk and eggs, beating firmly to ensure it remains smooth and lump free.

Pour the mixture, which will be quite runny, into a greased and lined 900 g/2 lb loaf tin and place in the centre of the oven for 50 to 60 minutes, or until a skewer inserted comes out cleanly. The cake will rise and then sink in the middle during cooking but don't worry, this is perfectly normal.

Allow to cool entirely in the tin, before turning onto a wire rack.

This cake is better kept for a couple of days in an airtight tin before slicing, during which time it will develop its characteristic sticky appearance.

IRISH GINGERBREAD

Serves 8

When I was looking for an Irish gingerbread, I felt that like so many gingerbreads there was not one traditional recipe that leapt out at you. But the one thing they all seemed to have in common was the inclusion of chopped preserved or crystallized ginger and sultanas.

It was also interesting to discover that gingerbreads were very much associated with mid-summer festivities in Ireland, these particular cakes being named 'Craebh', although gingerbreads in England and Scotland were, and are still eaten, as at Christmas as part of the traditional fayre.

115 g/4 oz butter	1 teaspoon ground ginger
115 g/4 oz muscovado sugar	1 teaspoon ground cinnamon
115 g/4 oz treacle	50 g/2 oz sultanas
115 g/4 oz golden syrup	115 g/4 oz chopped preserved ginger
225 g/8 oz wholemeal flour	2 large eggs, lightly beaten
1/2 teaspoon bicarbonate of soda	2 tablespoons milk

Preheat the oven to 160°C/325°F/Gas Mark 3.

Place the butter, sugar, treacle, and syrup in a large saucepan and stir over a low heat until dissolved. Set aside to cool.

In a large bowl sift the flour, soda and spices, stir in the sultanas and chopped ginger and making a well in the centre, beat in the egg and milk. Finally add the cooled butter mixture.

When thoroughly mixed pour into a greased and lined 900 g/2 lb loaf tin and bake in the centre of the oven for approximately 1 1/4 hours or until well risen and firm to touch. A skewer inserted into the centre should come out cleanly.

Leave to cool for 20 minutes before turning out onto a wire rack and leaving to become cold.

This cake improves, if you can keep it, for a day before eating – but you may not be able to manage it.

POTATO GINGERBREAD

Serves 6

Very similar to a recipe issued during the war by the potato board, which works very well indeed, but do be sure to grate the potato just before use or it will turn brown very quickly.

150 g/5 oz flour	50 g/2 oz chopped glace ginger
1 teaspoon baking powder	115 g/4 oz black treacle
1/2 teaspoon mixed spice	50 g/2 oz butter
2 teaspoons ground ginger	1 egg, lightly beaten
115 g/4 oz raw potato, grated	1 teaspoon bicarbonate of soda
50 g/2 oz sultanas	1 tablespoon milk

Preheat the oven to 180°C/350°F/Gas Mark 4.

Sift the flour, baking powder and spices into a bowl and add the grated potato, sultanas and glace ginger, stirring well.

In a small saucepan melt the black treacle and butter and allow to cool slightly. Add the beaten egg and stir, pouring almost immediately into the flour mixture.

Dissolve the bicarbonate of soda in the milk and beating, add to the cake mix.

Pour into a greased and lined 23 x 23 x 5 cm/9 x 9 x 2 inch tin and place in the centre of the oven and bake for about 35 minutes or until the cake is risen and firm to touch.

Allow to cool slightly before turning onto a wire rack to cool.

Cut into squares to serve.

GRASMERE GINGERBREAD

CUMBRIA   ***Makes 12 pieces***

When I first tasted this celebrated gingerbread, I was struck by the fact that it was quite unlike anything I knew as gingerbread. Bought from 'Sarah Nelson's Original Gingerbread Shop' in the village of Grasmere, the thin crisp squares of gingerbread, with their crumbly topping, are sold neatly wrapped in greaseproof paper, printed with a blue picture of the tiny little shop.

Sarah Nelson started baking in 1855 and the secret recipe continues to be stored in a bank vault, being made available only to the proprietors of the shop in Grasmere, where it all started a century and a half ago.

An excellent, similar result is achieved with the following recipe.

275 g/10 oz self raising flour	150 g/5 oz butter
1 teaspoon ground ginger	150 g/5 oz pale brown sugar
1 teaspoon cinnamon	

Preheat the oven to 180°C/350°F/Gas Mark 4.

Sift the flour and spices into a large bowl.

Rub the butter into the flour until it looks like fine breadcrumbs finally stirring in the sugar.

Grease a Swiss roll tin and put two thirds of the mixture into the bottom of the tin pressing down firmly. Scatter the remaining third over the top, spreading evenly without flattening.

Place the gingerbread in the centre of the oven and bake for 25 to 30 minutes or until golden brown. Remove from the oven and immediately cut the gingerbread into squares using a sharp knife, whilst still in the tin.

Leave to become completely cold before removing from the tin.

This gingerbread will become crisp as it cools, the top will remain crumbly. Should be stored in an airtight container.

WIDDECOMBE FAIR GINGERBREAD

DEVON   *Makes 12*

*Tom Pearse, Tom Pearse, lend me thy grey mare
All along, down along, out along lee
For I want to go to Widdecombe Fair
Wi' Bill Brewer, Jan Stewer, Peter Gurney,
Peter Davey, Dan'l Whiddon, Harry Hawk,
Old Uncle Tom Cobbleigh and all*

The link between gingerbread and country fairs is legendary, as this chapter confirms. One of the most famous fairs was of course, Widdecombe Fair in Devon, which also claims to be one of the oldest.

The small gingerbread cakes being a cross between a cake and a biscuit, would be hawked around the fair by vendors.

175 g/6 oz black treacle	350 g/12 oz plain flour
175 g/6 oz golden syrup	1 dessertspoonful ground ginger
350 g/12 oz dark muscovado sugar	1/2 teaspoon bicarbonate of soda
275 g/10 oz butter	1 tablespoon milk

Preheat the oven to 180°C/350°F/Gas Mark 4.

Place the treacle, syrup, sugar and butter into a medium sized saucepan and dissolve over a low heat. Set aside to cool slightly.

Sift the flour and ground ginger into a bowl and make a well in the centre. Pour in the treacle mixture, beating thoroughly.

Dissolve the soda in the milk and add to the other ingredients, stirring well.

Using a tablespoon, drop small heaps of the mixture onto a greased baking sheet, allowing space between them.

Bake in the oven for 10 to 15 minutes until golden brown.

Transfer to a wire rack and allow to cool.

PARLIES

SCOTLAND   *Serves about 9*

These wholesome ginger cakes were named after the members of the Scottish Parliament, who were reputed to have eaten them in considerable quantities. Baked either as individual cakes or rolled into a square and divided into smaller pieces, they are well worth trying, being simple to make and easy to eat.

Parlies were occasionally made without ginger, producing a plainer version.

450 g/1 lb plain flour	225 g/8 oz dark muscovado sugar
1 tablespoon ground ginger	115 g/4 oz black treacle
225 g/8 oz butter	115 g/4 oz golden syrup

Preheat the oven to 160°C/325°F/Gas Mark 3.

Sift the flour and ginger into a bowl, making a well in the centre.

Melt the butter, sugar, treacle and syrup in a medium saucepan, over a low heat and allow to cool.

Beat the melted ingredients into the flour using a wooden spoon until it forms into a ball.

Lift the ball onto a greased and floured baking sheet and roll gently into a square 5 mm/½ inch thick, marking it into portions. Alternatively, roll dessertspoonfuls of the dough into balls and place onto the baking tray, flattening slightly, leaving enough space between them for expansion.

Bake in the centre of the oven until golden brown, approximately 20 minutes. It may take a little longer if baked in one sheet.

Lift the Parlies carefully from the baking tray with a spatula and allow to cool on a wire rack.

If you have baked it in one square, it may be easier to cut it into smaller sections before moving onto the cooling rack, or loosen it underneath and slide it in one piece, from the tray onto the rack.

FOCHABERS GINGERBREAD

SCOTLAND   *Serves 16*

Fochabers, near Elgin in the North East of Scotland, lends its name to this delicious fruited ginger cake, distinguished by the addition of beer and although it is unclear as to its actual origins, it remains firmly connected to this small Scottish town.

As with all gingerbreads, it improves with keeping and the beer really does lend a unique flavour.

225 g/8 oz butter	2 teaspoons mixed spice
115 g/4 oz dark muscovado sugar	1 teaspoon cinnamon
225 g/8 oz black treacle	2 eggs, lightly beaten
300 ml/½ pint beer	75 g/3 oz ground almonds
1 teaspoon bicarbonate of soda	115 g/4 oz currants
450 g/1 lb plain flour	115 g/4 oz sultanas
1 tablespoon ground ginger	115 g/4 oz chopped mixed peel

Preheat the oven to 160°C/325°F/Gas Mark 3.

Cream together the butter and sugar until pale and fluffy.

In a medium saucepan, over a low heat, dissolve the treacle in the beer. Add the bicarbonate of soda.

Sift the flour and the spices into a large bowl. Beat the eggs into the butter and sugar mixture, and continue beating whilst adding them to the flour and spices together with the beer and treacle, finally folding in the ground almonds, fruit and peel.

Pour into a greased and lined 20 cm/8 inch square cake tin and bake in the centre of the oven for approximately 2 hours. Test with a skewer inserted into the centre, cooking a little longer if necessary, until the skewer comes out cleanly.

Cover the top with a layer of brown paper if you feel that the cake is beginning to darken too much.

Leave to cool in the tin for an hour before turning out onto a wire rack and allowing to become cold.

Cut into squares or oblongs before eating. Excellent buttered.

GRANTHAM WHITE GINGERBREAD

LINCOLNSHIRE   *Makes about 24*

The pale, light texture of the Grantham Gingerbread is quite unlike the dark, treacle based recipes we normally expect when we talk about gingerbread.

Its history, whilst a little uncertain, seems rooted in the Eggleston family shop in Grantham during the early 1800's. There, George Eggleston is said to have muddled up his ingredients during an evening bake, the resulting cakes being the Grantham White Gingerbread, a happy accident as it turned out, everyone thought them delicious.

Several recipes exist, all claiming to be 'the original' but certainly they are all very similar in content and result.

The following recipe avoids some of the more controversial ingredients such as bicarbonate of ammonia

115 g/4 oz butter	225 g/8 oz self raising flour
275 g/10 oz soft pale brown sugar	1 level tablespoon ground ginger
1 large egg	

Preheat the oven to 160°C/325°F/Gas Mark 3.

In a large bowl cream the butter and sugar together with a wooden spoon until light and fluffy and then beat in the egg. Sift the flour and ginger stirring into the butter mixture, until a firm dough is formed. Pull into a ball with your hands and turn onto a lightly floured work surface. Knead gently until smooth and then break the dough into 24 evenly sized pieces, rolling each into a ball and placing onto a greased baking tray, allowing space for them to spread a little.

Bake in the centre of the oven until very pale golden brown and crisp. This will take about 30 minutes. Remove from the oven, leave for 3 or 4 minutes and then, using a spatula, carefully transfer them onto a wire cooling tray.

BROONIE

Serves 6-8

Not unlike the Scottish Perkin, this gingerbread is rarely seen outside the Orkney Isles. Originally eaten at Celtic festivals, the Broonie is excellent served sliced and buttered.

Like all cakes in the Parkin family, the group of oatmeal based gingerbreads, it keeps very well, in fact improving if wrapped tightly in foil and stored in a tin for a few days before serving. Do try it.

225 g/8 oz self raising flour	115 g/4 oz pale brown sugar
2 level teaspoons ground ginger	2 tablespoons black treacle
115 g/4 oz medium or pinhead oatmeal	1 egg
115 g/4 oz butter	150 ml/¼ pint buttermilk

Preheat the oven to 160°C/325°F/Gas Mark 3.

Sift the flour and ground ginger into a bowl and stir in the oatmeal. Rub in the butter to the texture of fine breadcrumbs. Add the sugar and stir well.

In a small saucepan gently melt the treacle over a low heat and set aside to cool a little. Beat the egg into the treacle, and pour into the dry ingredients together with the buttermilk, continue beating thoroughly with a wooden spoon.

Pour into a greased and lined 900 g/2 lb loaf tin and bake in the centre of the oven until well risen and a skewer inserted into the centre of the cake, comes out cleanly. This should take approximately 1 hour.

Leave to cool in the tin.

PERKINS

Makes approximately 15

Perkins, whilst being traditionally Scottish, are very much the same as the oatmeal based Parkin, so loved in the North of England.

Originally made by dropping spoonfuls onto a hot griddle, they are now more commonly baked in the oven. But I would recommend that you try this recipe, baked in the traditional way, by cooking the Perkins on a griddle, resulting in ginger drop scones, which are absolutely delicious served warm and buttered.

225 g/8 oz plain wholemeal flour	115 g/4 oz butter
1 teaspoon bicarbonate of soda	50 g/2 oz golden syrup
2 teaspoons ground ginger	115 g/4 oz black treacle
1/4 teaspoon salt	1 large egg
115 g/4 oz coarse oatmeal	150 ml/1/4 pint milk
175 g/6 oz dark muscovado sugar	

Sift the flour, soda, ginger and salt into a large bowl, stirring in the oatmeal and sugar and make a well in the centre.

In a medium saucepan melt the butter, syrup and treacle over a low heat, do not allow to boil. Cool slightly and then add to the dry ingredients. Whisk the egg into the milk and stirring constantly, add to the mixture, continue beating to ensure that there are no lumps.

Heat the griddle and drop dessertspoonfuls of the mixture onto the hot surface, turning as they become brown and bubbles stop rising to the top.

Place on a clean cloth as they are cooked, covering them over; the steam will ensure that they remain soft until eaten.

Serve almost immediately, hot and well buttered.

PARKIN

YORKSHIRE   *Serves 16*

A wonderfully dark, spicy cake, originally eaten at Celtic or Christian festivals, although it is now traditionally served around the bonfire on Guy Fawkes Night. Always more popular in the North of England, it is made with coarse oatmeal and black treacle. Best baked at least a week ahead, by which time it will have become soft and sticky. The cake should be cut into squares before serving.

In keeping with its Celtic connections, the Parkin is also known as a Thor, Tharf or Thar Cake.

225 g/8 oz plain wholemeal flour	175 g/6 oz dark muscovado sugar
1 teaspoon bicarbonate of soda	115 g/4 oz butter
2 teaspoons ground ginger	50 g/2 oz golden syrup
1 teaspoon cinnamon	115 g/4 oz black treacle
1 teaspoon mixed spice	150 ml/^{1}/4 pint milk
^{1}/2 teaspoon salt	1 large egg
115 g/4 oz coarse oatmeal	

Preheat the oven to 180°C/350°F/Gas Mark 4.

Sift the flour, bicarbonate of soda, spices and salt into a large bowl. Stir in the oatmeal and sugar, making a well in the centre.

In a medium saucepan melt the butter, syrup and treacle over a low heat and then set aside to cool slightly before adding to the dry ingredients. Beat the milk and egg together in a jug and pour into the mixture, ensuring that you continue beating to eliminate any lumps that may form.

Immediately pour into a greased and lined 18 cm/7 inch square cake tin.

Place in the centre of the oven and bake for about 50 minutes or until firm to touch.

Allow to cool slightly before turning out onto a wire rack to become cold, when it should be wrapped in greaseproof paper and foil.

Store in a cool dry place to mellow, the cake will also change in texture, becoming sticky and inviting.

SCRIPTURE CAKE TRANSLATION

115 g/4 oz	almonds	Jeremiah	Chapter I	v11
350 g/12 oz	figs	Jeremiah	Chapter XXIV	v2
350 g/12 oz	raisins	I Chronicles	Chapter XII	v40
500 g/1lb 2 oz	plain flour	Leviticus	Chapter II	v2
2 teaspoons	baking powder	Galatians	Chapter V	V9
1 teaspoon	cinnamon	Solomon	Chapter IV	v14
Pinch	salt	St Matthew	Chapter V	v13
6	eggs	Job	Chapter XXXIX	v14
350 g/12 oz	butter	Isaiah	Chapter VII	v15
450 g/1 lb	sugar	Jeremiah	Chapter VI	v20
2 tablespoons	honey	I Samuel	Chapter XIV	v29
1/2 breakfast cup	milk	Solomon	Chapter IV	v11

SOURCES AND BIBLIOGRAPHY

Reference Section of Town Hall, Douglas Isle of Man; Bunratty Folk Museum, Co Clare, Southern Ireland; Reference Section, Rawtenstall Library; Reference Section, Ripon Library; Reference Library, Oxford; Reference Library, Aberdeen; Reference Library, Grantham; Reference Department, Oxford History Centre; Reference Library, Chorley; Local History Section, Canterbury Library; Reference Library, Tunbridge Wells; Reference Library, Bury St Edmunds; Best Foods, Unilever; Mr Roger Latter for his mother Mrs Gertrude Latter's Recipe Notes; Neville Peatman for his mother Ivy Peatman's handwritten recipes and sharing his knowledge; Gladys Pickard's recipes; The Manager, Drury Lane Theatre, London.

Jerome, Helen *Cake Making* 1932; Royal English Agricultural Society *Cottage Economy and Cookery* 1843; Acton, Eliza *Modern Cookery for Private Families*; David, Elizabeth *English Bread and Yeast Cookery*; Raffald, Elizabeth *The Experienced English Housekeeper* 1769; Markham, Gervaise *The English Huswife* 1615; Black, Maggie and Le Faye, Deirdre *Jane Austin Cookbook*; Fairclough, M A *The Ideal Cookery Book*; Mrs Beeton's *Book of Household Management* 1861; Bright, T *Treatise of Melancholy* 1586; *The Cookery Book of Lady Clark of Tillypronie* 1841.

USEFUL SUPPLIERS OF BAKEWARE AND SPICES

Alan Silverwood Ltd – tel 0121 454 3571. Superb cake tins in all shapes and sizes. Call for nearest stockist.

Nisbets Catering Equipment – tel 01454 855555. Comprehensive mail order catalogue.

Lakeland Limited – tel 015394 88100. Baking equipment by mail order catalogue or branches countrywide.

Fox's Spices Limited – tel 01789 266420. Superb spices including many uncommon ones such as sweet mixed spice by mail order catalogue.

INDEX

Regional Cakes

CONTENTS

FOREWORD

Regional, historical and traditional cakes, Scottish cakes, Irish cakes and Welsh cakes, cakes baked in castles, grand houses and cottages, using local ingredients, often enhanced with exotic spices and vine fruits – these together with a vast treasure-trove of English cakes, create an irresistible challenge to any cake maker.

Cakes come in all guises; baked in the oven or on a griddle, involving a wide variety of delectable ingredients: free range eggs, fresh butter, organic stone ground flour and raw sugar so full of flavour that it is like eating toffee or fudge. The vine fruits, which fill you with wonder at their magical journey from the other side of the world to our homes, together with cherries and any one of the enormous selection of mouth-watering nuts.

Add to this the care and love taken in preparation, sometimes using yeast to enable cakes to rise as in the case of the Saffron Cake and Tea Cakes or simply the addition of hard work to add the air needed to make a sponge cake rise. Cakes, which are so packed with fruits that they rise very little. The rewards of making a glorious fruit cake, fill a baker's heart with joy, as they are taken from the oven, so aromatic and visually stunning in an honest way. Just start a conversation about cakes with any dedicated, enthusiastic cake maker and you are guaranteed to brighten any dreary day.

The one thing all these cakes have in common is that they have the propensity to give inescapable *pleasure*, whether eaten in restrained slices with a cup of tea on a Sunday afternoon, or displayed as the awe-inspiring centre piece at a special festivity or celebration.

Cakes are sometimes best eaten in large wedges by hungry workers or as an eagerly awaited finale to a summer picnic. But the most important aspect of cakes is that they give *pleasure* in every way, *pleasure* to the cook, *pleasure* whilst cooking, the smell is divine, and *pleasure* whilst eating. What more can you ask for from a cake?

INTRODUCTION

When I first began researching traditional cake recipes I had simply no idea that it would become such a passion. Delving into second-hand bookshops, charity shops, book stalls, in fact any corner where an old book might linger, it did not take long before I realized that what was contained in the often musty, always stained, pages of well used and loved cookery books, was in reality a social history. It was the history of local produce, imported fruits and spices, of regional alcohol such as ales and cider and most importantly the story of wholesome honest food. With just a little imagination it was easy to picture the kitchens in which the cakes were produced with such loving care; the recipes reflecting the lives of generations of cake makers were a fascinating record of social conditions and attitudes, never just words in books.

The more enthralled I became, the more important it was to change my concept of the word 'traditional'; it did not necessarily mean old, it spanned time. A Blitz Cake (almost identical to Ration Book Cakes) which was a flour and sugar sponge loaf made with dripping but without eggs, says much about the ingenuity of cooks in war-torn cities where eggs were precious. The many versions of griddlecakes, cooked in cottages from simple ingredients, often over open grates or on ranges, and the iron pot cakes, which I saw so eloquently demonstrated in a living museum in Southern Ireland, all reflected the best use of ingredients and basic kitchen equipment.

The names alone conjure up pictures, Welsh Bara Brith, Cornish Saffron Cakes, Northumberland Singin' Hinnies, Norfolk Vinegar Cake, Dorset Apple Cakes, Westmorland Pepper Cake and Yorkshire Parkin, the list is endless. What they all have in common is the inclusion of good local food and a lack of pretentious ingredients, something that we strive for today in our attempts to use the very best of everything, in order to bake the very best of cakes. There really are no shortcuts; a cake represents the amount of care put into it, the quality of the ingredients and the love added freely by the baker. It may take a little more time but it is always indisputably worthwhile.

Some of the older recipes are surprisingly extravagant, even rather romantic. Who could resist the sound of the Gold Cake, the Silver Cake, or the oddly named Sand Cake? But all share an ability to entice us to try. Although I do admit to being slightly less than excited at the prospect of baking Cat's Tongue Cakes despite the fact that they perfectly illustrate the vagaries of cake making as they are actually really delicious.

Sometimes the stories surrounding the cakes develop a life of their own, often with a dubious element of truth, but never failing to add to the interest of the subject. Add to this the question of a cake's regional claims and bakers fighting fiercely, with each claiming to have the rights to an 'original recipe', and it's not difficult to see why regional cakes are a serious subject.

In an odd way, these cakes reflect the aims of today's cake makers and give us an opportunity to use wonderfully wholesome ingredients, with the added pleasure of preparing, baking and eating a slice of history.

How much better a worker might feel if their morning coffee or afternoon tea is accompanied by a good wholesome piece of cake rather than an industrially produced snack. The delight of a little child at opening a lunchbox and finding one of the individual fairy cakes, they had helped to bake and decorate the day before, nestling in with the sandwiches. Or perhaps the memories of a pleasant picnic by the sea or in the countryside during long summer days – when eating pieces of cake in the open air and licking your sticky fingers is an unsurpassed treat – will be recalled during the long working week. Just don't try to tell me that equal pleasure will be obtained from unwrapping and cutting a shop bought slab of cake where reading the list of ingredients often becomes more akin to a science lesson.

By the way, did you know that the word 'picnic', thought to have been derived from the French *piquenique* which is a combination of *piquer* (to pick) and *nique* (trifle), came into being from the Pic-Nic Society, which was formed by music lovers who took pies and cakes along to organised musical evenings during the very early part of the 19th century? Great fun was had during these evenings of feasting and merry making and the word 'picnic' remains the term used for portable 'banquets' to this very day. I like to think of this scenario when eating in the open air, because so many of our words and terminologies, particularly in cookery, have wonderful histories of their own, but perhaps that is another book?

The cooking of a particular area of Great Britain often clearly reflects both the ingredients available and the facilities used to cook on and inevitably perhaps even the wealth of a community. Therefore whilst at first glance the Regional Cakes sections may look as though I have outrageously favoured English cakes that simply isn't so.

The enormous variations in baking were often as a result of something as simple as the landscape surrounding a village, town or city. Where cattle were able to graze on lush grass, butter and milk would be readily available and this would naturally reflect in the cakes baked. Coastal areas of Britain throughout history suffered invasions from overseas, both through war and pirates. Add to this the traders who visited the larger ports and you ensured that the coastal populations had easier access to spices, almonds, figs, dates and fruits brought over from the warmer lands, and these goodies then quickly found their way into the cities.

Colder rockier areas of Britain, where cereals were less easily grown and fruits difficult to cultivate, produced wholesome warming foods such as oats, barley and potatoes which provided staple diets for many poorer families, supplemented by access to dairy products for the more fortunate. Scottish cooking in particular reflects this with a propensity towards oatcakes, bannocks and tea breads often utilising just such ingredients. Simple honest food typified by cakes cooked on the griddle or girdle, are much loved in Scotland.

The Scots, always famed for their hospitality, would produce wonderful scones, ginger cakes and drop scones as the mainstay of their tea table and I can well remember being invited for a cup of tea and blether, on the second day of my new life in Scotland. Carrying my baby son Andrew and leading my two-year-old daughter Sian by the hand through the snow, we arrived for tea at the appointed hour. The array of goodies was impressive and it was as I sipped my hot tea that I asked, pointing at the fare in front of me, 'which one is the blether?' A look of incredulity crossed Morag's face as she realised that I was perfectly serious. Patiently she then explained to me that 'blether' was a 'chat' not a scone or slice of tea bread. We still laughed about it years later over our tea and blether.

Larger Scottish cakes are wholesome and straight forward fruit cakes, just think of the world famous Dundee Cake, the aromatic and alcoholic Sultana Cake steeped in whisky and of course, the famous Black Bun so customary for the New Year celebrations, all reflective of the foods of this hardy country. Only in the 'big house' where life was easier, usually fully staffed and with more up to the minute kitchen ranges and facilities, were elaborate cakes baked and served.

Irish baking has a similar history, except that in the 'big house' it was usually an Anglo-Irish family, the children often having been sent to boarding schools in England, thus encouraging the influence of English baking into such homes. Again here the best of cooking equipment made delicate cakes easier to cope with and from these households we have the Lemon Cake so beloved at shooting teas.

The average Irish farmer or peasant had few such glamorous facilities but ingeniously baked wonderful cakes in an iron pot oven by the fire, and with its lid covered with ashes, the pot cooked a remarkably good cake. These recipes are still being baked today by the older generation. The griddle was an essential piece of baking equipment and like Scotland, Wales and the North of England, was widely used in Ireland, as is reflected in the range of Soda Cakes and fruited breads baked in this way, the recipes being legion and all well worth trying.

In Elizabethan times the introduction of potatoes to the Irish diet was quickly reflected in the recipes. They were often included in cakes, not least the famous Fadge Cakes, Irish Chocolate Cake and Irish Apple Cake, all delicious, all including potatoes and with a very Irish feel about them. More recently however, the increasing tourist trade has encouraged the baking of traditional recipes and certainly on our trips to Ireland, we have actively sought out Porter Cakes, Barmbrack, Spotted Dog and Irish gingerbreads.

The English in contrast baked a wider range of regional cakes, usually closely linked to a festival, fair or simply to use local surplus produce. But from the 18th century, European chefs and in particular French ones, became a status symbol in the big houses and whilst not particularly affecting regional cakes, they did add to the already wide range of country cakes baked in English homes. Who are we however, to say that the cakes baked here over several centuries since their introduction from Europe, have not become truly British over such a long period of time? Hence the inclusion of popular cakes such as the Battenburg or the Swiss Roll, which over the years have become so much part of our lives.

All this is so very different to the Welsh who rarely baked the elaborate cakes favoured by the English and much in the same way as the Puritans had done in England, the Methodists influenced the Welsh in their baking by firmly opposing any rich extravagant foods in their community. Cakes were kept for weekends and in particular teatime on Sunday, which is really the case right up to this day.

What the Welsh are famous for are the griddle or bakestone cakes, cooked using produce that in the past would have been readily available, such as lard and dripping which together with buttermilk provided the basis for such cakes, perhaps occasionally with the enrichment of a few currants or some caraway seeds.

I do hope that you will enjoy reading and trying some of the recipes I have compiled. There are certainly lots more I have been unable to include, indeed it often seems that every day I find another cake or gingerbread, which sounds delicious, but I had to stop somewhere. The stories surrounding some of the cakes are fascinating and even where the origins have been untraceable, it makes them no less genuine or fun to eat and I like to think that like me, you will feel tempted to try baking a little bit of history.

ESSENTIAL INFORMATION

THE GOLDEN RULES OF BAKING

Baking is something to enjoy, but unlike a lot of cookery, it cannot be stressed enough how important it is to follow the recipe. I often hear people say 'I just throw in the ingredients', well they may do, but they are taking a chance because when making a cake you need to **weigh all the ingredients precisely** and although I personally don't, some bakers even weigh their eggs. (I find that with graded eggs this is not really as necessary as in the past.)

It is also very important to use the **size of tin** recommended in the recipe, as too small a tin or too large a tin, will result in a very different cake to the one intended. I always line tins with greaseproof paper and in the case of fruit cakes, or cakes which require a long baking time, I also tie a double layer of brown paper around the outside of the cake tin. I have written more about this in the section on lining cake tins.

Ovens are the devil's own problem, few cook at identical temperatures or speeds, whatever the dials may say. I was once told that it was impossible to cook a fruit cake in a fan oven, but proved the rule wrong by winning a Gold Award and Bronze Award for fruit cakes, which had been cooked in just such an oven. In fact I think I was more pleased with the Bronze Award as it proved the Gold was not a fluke. So although a recipe will give a time and temperature, do check the cakes after a while to ensure that they are not cooking too quickly and turn your oven down a little if necessary. Cooking times can only be recommendations.

It is possible to **freeze** all cakes successfully, especially sponge based ones which you may need to make in large batches for special occasions, parties etc. It's not necessary with fruit cakes though because they have excellent keeping qualities and some cakes do improve and mature with keeping.

I have found the best way is first to 'open' freeze, that is unwrapped; this eliminates any possible damage to both cake and icing. Then when the cake or cakes are frozen you can pop small ones together in a freezer bag or wrap large ones in cling film. By freezing small cakes you can also remove the desired quantity a few at a time. Whilst it is possible to ice, decorate or fill with jam before freezing it is best to do this after a cake has thawed.

The following sections attempt to outline the basic rules and equipment needed before delving into the art of cake baking. I have added some measurements, which may prove useful, particularly if like me you still think in inches, pounds and ounces, or at least still need to check.

I guess we can only marvel at how people managed centuries ago, with little of the above items to make life easier. One thing is certain, creaming and beating could mean 1 or 2 hours of work before the right texture or consistency was reached and ovens, when available, were often difficult to regulate, the method of regulation depending on the amount of fuel added and what had been previously cooked that day.

Finally, do remember that the art of baking is a science, the process is simply chemistry, the reacting of one ingredient with another and that those ingredients should always be the very best you can buy.

So good luck, take care with the measuring and weighing and don't forget to add a lot of LOVE, that most important of sentiments, which no money can buy. I promise you will reap the rewards.

MIXING METHODS

In the book you will find several different methods of mixing which I will explain very briefly:

Creaming: Put the fat and sugar into a large bowl and using either a wooden spoon or hand mixer, beat until the two ingredients are thoroughly mixed together. The texture of the fat and sugar will become lighter and the colour paler. This is the way of adding air to most basic cake recipes.

Rubbing In: Generally this method is for rubbing fat into flour. Sift the flour and other ingredients as stated in the recipe, cut the fat into pieces adding it to the flour. Using only your finger tips and thumbs, to keep the ingredients cool, rub the ingredients together – you will see that the fat pieces become smaller and smaller until the mixture resembles fine breadcrumbs in texture.

Melting: This method is used in particular for gingerbreads, where the ingredients such as butter, sugar, treacle, syrup are melted gently over a low heat until they become completely amalgamated. It is, however, important that the mixture is allowed to cool slightly before adding to the other ingredients so that it does not cook them.

In many recipes it is suggested that eggs are beaten into the melted mixture, again you can see how important it is to allow it to cool slightly before adding them or you will end up with scrambled eggs in the butter mixture.

Mixers: It is possible with some recipes to put all the ingredients into your mixer, switch on and hey presto – but the quality is never as good – sponges having quite large air holes and generally a poorer texture – but for some cakes this will simply be a matter of your preference and is unimportant. In the case of shortcrust pastry, the base for several cakes, I find using the mixer method is excellent, particularly if like me you have warm hands, which are rather the death knell for good pastry.

EQUIPMENT

It is actually possible to bake with very little equipment since the art of baking is basically a hands-on procedure, but some items such as the following, are essential.

Scales: A good set of scales is absolutely essential to enable careful weighing of the ingredients.

Wire Cooling Rack: It is important to own at least two of these and I find that generally the oblong ones are the most useful, as they are suitable for both large cakes and lots of smaller buns. Quality is important. The main thing to look for is that they are sufficiently strong to take the weight of large fruit cakes.

Sieve: A sieve is essential and a flour/icing shaker will be very useful.

Spoons: Although you can use the spoons from your kitchen, it is possible to purchase very inexpensively a set of measuring spoons and I do think they are invaluable, I cannot imagine baking without a set. Try to buy sets incorporating $1/4$ and $1/2$ teaspoon sizes. In addition a metal tablespoon is necessary for some of the folding in procedures.

Knives: Knives, including large and small pallet knives, are available from most cookery or kitchenware departments.

Wooden Spoons: Inexpensive and easily available; you will need two or three in different sizes.

Lemon Juicer: My favourite and certainly the simplest form of juicing a lemon, is a wooden squeezer, simply cut the lemon or orange in half and press and turn it in the middle of the flesh.

Grater: A multipurpose grater is indispensable and can be used for many tasks including grating nutmeg, so try to buy a four-sided grater as these will give you the most options.

Finally greaseproof paper, cling film and foil complete the essentials. You may want ribbon and gold band to tie round celebratory and festive cakes such as those seen in the pictures for Simnel Cake and Fresh Orange Fruit Cake, these can be bought at cake decorating shops. Simply cut to the required length and secure with double sided sticky tape.

Apart from the above items it is unlikely that with a normal supply of things like bowls and saucepans which are found in all kitchens, you will need to purchase anything specifically for baking cakes.

CAKE TINS

Firstly, I can say at this stage that like most things in life, you really do get what you pay for with cake tins. It is important to buy good quality, solid, well-made tins, (although they need not necessarily be heavy) which will not only reward you with baking your cakes in superb style, but also last a lifetime if looked after properly.

Cake Tins: A selection of tins will be useful and I suggest one 15 cm/6 inch, 18 cm/7 inch and 20 cm/8 inch round tin, together with a 900 g/2 lb loaf tin, plus 2 sandwich tins, say 15 cm/6 inch will be a good basic selection to which you can add.

Non-stick linings are good but personally I do not find them necessary, I like to line my tins with greaseproof paper anyway, giving the cake a little more protection. But if they are your preference, I would even suggest lining them to ensure there is no possibility of sticking.

For fruit cakes I find loose-bottom tins preferable as removing the cake is made much simpler, lessening the risk of damaging your hard work.

Choosing the correct size of tin is probably one of the most important details in baking, too small a tin will cause problems as the cake will not have enough space to expand as it cooks, but too large a tin will result in a thin, rather overcooked cake if care is not taken.

When deciding whether to use a round or square cake tin, it is important to note that the quantity of mixture prepared for a round tin, if using to fill a square tin, should be an inch smaller i.e: 18 cm/7 inch round tin has the same capacity as a 15 cm/6 inch square.

Baking Trays: You will really need at least two good baking trays, recipes often require room for cakes to expand a little as they cook. Be sure to buy baking trays, which are quite heavy and will not bend easily. They will conduct the heat better and lessen the chances of burning your cakes.

Just one note, do be sure that they will fit into the oven before you buy them. This may seem common sense but I am the person who once bought a table, which would not come through any door or window in the house. It remains in the garage to this day; a reminder of a 'bargain' turned into an embarrassment. We pot up plants on it.

Bun Tin: You will find mention of bun tins in this book. These are the tins, which are normally sectioned into 12, suitable for making little fairy cakes, buns or cakes lined with pastry. They can be greased and used unlined, and indeed for pastry based cakes should be, but for buns and fairy cakes etc they can be lined with easily purchased greaseproof cake/bun tin liners. It is generally better to own at least two as most recipes make at least 18 cakes.

Swiss Roll Tin: A useful tin, oblong and shallow, not only suitable for making a Swiss roll, but you will find the shape recommended in several recipes throughout the book.

Dariole Moulds: Small individual tins, specifically for the baking of Madeleine Cakes. They are easily obtainable from any good kitchen equipment store.

Griddle (Girdle): Rather less used nowadays, a griddle is a brilliant piece of equipment to own. I have always enjoyed making drop scones, ever since I lived on a moor in the Highlands of Scotland.

Nothing seemed more enjoyable whilst looking out at the falling snow than watching the bubbles rise on the cooking mixture before flipping over the really delicious little cakes, to allow them to brown on the other side. Less commonly used the further south you go, I do think the griddle should enjoy a revival and lots of the recipes in this book, particularly the really old ones, require little imagination to picture cakes being baked on old ranges and over open fires.

That said a flat, heavy frying pan is a suitable alternative and you can always buy a griddle if you find yourself an enthusiast of griddle cakes.

LINING CAKE TINS

As you will see from the recipes in this book, I have detailed most of the cake tins to be greased and lined and feel that I should briefly explain this procedure.

Firstly, it is very important when baking a cake which requires a long slow baking time in the oven, such as a rich fruit cake, to not only grease and line the tin with greaseproof paper, but also to tie a double layer of brown paper, with string, around the outside of the tin. This quite simply, stops the outer edge of the cake from cooking too quickly, which often results in a cake, which is dry on the edges, before it has finished cooking in the centre.

This is also why with the richer fruit cakes and cakes requiring some time in the oven, it may also be necessary to not only turn down the oven a little but to lay a piece of brown paper over the top of the cake tin, if the cake appears to be browning too rapidly.

900 g/2 lb Loaf Tin or Bun Tins: It is probably best to look in your local cookware shop or supermarket for ready-made greaseproof liners in the shape of these particular tins, they are readily available and save a lot of difficult juggling around.

Round or Square Deep Cake Tin: Cut a double piece of greaseproof for the base by using the tin as a template, drawing around it and cutting it to fit snugly into the bottom of the tin. Then cut a strip of greaseproof paper long enough and deep enough to fit around the outer edges, allowing about 2.5 cm/1 inch extra in depth. Lay the strip of greaseproof on the work surface and cut slits in one of the long edges to a depth of 2.5 cm/1 inch approximately 1 cm/$\frac{1}{2}$ inch apart. Lightly grease the cake tin and position the long strip around the inner edge of the tin, allowing the slits to sit on the bottom of the tin. Over these slits, position the double layer cut for the base of the tin. Now your tin will be fully lined and you will find that the slits you cut in the edging strip will have allowed the greaseproof paper to sit neatly around your tin.

It is generally best to peel lining paper carefully from a cake once it is cold, unless your recipe states otherwise, as it will help to prevent breaking the cake edges.

Sponge Cake Tins: These are generally shallow round tins or occasionally I like to use a ring tin but the preparation for both is the same.

Lightly grease the surface of the tin and sprinkle it with a little flour. Then tip the tin from side to side to ensure that the surface is covered and that there are no gaps, otherwise your cake mixture will stick to the tin. Tip out any surplus flour, banging the tin gently. You can if you wish, lay a greaseproof circle in the base of the sandwich tin. I generally do, but it is not essential.

Baking Trays: The preparation of these depends on what you are about to bake. A bun mixture can be baked on a lightly floured baking tray, but a sticky mixture such as ginger cakes and rock cakes, which are dropped or spooned onto the tray, will benefit from lightly greasing the tins first.

BASIC INGREDIENTS

Yeast: A living plant, which in its low life form, produces carbon dioxide during fermentation and it is this gas which causes dough to rise by the formation of tiny bubbles. Helped by the addition of a little sugar, which if creamed gently with the yeast and then set into a warm place, enables it to grow more quickly. It needs to be remembered however that too much heat will kill the yeast, as it does during cooking, whilst too low a temperature slows the growth.

It is widely believed that the ancient Egyptians were responsible for discovering the power of yeast, as before then all breads would have been unleavened. It was however, the French biologist Louis Pasteur in the 19th century who really studied yeast and discovered the many other uses to which it could be applied, such as medicinally in the manufacture of antibiotics and as a rich source of vitamin B.

Whilst the use of yeast is strongly associated in our minds with bread making, it should be remembered that a great many of our traditional cakes are yeast based and there is an almost indistinguishable blurring between tea cakes and tea breads, some of the best known being Sally Lunn Cake, Saffron Cake and Bath Buns, all indisputably 'cakes'.

Yeast-based cakes have appeared in so many cookery books and story books over the years that their place in history is undeniable. The famous Simnel Cake was yeast based and of course, many Harvest Cakes were dough based, so historically yeast cakes were the forerunners of many of our modern cakes.

Brewers Yeast: Also known as Ale Barm or Beer Barm, the yeast being the froth which forms on top of the liquid as it ferments. This is the oldest type of 'Bakers' yeast. It can however, be very bitter, being the product that is discarded during the making of beer or ale. The fermented liquid is the part we enjoy drinking.

Compressed Yeast: These are yeast plant cells compressed into a block and bound together with the addition of a little starch. Perhaps the best form of yeast to use in the baking of cakes, giving an excellent flavour and being simple to use.

Dried Yeast: This form of yeast is relatively modern; convenient to use and sold in packets which have a long shelf life.

Baking Powder: The combination of alkaline and acid substances found in baking powder, when moistened produce carbon dioxide, which will make a cake rise. These substances are bicarbonate of soda and cream of tartar or tartaric acid, which when mixed with a stabilizing ingredient such as arrowroot, cornflour or ground rice, enables it to be stored ready for use. It is also possible to use bicarbonate of soda and vinegar as the acid substance. The eggless vinegar cakes from Norfolk are a perfect example of this combination.

It is not difficult to imagine how, when this product first became available in 1846, it must have seemed truly remarkable, totally transforming the cook's cake-making sessions, as before that time the only way to make a cake rise without the use of yeast, involved arm-aching whisking of eggs and sugar, sometimes for an hour or more.

Bicarbonate of Soda: A raising agent which is often used in cakes which include honey or treacle, such as gingerbreads. It also works well with buttermilk or sour milk.

Buttermilk: Often found in Welsh or Irish cookery, it helps to lift heavier recipes. It can be found in delicatessens or some of the larger supermarkets.

Sour Milk: This can be made at home easily by adding a teaspoon of lemon juice to milk and allowing it to curdle. Alternatively, the milk can be simply left in a warm atmosphere until it becomes sour, when it should be placed in a refrigerator until needed. Sour milk, like buttermilk, helps to lift heavier recipes.

Eggs: I place importance on the eggs I buy and personally I always try to use free-range eggs, simply because I feel a lot happier if I know that the welfare of the hen has been taken into consideration, by allowing them to run around in conditions which ensure a happy chicken.

The important thing however is that you use large (size 1 or 2) for most recipes unless otherwise stated and always lightly beat them before using. Whether you simply keep your eggs in a cool place or the refrigerator, they should always be at room temperature before using in a recipe, as very cold eggs are likely to cause the mixture to curdle.

Sugar: It was during Elizabethan times that sugar became more widely available at least for the more affluent families; honey had been the most common sweetener up until then, with sugar available only in limited quantities and at a very high price.

Sold mainly in cones, a little tool called a Nipper was used to cut off portions of the cone, which was then pounded. It was not however, until much later at the end of the 17th century that sugar came into its own being used to sweeten tea and other food items.

Coming mainly from sugar cane and sugar beet, the largest source is the cane variety, grown mainly in tropical climates. Sugar beet, which is often fed to animals in Britain, is grown in temperate climates but the resulting extracted sugars from either cane or beet are absolutely identical.

Caster Sugar: Fine white sugar, excellent for sponges. Particularly suitable for creaming methods.

Granulated Sugar: A coarser sugar, which can be used for cakes and will cream quite well, but the texture will result in speckled cake tops if used in sponges. It is most commonly used for sweetening drinks and sprinkling over food.

Demerara Sugar: A very coarse pale brown sugar, with good flavour. Rubs in well and is particularly suited for use in the making of gingerbreads.

Soft Brown Sugars: Either dark brown or pale brown, they give a good flavour and cream well, not unlike fudge or caramel to taste.

Muscovado Sugar: Dark brown or pale brown, it is strongly flavoured and excellent for fruitcakes.

Plain Flour: The most common variety used in fruit cakes, it has a low gluten content, which produces softer textured cakes. Plain flour having no added raising agent is particularly suited to the cakes which are not required to rise very much, such as a fruit cake. A raising agent can be added, according to the quantity in any particular recipe and this method does at least give you complete control. Generally the raising agent used will be baking powder.

Strong plain flours are more suitable for use in fruit tea breads and buns as it has very high gluten content, but is unsuitable for cakes in general.

Self Raising Flour: This is simply plain flour to which a raising agent has already been added, so baking powder is generally unnecessary. However, unless recommended care should be taken when using this flour, as you have no control over the amount of rise it will give to a cake.

Wholemeal or Wheatmeal Flour: Particularly suitable for wholefood cakes having a lot of the husk of the grains retained, they are therefore considered healthier. They can be bought in both plain and self raising flour varieties.

There are many other types of flours, rye, buckwheat, cornflour, rice flour being just a few but not that many are used in the making of cakes, they are more suited to breads.

Do note: It is particularly important to sift flour when adding baking powder, bicarbonate of soda, spices or other such ingredients, as this is the only way of ensuring they are evenly distributed.

Finally, flour must be kept sealed or in an airtight container and stored in dry conditions.

Fats: Butter or soft margarine are the most widely used fats for cakes, but in this book you will come across many recipes using lard or pork dripping and even in one or two cases 'flead' which are the small droplets of fat, lining the stomach of a pig, albeit they are very old recipes. However, where such fats are used, they are intrinsic to the particular recipe.

Personally I prefer butter for cakes because I think it gives an excellent flavour and certainly for fruit cakes, it adds to the texture and keeping qualities. However, many of the soft margarines on the market now, do make really good cakes and are less expensive for everyday cooking.

Butter should always be used at room temperature for baking, unless otherwise specified.

Black Treacle: Very dark, very strong and can dominate cakes, it is ideal for some gingerbreads, and rich dark fruit cakes. The flavour mellows over a period of time.

Golden Syrup: Lighter and stickier. Very sweet, ideal for use in gingerbreads, I often use it half and half with black treacle, which gives a more delicate flavour.

Nuts: When purchasing and storing nuts, it is important to not only buy the best quality you can find, but also adhere strictly to the best before date and storage instructions as nuts have relatively short shelf lives and go rancid quickly.

Vine Fruits: The varieties are endless but again, try to seek out the best, it will always be worthwhile.

SPICES

Here I aim to give a little detail about some of the more commonly used cake spices, despite the temptation to enthuse about each and every spice known to man.

I always find the very word 'spices' incredibly evocative, just the mention of cinnamon, nutmeg, mace, pepper, saffron, ginger and the many others widely used, brings to mind the Spice Trade which began as early as 2000 BC – almost incomprehensible to the modern mind. But it was as far back as 3500 BC that the Ancient Egyptians began to use spices in cooking, and mummified bodies have been found to contain spice seeds.

But not until the 11th century did spices begin to reach the shores of Europe, Venice becoming a particular centre, indeed controlling most of the trade, which resulted in its considerable wealth, and on which the Italian Renaissance was born.

During the Middle Ages spices reached these islands, but they were always expensive and never enough. In 1180 during the reign of Henry II, the Pepperers' Guild was formed in London and it became possible to buy some of the most expensive items in the world; with a pound of saffron costing as much as a horse and mace about the same price as a cow. So it is easy to see the importance and status that spices bestowed upon a household.

In 1600 Elizabeth I granted a Royal Charter to the East India Company, which was to become one of the largest and most formidable trading companies ever known, even to this day. But it did mean that rather than the odd drib and drab, we began to receive quantities of spices which were to transform our cuisine. Certainly cakes benefited enormously and banquets must have taken on a flavour, which even Tudor meals could not display.

Allspice *Pimenta dioica*
Also known as Jamaican Pepper, this spice, smelling of cloves, cinnamon and nutmeg, is widely used at Christmas time, and being rather pungent is well suited to Christmas cakes, puddings, mincemeats and mulled wine.

The Allspice tree is a member of the Myrtle family and grows to about 35 feet in height. It grows best in the West Indies or South America. The Allspice 'orchards' are famed for the aromatic scent that fills the air, from the white flowers of the blossom producing the green berries which become purple as they ripen. Later during drying they lose their purple sheen and form the characteristic rather dull brown appearance.

Allspice is also said to have preserving powers and was widely used during the 17th century to preserve meat and fish, particularly for travellers.

Caraway *Carum carvi*
Caraway is one of the world's oldest spices as shown by its popularity in cakes throughout the centuries, indeed in the 16th century there was hardly a cake or bread which did not

include this most pungent of spice.

Not unlike aniseed in flavour, caraway bears a resemblance to a large parsley plant, being about 2 feet in height, with the seeds forming in the large cream flower heads.

Probably the most famous cake was the Caraway Seed Cake, an old fashioned cake which sadly like most of our caraway recipes, has lost popularity, but used in moderation this is an interesting and very different spice, still very widely used in Europe.

Cinnamon *Cinnamomum zeylanicum*
One of the most evocative of winter spices, bringing to mind mulled wine and the scent of Christmas festivities. In the Bible, there are many references in the Old Testament, which illustrate how very precious this spice was even before the birth of Christ.

Coming from an evergreen tree of the Laurel family, the slim new branches are peeled and the bark rolled by hand to form the cinnamon quills with which we are so familiar. They are dried in the warm sunshine and it is a delight to try to imagine the aromatic atmosphere which surrounds thousands of quills drying outdoors in the summer.

Used in cakes, puddings, mulled wines, punches and indeed many other culinary treats, cinnamon can also be purchased ground, making it easily added to cakes. It is in fact very difficult to grind cinnamon at home as the quills do not break evenly, tending to splinter.

Cloves *Eugenia caryophyllus*
Reminiscent of childhood; apple pies and apple cake never seemed quite right without the addition of a small amount of clove. In fact even writing about them here takes my mind straight to the evocative smell of my mother's Sunday apple pies.

It is important to use them with care as they can be overpowering, but that does not make them unpleasant, it is just that a hint seems somehow best with this particular spice.

Grown mainly on the islands of the East African coast, Zanzibar and Pemba being the world's largest producers, the cloves are the unopened flower buds of the tree, which are hand picked before the little buds have the chance to form into flowers. The trees are about 30 to 40 feet high so this is quite a task, and although I have never had the fortune to be near to one of them, I understand that the smell is quite sensationally heady.

Coriander *Coriandrum sativum*
Like caraway, coriander is a member of the parsley family; the plant grows to about 2 feet high with small pinkish flowers.

Not unlike peppercorns, coriander grows almost anywhere where the sun shines. The seeds are very pale brown but grind into a surprisingly dark spice. Coriander adds a wonderful flavour to orange or lemon cakes having a slightly 'citrus' aroma and flavour itself. I understand that before toothpaste coriander seeds were chewed to freshen the breath – not much to do with cakes but interesting nonetheless.

Ginger *Zinigiber officinale*
The root or rhizome of the ginger plant can be used fresh, dried, preserved in syrup, crystallized or ground with the finest ginger coming from Jamaica.

The ginger plant grows to about 3 feet high, with tall slender leaves and yellow flowers, which need a tropical climate to grow well.

I can still remember the first experience of the amazingly delicate almost citrus smell of a freshly sliced piece of root ginger, in contrast to the strongly aromatic smell of ground ginger and frankly finding the rather wrinkled root of the ginger plant, extraordinarily unattractive.

Traditionally ground ginger, crystallized or stem ginger has been used in Britain to make our very oldest of cakes – the gingerbread. It is also good to know that ginger cakes can be eaten with the clearest of conscience as it is said to aid digestion.

Mace *Myristica fragrans* and Nutmeg *Myristica fragrans*
The mace and nutmeg grow together on the same tree; the blades of mace wrapped around the outer shell of the nutmeg. Both spices are incredibly aromatic and wonderfully warming, although I always think mace is rather more 'citrus' and like to add it to lemon cakes.

The nutmeg tree grows to around 60 feet, with a large apricot-like fruit surrounding the nut. Mace retains this lovely apricot colouring, whilst the nutmeg itself is dark brown.

Nutmeg is best freshly ground, as needed, the flavour being far superior to any which has been stored ready ground.

Mixed Spice
This combination of spices is most commonly used for cakes and puddings, and has become a very typically British mixture. Although it varies a little from retailer to retailer, the most common spices used are ground allspice, cinnamon, cloves, nutmeg and ginger.

Mixed spice is a quick and easy way of keeping some ready to use cake spices to hand. However, it is worth buying mixed spice in smallish quantities as it does not keep well and is infinitely better the fresher it is.

Saffron *Crocus Sativus*
Saffron, an aromatic, deep orangey-red spice was brought to Cornwall by the Phoenicians who exchanged it for tin, although it may actually have arrived here much earlier, the Arabs having first introduced it into Europe in the 10th century.

Saffron Walden in Essex (Walden is Anglo-Saxon for field) was a flourishing centre for its growth as was Cambridgeshire where large fields of the purple saffron crocus (*crocus sativus*) were cultivated. It is a highly labour intensive job which involves extracting the bright orange stamens by hand and spreading them out to dry and the workers who spent their days tending the flowers became known as 'Crockers'.

It is the most expensive and highly treasured spice in the world as it takes over 200,000 dried stigmas from around 70,000 crocus flowers to make a pound of saffron. Sold in very small packets it is almost as expensive as gold.

Although costly it is still worthwhile buying the very best saffron you can find. If you consider how very little saffron you need to infuse in a small amount of water to achieve a delectable aroma and distinctive colour, it will seem slightly less extravagant

Vanilla *Vanilla fragrans*
A native of Mexico, vanilla is the pod of a climbing orchid. Production is a very hands-on process and the pods which are green initially, become the characteristic brown during curing which in turn brings out the aroma and flavour, with the whole procedure taking several months.

Originally the Aztecs blended vanilla with the beans from the pod of the cocoa plant, making chocolate rather as we know it today, but in 1520 when the Spanish conquered the Aztecs they named the pods 'Vanilla' meaning 'little scabbard'. Although there have been many attempts to grow the pods outside of Mexico, none have been as successful, although I have to admit to preferring Bourbon vanilla from Madagascar, which has a truly sensational deep, dusky aroma.

One of the best ways to use the pods is to fill an airtight jar with caster sugar and tuck in 2 or 3 pods. They can be re-used many times; just keep topping up the jar as you use the vanilla sugar in sponges or cake recipes.

CONVERSION TABLES

OVEN TEMPERATURES

120°C	250°F	Gas Mark $1/2$
140°C	275°F	Gas Mark 1
150°C	300°F	Gas Mark 2
160°C	325°F	Gas Mark 3
180°C	350°F	Gas Mark 4
190°C	375°F	Gas Mark 5
200°C	400°F	Gas Mark 6
220°C	425°F	Gas Mark 7
230°C	450°F	Gas Mark 8
240°C	475°F	Gas Mark 9

Note: When using a fan oven, they can be a bit of a law unto themselves and I find with mine that setting the Centigrade about 10 degrees lower than suggested in the recipe, gives the right result.

VOLUME

2 fl oz	50 ml
3 fl oz	75 ml
4 fl oz	100-125 ml
5 fl oz/$1/4$ pint	150 ml
10 fl oz/$1/2$ pint	300 ml
15 fl oz/$3/4$ pint	425 ml
20 fl oz/1 pint	600 ml
$1 1/4$ pints	725 ml
$1 3/4$ pints	1 litre
2 pints	1.2 litres
$2 1/2$ pints	1.5 litres
4 pints	2.25 litres

MEASUREMENTS

$1/8$ inch	3 mm
$1/4$ inch	5 mm
$1/2$ inch	1 cm
$3/4$ inch	2 cm
1 inch	2.5 cm
$1 1/4$ inch	3 cm
$1 1/2$ inch	4 cm
$1 3/4$ inch	4.5 cm
2 inches	5 cm
$2 1/2$ inches	6 cm
3 inches	7.5 cm
$3 1/2$ inches	9 cm
4 inches	10 cm
5 inches	13 cm
$5 1/4$ inches	13.5 cm
6 inches	15 cm
$6 1/2$ inches	16 cm
7 inches	18 cm
$7 1/2$ inches	19 cm
8 inches	20 cm
9 inches	23 cm
$9 1/2$ inches	24 cm
10 inches	25.5 cm
11 inches	28 cm
12 inches	30 cm

WEIGHTS

$1/2$ oz	10 g
$3/4$ oz	20 g
1 oz	25 g
$1 1/2$ oz	40 g
2 oz	50 g
$2 1/2$ oz	60 g
3 oz	75 g
4 oz	100-125 g
$4 1/2$ oz	125 g
5 oz	150 g
6 oz	175 g
7 oz	200 g
8 oz	225 g
9 oz	250 g
10 oz	275 g
11 oz	300 g
12 oz	350 g
1 lb	450 g
$1 1/2$ lb	700 g
2 lbs	900 g
3 lbs	1.35 kg

THREE BASIC RECIPES

As the following will be used frequently within the book as a standard part of cake making, I have detailed them here for you to refer to:

PUFF PASTRY   *Makes 450 g/1 lb*

450 g/1 lb plain flour
1/2 teaspoon salt

450 g/1 lb butter
100 ml/4 fl oz very cold water

Sift the flour and salt into a large bowl and add 50g/2 oz of the slightly softened butter, rub into the flour until it resembles fine breadcrumb texture.

Add enough water to form a soft dough and turn the pastry out onto a lightly floured board, kneading gently until smooth.

Roll the pastry into an oblong and dot half the remaining butter onto one half. Fold the other half of the pastry over the buttered area and roll out the pastry again into an oblong, repeating the process with the remaining butter. Wrap the pastry in cling film and leave in a cool place such as the refrigerator for about 30 minutes to allow it to settle.

Next stage:

Roll the dough into an oblong again, being careful not to let any of the butter break through the surface of the pastry and then fold it into three and return in cling film to the refrigerator for a further 45 minutes, it is this folding which gives the pastry its characteristic layers.

Repeat the process twice more and then the pastry is ready to use. You will be able to see the layers you have formed in the pastry dough, during all the folding and rolling.

Bake in accordance with the recipe you are following.

Note: I feel compelled to say at this stage that there is absolutely no crime however, in buying one of the excellent frozen or chilled packs of puff pastry which are readily available in supermarkets today, as it is simply impossible to make a good puff pastry without taking considerable time and trouble.

SHORTCRUST PASTRY

Makes 450 g/1 lb

450 g/1 lb plain flour
1/2 teaspoon salt
175 g/6 oz butter, chilled

50 g/2 oz white vegetable fat or lard, chilled
3 to 4 tablespoons very cold water

Sift the flour and salt into a bowl and add the butter and vegetable fat or lard, which should be chilled and cut into small pieces. Rub it lightly with your fingertips into the flour until it resembles fine breadcrumbs and then add a little of the water, stirring with a pallet knife. Add a little more water until the mixture forms into soft (but not sticky) dough.

Wrap the pastry in clingfilm and store in the refrigerator until required.

Note: It is important when making shortcrust pastry to keep your hands as cool as possible. The surface on which the pastry is prepared and rolled should also be cold; marble or stainless steel is particularly suitable. In addition the pastry dough should be handled as little as possible, otherwise you will end up with very heavy pastry.

YEAST DOUGH

Makes approx 450 g/1 lb

20 g/3/4 oz fresh yeast
2 teaspoons caster sugar
175 ml/6 fl oz lukewarm milk

450 g/1 lb plain flour
(white or wholemeal depending on recipe)
1/2 teaspoon salt

Cream the yeast and sugar together in a small bowl and add the lukewarm milk, stirring thoroughly. Set aside in a warm place to allow the yeast to work and froth to develop. About 10 minutes.

Sift the flour and salt into a large warm bowl, making a well in the centre.

Pour the yeast mixture into the flour, stir with a pallet knife and then using your hands, mix the dough together until a ball is formed.

On a lightly floured surface, knead thoroughly for 5 minutes until the dough is smooth and elastic. Then use as required.

Note: It is important when preparing dough not to allow any of the ingredients to become cold, yeast dies if it becomes either too hot (as in cooking) or if it becomes very cold it slows down the active ingredient.

Of all the categories, this is probably my favourite, simply because there are not only some really delectable cakes but also some wonderful stories attached to them.

Probably the most difficult task has been selecting particular recipes, since so many of the cakes have several versions all claiming to be the 'original'. Whilst there may be some truth attached to such claims, I suspect that over many hundreds of years the origins of such cakes became blurred and many good and adventurous bakers have added their own little touches, which in turn became 'regional'.

Of course, a great many small cakes have their origins in festivals, fairs and wakes all of which were celebrated and enjoyed regionally. One which fits perfectly into this category would be Eccles Cakes, originally part of the food baked for wakes in the town of Eccles. Wakes were linked to various Church anniversaries, even though in the 16th and 17th centuries the Puritans verbally 'attacked' wakes and other noisy celebrations as they involved drinking and merry making on a disorderly scale, and would have included the eating of regional cakes. I have to admit they sound rather fun and no doubt the housewives and bakers thoroughly enjoyed preparing the 'traditional' edible delights.

Other such cakes are the Queen Cakes of England and the Queen Cakes of Ireland, which whilst having the same name, are actually completely different in appearance and character. The Irish Queen Cakes are very similar to Fairy Cakes, little sponge cakes cooked in a bun tin and finished with glace icing, whereas the English Queen Cakes, very popular in the 19th century, were traditionally baked in heart-shaped tins and un-iced but with the inclusion of a little lemon zest and fruit.

I hope you will enjoy some of the stories in this section, which in turn will tempt you to try baking them – although you could be forgiven if you choose to forego the Flead Cakes, that is unless you keep pigs in which case you have very little excuse.